# Sustainability in Agribusiness

Accomplishing sustainability in the agribusiness sector is a significant, yet time-sensitive, challenge, especially when balanced with the need to grow sufficient quantity and quality of food to keep the growing global population healthy.

Through both quantitative and qualitative methods, this book explores the extent to which the agribusiness sector is already evolving to become sustainable and the ways in which innovation in the industry can help address sustainable development goals, particularly around zero hunger, gender equality, decent work, responsible consumption and production, and climate action. The contributors to this volume address the following key questions: What are the drivers and barriers for the agribusiness sector to become sustainable? Which business models best facilitate the implementation of sustainable goals? How can we measure the extent to which the agribusiness sector is becoming more sustainable? How can the agribusiness sector leverage recent technological advancements to achieve its sustainability goals? The analysis of the sustainability challenges for the sector ranges across various facets of the industry including employment, pre-production industries, agriculture, food processing, distribution, and trade.

This book will be of significant interest to readers in agribusiness, innovation management, and sustainability.

**Maria Carmela Annosi** is Senior Assistant Professor of Innovation Management and Organizational Behavior at the School of Social Sciences, Wageningen University and Research, The Netherlands. She is a member of the Research Centre for Strategic Change "Franco Fontana" of Luiss University. She is co-founder of DigiMetis network of WUR research experts on the analysis of socio-ecological systems in a digitalized era, inside Wageningen University and Research and she is an academic external collaborator of McGill Centre for the Convergence of Health and Economics (MCCHE). She is a Board Member of the International Food and Agribusiness Management Association (IFAMA).

**Francesco Paolo Appio** is Associate Professor of Innovation at SKEMA Business School (Campus Grand Paris, France) and Executive Committee member of the SKEMA AI Institute. He received a PhD in Management at Scuola Superiore Sant'Anna (Italy) and visited important international institutions such as MIT Sloan, Bocconi University, and KU Leuven, among others.

**Federica Brunetta** is Associate Professor of Management and Strategy at the Luiss Business School and at the Department of Business and Management of Luiss University, in Rome. She is Vice Director of the Research Centre for Strategic Change "Franco Fontana" of Luiss University and Academic Coordinator of Luiss Business School Executive Education. She received her PhD from the Catholic University "Sacro Cuore" (Italy).

# Routledge Studies in Agricultural Economics
Series Editor: Ashok Mishra
*Arizona State University, USA*

**Public Policy in Agriculture**
Impact on Labor Supply and Household Income
*Edited by Ashok K. Mishra, Davide Viaggi and Sergio Gomez y Paloma*

**Agricultural Development in Brazil**
The Rise of a Global Agro-food Power
*Edited by Antonio M. Buainain, Rodrigo Lanna and Zander Navarro*

**The Economics of Food Loss in the Produce Industry**
*Edited by Travis Minor, Suzanne Thornsbury, and Ashok K. Mishra*

**Transforming Agriculture in South Asia**
The Role of Value Chains and Contract Farming
*Edited by Ashok K. Mishra, Anjani Kumar and Pramod K. Joshi*

**Sustainability in Agribusiness**
The Impact of Societal Challenges, Technological Advancements, and Development Goals
*Edited by Maria Carmela Annosi, Francesco Paolo Appio, and Federica Brunetta*

For more information about this series, please visit: www.routledge.com/Routledge-Studies-in-Agricultural-Economics/book-series/RSAG

# Sustainability in Agribusiness
The Impact of Societal Challenges,
Technological Advancements,
and Development Goals

Edited by Maria Carmela Annosi,
Francesco Paolo Appio
and Federica Brunetta

LONDON AND NEW YORK

First published 2023
by Routledge
4 Park Square, Milton Park, Abingdon, Oxon OX14 4RN

and by Routledge
605 Third Avenue, New York, NY 10158

*Routledge is an imprint of the Taylor & Francis Group, an informa business*

© 2023 selection and editorial matter, Maria Carmela Annosi, Francesco Paolo Appio, and Federica Brunetta; individual chapters, the contributors

The right of Maria Carmela Annosi, Francesco Paolo Appio, and Federica Brunetta to be identified as the authors of the editorial material, and of the authors for their individual chapters, has been asserted in accordance with sections 77 and 78 of the Copyright, Designs and Patents Act 1988.

All rights reserved. No part of this book may be reprinted or reproduced or utilised in any form or by any electronic, mechanical, or other means, now known or hereafter invented, including photocopying and recording, or in any information storage or retrieval system, without permission in writing from the publishers.

*Trademark notice*: Product or corporate names may be trademarks or registered trademarks, and are used only for identification and explanation without intent to infringe.

*British Library Cataloguing-in-Publication Data*
A catalogue record for this book is available from the British Library

*Library of Congress Cataloging-in-Publication Data*
Names: Annosi, Maria Carmela, editor. | Appio, Francesco Paolo, editor. | Brunetta, Federica, editor.
Title: Sustainability in agribusiness: the impact of societal challenges, technological advancements, and development goals/edited by Maria Carmela Annosi, Francesco Paolo Appio, and Federica Brunetta.
Description: Abingdon, Oxon; New York, NY: Routledge, 2023. | Series: Routledge studies in agricultural economics | Includes bibliographical references and index.
Identifiers: LCCN 2022034597 | ISBN 9781032122250 (hardback) | ISBN 9781032122274 (paperback) | ISBN 9781003223672 (ebook)
Subjects: LCSH: Agricultural industries—Environmental aspects. | Sustainable development.
Classification: LCC HD9000.5 .S823 2023 | DDC 338.1—dc23/eng/20220721
LC record available at https://lccn.loc.gov/2022034597

ISBN: 978-1-032-12225-0 (hbk)
ISBN: 978-1-032-12227-4 (pbk)
ISBN: 978-1-003-22367-2 (ebk)

DOI: 10.4324/9781003223672

Typeset in Bembo
by Apex CoVantage, LLC

# Contents

*List of contributors*     x

**Introduction**     1
MARIA CARMELA ANNOSI, FRANCESCO PAOLO APPIO, AND FEDERICA BRUNETTA

*Introduction 1*
*Presentation of the chapters 2*
  *Theories, concepts, and definitions 3*
  *The role of business models and ecosystems 5*
  *The role of innovative technologies in sustainability 6*
*Conclusion 7*

## PART I
## Theories, concepts, and definitions     9

**1 State-of-the-art and conceptual issues: agribusiness and sustainability**     11
MARIA CARMELA ANNOSI, MARIA JOSE MURCIA, AND MARIA CRISTINA ZAGAME

*Introduction 11*
*Method for literature review 12*
*Disciplinary, methodological, and contextual orientation of agribusiness sustainability research 14*
*Theoretical underpinnings and major themes 15*
  *Institutional change and legitimacy 15*
  *Organizational change 17*
  *Sustainable value chains 18*
  *Viability of sustainable enterprise 19*

vi  Contents

    Contributing to sustainable development  20
    Sustainability and agribusiness: a future research agenda  21
    Conclusion  26
    References  27

2  **The role of agribusiness in achieving sustainable development goals: technologies, strategies, and ecosystems**  32
VIVIANE FILIPPI AND VIVIANA D'ANGELO

    Introduction: the impact of agribusiness on the sustainable development goals (SDGs)  32
    The importance of agriculture in fighting poverty and improving living conditions: technologies and innovative approaches  34
        The role of agriculture in fighting poverty  35
        The role of technological innovation in agriculture  36
        The impact of agribusiness in fighting poverty: technological revolution, climate-smart agriculture, and genetic enhancement  37
        The role of frugal innovation in democratizing agricultural innovation  38
    The role of agribusiness in empowering women: reducing inequalities and improving work conditions  39
    Natural resource depletion and greenhouse gas emissions pose questions about the sustainability of current food consumption and production models  40
        Agribusiness and the increasing pressure on natural resources  41
        The role of agriculture in GHG emissions  42
        Climate change, ecosystems, and agricultural productivity  43
        Carbon footprint, life cycle assessment techniques, and other tools to measure agribusiness sustainability  44
    How food systems should be reformed to achieve sustainability and become instrumental for climate action  45
        The role of agribusiness in the food system: a holistic versus an atomistic view  45
        Transition to sustainable food systems  46
        Agri-enterprises, circular production, zero waste, and other sustainability paradigms  46
        The agri-food industry toward sustainability: agricultural research, GIS technologies, and renewable energies  48

*Conclusion: future directions for agribusiness in the framework of the SDGs 50*
*References 53*

## 3 The sustainability disclosure on gender equality: insights from Italian agri-food listed companies     64
FILOMENA BUONOCORE, DAVIDE DE GENNARO, CONCETTA METALLO, AND SABRINA PISANO

*Introduction 64*
*Gender equality and SDGs in agri-food 66*
*Gender equality in sustainability disclosures 67*
*A study of listed agri-food companies in Italy 69*
  *Sample and data source 69*
  *Research method 70*
  *Results 71*
*Emerging drivers for gender reporting in the Italian agri-food sector 75*
  *Practical implications 75*
*References 76*

## PART II
## The role of business models and ecosystems     83

## 4 Inclusive value creation in the coffee industry: a framework of blockchain-enabled dynamic capabilities for sustainable international supply chain transformation     85
MARIA JELL-OJOBOR AND MICHAEL PAUL KRAMER

*Introduction 85*
*Sustainable supply chains 86*
  *Coffee supply chains 87*
*Blockchain technology in agri-food supply chains 88*
*Theoretical framework 90*
  *Sustainable coffee supply chain management practices and inclusive value creation 91*
  *Blockchain-enabled dynamic capabilities for brand differentiation and long-term competitive advantage 92*
*Discussion 95*
*References 97*

## 5 Associativism as a promoter of sustainability in farmers and a driver for creating value for sustainable practices: the case of Socicana 101
RAFAEL BORDONAL KALAKI AND MARCOS FAVA NEVES

Introduction 101
The sugar-energy sector as a promoter of sustainability 102
Socicana 103
  History of Socicana 103
  Members 103
  Sector of activity, representativeness, and geographical scope 104
  Services provided 104
  Governance and organizational structure 104
  Associative fee 104
Promoting sustainable development 105
  Top Cana Program 106
    Operational aspects 107
    Main results 107
  Bonsucro certification program 108
    Operational aspects of the program 108
    Main results 109
  RSB certification program 109
    Operational aspects of the program 110
    Main results 111
Creating value through sustainability 111
  Crédito Rural Verde 111
    Operational aspects of the program 112
    Main results 113
  Bonsucro credits 113
    Operational aspects of the program 114
    Main results 115
Conclusion 115
Teaching notes 115
  Overview 115
  Statement of relevance 116
  Target market statement 116
  Suggested assignment questions 116
Annexes 116
  COP 21 and the possible impacts on the Brazilian sugar-energy sector 116
  Socicana services provides 117
  Top Cana general results 120
    General data 121

Contents ix

6 **Social business models in agri-food: an interview with Sara Rajabli, founder of Buta Art & Sweets** 128
LAMAN BAGHIROVA, ELENA CASPRINI, NICCOLÒ FIORINI, AND MARIA CARMELA ANNOSI

*Introduction 128*
*Background 129*
*Interview with Sara 130*
*Discussion 142*
*Conclusion 144*
*References 145*

## PART III
## The role of innovative technologies in sustainability 147

7 **The role of innovative technologies in sustainability** 149
FRANCESCA CHECCHINATO, CINZIA COLAPINTO, VLADI FINOTTO, AND ALENA MYSHKO

*Introduction 149*
*Theoretical framework 151*
*Methods 156*
*Discussion 158*
  *Description of results 158*
  *Factors behind innovative technological implementations 159*
  *Mapping the sector: nodes of the agri-food supply chain 161*
  *Mapping the sector: the role of actors 163*
  *Sustainability: toward a comprehensive approach 165*
*Conclusion 168*
*References 170*

8 **Sustainability in agribusiness: what is still in the works** 173
MARIA CARMELA ANNOSI, FRANCESCO PAOLO APPIO, AND FEDERICA BRUNETTA

*Concluding remarks and what is still in the works 173*
*References 176*

*Index* 178

# Contributors

## Chapter 1

**Maria Carmela Annosi**
*Wageningen University & Research, The Netherlands*
Maria Carmela Annosi is Senior Assistant Professor of Innovation Management and Organizational Behavior at Wageningen University & Research. Her research interests are diffusion and institutionalization of existing practices and genesis of new practices.

**Maria Jose Murcia**
*Facultad de Ciencias Empresariales and IAE Business School, Austral University, Argentina*
Maria Jose (Majo) is Assistant Professor at Austral University. She is also Visiting Professor at the University of British Columbia, Canada. She conducts research in the broad fields of strategy and sustainable business management and is Director of the Center for Sustainability and Social Innovation (CESIS) at Austral University.

**Maria Cristina Zagame**
*IAE Business School, Austral University, Argentina*
Maria Cristina is a professional in the Argentinean agribusiness sector. She earned an MBA from IAE Business School and a BA in Agricultural Engineering from the National University of Mar del Plata, School of Agricultural Sciences, Argentina.

## Chapter 2

**Viviane Filippi**
*International Fund for Agricultural Development (IFAD), Italy*
Viviane Filippi is a development practitioner working in agricultural research at the International Fund for Agricultural Development (IFAD) of the United Nations. Her main professional and research interests are agricultural innovation, biotechnologies, environmental sustainability, climate change, agroecology, circular economy, governance, aid effectiveness, and public policy.

## Viviana D'Angelo
*Università Cattolica del Sacro Cuore and Luiss University, Italy*
Viviana D'Angelo is Assistant Professor in the Department of Economics and Business Management at Università Cattolica del Sacro Cuore. Her main research interests are technological innovation, innovation in the pharmaceutical sector, innovation and technological changes, sustainable and frugal innovation, and circular economy.

## Chapter 3

### Filomena Buonocore
*Department of Law, University "Parthenope" of Naples, Italy*
Filomena Buonocore is Full Professor of Organization Studies at the University "Parthenope" of Naples. She has taught undergraduate courses and master's and PhD level courses on Human Resource Management and Organizational Behaviour. She published articles in Journal of Management, Human Resource Management Journal, Journal of Managerial Psychology, and other scholarly journals.

### Davide de Gennaro
*Department of Business Science – Management & Innovation Systems, University of Salerno, Italy*
Davide de Gennaro is Assistant Professor of Organization Studies at the University of Salerno. He also works as Temporary Professor at the Italian National School of Administration (SNA) in Rome. He published articles in Journal of Vocational Behavior, Human Resource Management Journal, Management Research Review, and other scholarly journals.

### Concetta Metallo
*Department of Science and Technology, University "Parthenope" of Naples, Italy*
Concetta Metallo is Associate Professor of Organization Studies at the University "Parthenope" of Naples. Her research interests focus on technology and usage behaviors. She published articles in Technological Forecasting and Social Change, Production Planning & Control, The Information Society, BMC Health Services Research, Government Information Quarterly, and Behaviour & Information Technology.

### Sabrina Pisano
*Department of Law, University "Parthenope" of Naples, Italy*
Sabrina Pisano is Associate Professor of Business Administration at the University "Parthenope" of Naples. She teaches "Accounting and annual report" and "Human resources administration and economics." She published articles in Journal of Management and Governance, Journal of Intellectual Capital, Corporate Governance: The International Journal of Business in Society, and Socio-Economic Planning Sciences.

## Chapter 4

**Maria Jell-Ojobor**
*Luiss University, Italy*
Maria Jell-Ojobor is Assistant Professor of International Business and Strategy at Luiss University in Rome. Her research areas are international strategic networks and sustainable business model transformation. Before entering academia, she worked as a project manager at multinational healthcare companies and international organizations in Europe and Africa.

**Michael Paul Kramer**
*Hochschule Geisenheim University, Germany*
Michael Paul Kramer, born in Berlin, is a PhD candidate at the Hochschule Geisenheim University, Germany. He researches on the potential impacts of disruptive technologies on wine supply chains. Since 2020, he also teaches Information Technology Management at the International Wine Business and Fresh Produce Logistics programs at Geisenheim University.

## Chapter 5

**Rafael Bordonal Kalaki**
*Socicana, Brazil*
Rafael Bordonal Kalaki is CEO at Socicana and member of the Bonsucro Members Council. He is graduated in Agronomic Engineering, master's and PhD in Business Administration. He is expert in strategic planning in agribusiness systems and author of 16 books about agribusiness chain in Brazil, and numerous scientific articles on this topic.

**Marcos Fava Neves**
*University of São Paulo and Fundação Getulio Vargas, Brazil*
Marcos Fava Neves is an international expert on global agribusiness issues and a part-time professor of planning and strategy at the School of Business (FEA-RP) of the University of São Paulo (USP) and FGV Business School. He is the author and coordinator of 67 books published and more than 200 in scientific journals.

## Chapter 6

**Laman Baghirova**
*University of Siena, Italy*
Laman Baghirova graduated in International Accounting and Management (University of Siena, Italy) in 2020. Currently, she is working as an assistant business developer at Caldia Fiduciare in Luxembourg. Her research interests are social entrepreneurship, female entrepreneurs, and marketing.

### Elena Casprini
*University of Siena, Italy*

Elena Casprini is a senior researcher in Management at the University of Siena, Italy. Her research interests are family firms, business model innovation, and open innovation.

### Niccolò Fiorini
*University of Siena, Italy*

Niccolò Fiorini is a post doc researcher at the University of Siena. His research interests are technology transfer, Industry 4.0, marketing, and entrepreneurship.

### Maria Carmela Annosi
*Wageningen University & Research, The Netherlands*

Maria Carmela Annosi is a senior assistant professor of Innovation Management and Organization Behavior at Wageningen University & Research. Her research interests are diffusion and institutionalization of existing practices and genesis of new practices.

## Chapter 7

### Francesca Checchinato
*AgriFood Management & Innovation Lab, Department of Management, Ca' Foscari University of Venice, Italy*

Francesca Checchinato, PhD in Management, is Associate Professor of marketing at the Department of Management, Ca' Foscari University of Venice. Her main research fields concern digital marketing, digital transformation and adoption, and impact of digital technologies on company's corporate and brand awareness.

### Cinzia Colapinto
*AgriFood Management & Innovation Lab, Department of Management, Ca' Foscari University of Venice, Italy*

Cinzia Colapinto, PhD, is Associate Professor at the Department of Management, University of Venice (Italy). Her research interests focus on entrepreneurship, innovation, and strategy: she is interested in the role played by digital technologies on business model transformations and on their impact on the achievement of sustainable development goals by SMEs.

### Vladi Finotto
*AgriFood Management & Innovation Lab, Department of Management, Ca' Foscari University of Venice, Italy*

Vladi Finotto, PhD in Management, is Associate Professor of Entrepreneurship and Strategy at the Department of Management, Ca' Foscari University of Venice. He is the delegate for technology transfer, entrepreneurship, and industrial liaisons and coordinates a variety of industry–university initiatives.

**Alena Myshko**

*AgriFood Management & Innovation Lab, Department of Management, Ca' Foscari University of Venice, Italy*

Alena Myshko, PhD in Urban Studies and industry experience in transport and logistics, is Research Fellow on a project on the digitalization of wholesale agri-food markets at the Department of Management. She is interested in local and regional development; mobility, transport, and logistics; and complex institutional analysis of agri-food sector.

## Chapter 8

**Maria Carmela Annosi**

*Wageningen University & Research, The Netherlands*

Maria Carmela Annosi is Senior Assistant Professor of Innovation Management and Organizational Behavior at Wageningen University & Research. Her research interests are diffusion and institutionalization of existing practices and genesis of new practices.

**Francesco Paolo Appio**

*SKEMA Business School, France*

Francesco Paolo Appio is Associate Professor of Innovation at SKEMA Business School (Campus Grand Paris, France) and Executive Committee member of the SKEMA AI Institute. His research interests are digital transformation at multiple levels, artificial intelligence for business, and sources of innovation.

**Federica Brunetta**

*Luiss University and Luiss Business School, Italy*

Federica Brunetta is Associate Professor of Management and Strategy at the Luiss Business School and at the Department of Business and Management of Luiss University, in Rome. She is the Vice Director of the Research Centre in Strategic Change of Luiss University. Her research interest are strategies in highly-regulated settings and strategic change, including digitalization and business model innovation.

# Introduction

*Maria Carmela Annosi, Francesco Paolo Appio, and Federica Brunetta*

## Introduction

Industrial and technological developments have led to significant ecological degradation and the emergence of new world challenges, such as global warming, ozone depletion, deforestation, and desertification, among others. The usage of the earth's resources is central to agriculture and justifies the recent attention on new agribusiness practices in the search for resource optimization and new agribusiness management approaches, such as the circular economy and sustainable development. Many firms have deployed or adopted technological solutions to address the ecological issues they face, with the aim of producing and selling more goods to more people with less energy and fewer resources and waste.

However, to achieve these new goals, firms have to be re-organized, redesigned, and restructured, which will lead to reduced ecological impacts. In fact, the transformations of these firms demand the integration of new moral responsibilities into their strategy creation and implementation processes as technological advancement alone would not be sufficient to stabilize the impact these firms have on the planet. What's more, sustainable-development actions embraced by firms have to include social and economic elements in addition to environmental factors, with the first two elements as secondary goals because everything else is conditional on learning to live sustainably within the Earth's systems and limits. Following the definition given in Starik and Rands (1995: 909)[1], we see ecological sustainability as the ability of firms, either individually or collectively, "*to exist and flourish (either unchanged or in evolved forms) for lengthy time frames, in such a manner that the existence and flourishing of other collectivities of entities is permitted at related levels and in related systems.*" Accordingly, firms that follow the principles of ecological sustainability should not "*alter physical, chemical, and biological factors (or political, economic, social or cultural conditions), such that the carrying capacity for otherwise sustainable entities would be dramatically reduced or eliminated*" (Starik and Rands, 1995).

There are various reasons why so few firms have achieved good ecological sustainability performance despite its desirability as a goal. In some cases, new moral responsibilities have been seen as the solutions to novel cost reduction

DOI: 10.4324/9781003223672-1

and market-differentiation strategies, with organizations going beyond the traditional economic value chain and focusing their strategies on the entire ecological life cycle, including reducing resource use, energy use, pollution, and waste, as well as producing more environmentally sensitive products that pollute less and are more durable, recyclable, reusable, and so on; making economic investments in developing parts of the world; and forming collaborative relationships with other organizations of various types in order to effectively manage common resources.

The idea of sustainable management has recently been the focus of growing attention in the agribusiness sector. This is mainly due to widespread dissatisfaction with the industrialization of agricultural production and food processing and growing public pressure on agribusiness firms to implement more sustainable management practices. The most relevant arguments for implementing sustainable management practices require multiple levels of analysis; ecosystems (macro-level), organizations (meso-level), and individuals (micro-level), all have to make sure that their practices converge toward a more sustainable approach to agribusiness. It is particularly important to understand how and to what extent changes and innovations in agribusiness can contribute to solving urgent societal challenges, accomplishing the largest number of sustainable development goals, and leveraging the most recent technological advancements.

In this book, we will analyze the implementation of new eco-enterprise strategies in the agri-food sector by examining how the technology has helped in the realization of new sustainability goals, offering a look at the different technological solutions used. It also illustrates examples of new social enterprises by explaining the fundamentals of new social business models and also placing an emphasis on new social goals with a presentation of the problem of gender equality in agribusiness.

By so doing, we provide a multilevel perspective on the phenomenon of sustainability: (1) strategical, as we report on how new strategies are identified to achieve either cost reduction or market differentiation; (2) social as we discuss the issue of inequality in agriculture; and (3) ecologic, as we offer an overview of the organizational and technological solutions and practices enacted by firms to address ecological problems

We have maintained the organizational focus across all of these perspectives, which should allow for a fine-grained analysis of the implications of ecological sustainability for firms in the agricultural sector

## Presentation of the chapters

Accomplishing sustainability in the agribusiness sector is a timely challenge that many developing and developed countries are facing. Agribusiness is one of the world's largest manufacturing sectors in terms of output value, employment, and international trade, involving pre-production industries, agriculture, food processing, distribution, and trade. The production of enough quality food to keep the population healthy is the main scope of the agribusiness sector. However, a closer look at the sector shows that it is becoming increasingly complex and multifaceted, and it has broad implications when it comes to achieving more sustainable outcomes. The agribusiness sector is certainly evolving to become more sustainable. The main challenge is in understanding to what extent this is happening and the multiple ways it can help address the sustainable development goals (e.g., SDG 2 = zero hunger, SDG 5 = gender equality, SDG 8 = decent work, SDG 12 = responsible consumption and production, SDG 13 = climate action).

The purpose of this book is to provide an analysis of what makes the agribusiness sector sustainable, advancing knowledge on the drivers, barriers, approaches, nature of the societal challenges, variety of technological advancements, and relevance of the development goals.

The chapters in this book are grouped into three sections, recalling the different interdependent perspectives emphasized earlier:

- **Theories, concepts, and definitions.** In this first section, authors focus on existing contributions to highlight how extant literature has analyzed these issues and set the discourse for future research and for the subsequent chapters.
- **The role of business models and ecosystems**. This section examines how business models can be innovated to achieve sustainability goals. The authors have analyzed this issue theoretically and empirically, with the description of two cases from agribusiness companies.
- **The role of innovative technologies in sustainability.** This section deepens the understanding of the application of innovative technologies in order to implement sustainable practices and increase economic and environmental sustainability.

## *Theories, concepts, and definitions*

The first contribution in the book is presented by Annosi, Murcia, and Zagame. The objective of this introductory chapter is to provide an overview of theories and set the tone for subsequent conversations in the book.

Through a systematic literature review of managerial and organizational studies, the authors have examined extant research contributions on agribusiness sustainability and emergent themes in agribusiness, organizing them into a comprehensive, multilevel framework comprising the analysis of antecedents, processes, and outcomes of sustainability in agri-food.

More specifically, their work starts by presenting, as part of collected and systematically revised contributions, an analysis of those focused on changing paradigms that define agribusiness legitimacy, linking institutional changes (e.g., certifications) and new social norms as antecedents of sustainability-related activities. Second, they focus on organizational change and how the development of emerging institutional demands influences organizational responses and practices, and on how sustainable value chains are emerging in response to the need for extending sustainable activities beyond organizational boundaries; taken together, these studies represent evolving conversations on processes related to sustainability. Finally, they look at studies that contribute to the understanding of the outcomes and performance implications of engaging with sustainability.

As the authors point out, these topics have been developed in literature but still require additional investigation. For this reason, they've outlined a future research agenda, for both academia and policymakers. This is done through a sound analysis of the avenues identified by the authors of the analyzed contributions, and by focusing on the opportunities and limitations of existing studies.

The second chapter, authored by Filippi and D'Angelo, puts the focus on core theories, concepts, and definitions related to the impact of agribusiness on the sustainable development goals (SDGs). The impact concerns more than 50% of the SDGs: SDG 1 – no poverty, SDG 2 – zero hunger, SDG 3 – good health and well-being, SDG 5 – gender equality, SDG 8 – decent work, SDG 10 – reduced inequalities, SDG 12 – responsible consumption and production, SDG 13 – climate action, and SDG 15 – life on land. Agribusiness is the major cause of the lower economic status of the majority of the world's poor; it also provides food, feed, consumption goods, and industrial inputs. It occupies over 40% of the planet's land surface and is responsible for about 25% of annual greenhouse gas emissions. Authors specifically focus *on the ways agribusiness can transition toward more sustainable approaches*, by reviewing and exploring how agribusiness is contributing to the achievement of the SDGs. Filippi and D'Angelo provide a comprehensive view of the technologies, ecosystems, and strategies serving this purpose in relation to the challenges, obstacles, and opportunities found on the path toward sustainability. It is particularly interesting how they argue for a holistic, rather than atomistic, view of farming systems to enable the uptake of biotechnologies, ICT, GIS, and good agronomic practices, with the aim of increasing sustainability. They also provide paths for future research and policy directions in the framework of the SDGs, with the latter being recognized as key to reorganizing food systems. The main takeaway from this chapter is that agriculture undoubtedly plays a fundamental role in the development of human prosperity, and as such, it is pivotal to the pursuit of the SDGs.

While the SDGs take a balanced view of the three dimensions of sustainable development – economic, social, and ecological – the last chapter included in this section, Chapter 3, focuses specifically on SDG 5, which targets the achievement of equal opportunities for women and men in economic development, the elimination of all forms of violence against women and girls, and equal rights at all levels of participation. The authors of Chapter 3, Buonocore, de Gennaro, Metallo, and Pisano, discuss the issue of gender equality in the agribusiness industry, a field in which gender sustainability is at risk. There is a need for deep reflection and urgent action. Buonocore et al. start by providing core theories and definitions emphasizing through their analysis the importance of gender equality and the role of sustainability disclosures, which are expected to promote additional accountability and transparency but appear to still be partially neglected in this industry. They then present the result of the analysis of case studies of Italian listed companies working in the commodities sector – food, beverages, and tobacco – suggesting a still limited level of disclosure in terms of gender equality, despite the increasing requirement for gender equity in agri-food.

## *The role of business models and ecosystems*

In this section, the authors examine whether and how business models can be innovated to achieve sustainability goals. In order to do so, the presented evidence also highlights the role of business ecosystems, and how they enact SBMs by integrating diverse entities coherently, through collaboration and coordination.

In order to provide empirical grounding for business models and business ecosystems in the agri-food sector, this section presents different perspectives along with contributions that were all developed by looking at real-case scenarios. Specifically, two cases are presented. The first one is an overview of Inclusive value creation in the coffee industry through the use of blockchain solutions. The second one, which can also be used as a teaching case, takes a look at Socicana, a Brazilian association for the sugarcane industry. Finally, the opportunities and challenges of sustainable business models are discussed in the vibrant and engaging interview with Sara Rajabli, founder of Buta Art & Sweets, a social enterprise based in Azerbaijan.

Chapter 4, authored by Jell-Ojobor and Kramer, gets into specifics, describing how the elements at the basis of sustainable business models in the coffee industry (i.e., fair prices, conducive working conditions, sustainable production, and ecological protection) may hinder the financial performance of coffee manufactures, unless the emerging sustainable business model is more competitive than the traditional one. To this end, they argue that strategic choices related to technology adoption, and, in particular, investment in blockchain technology, support the development of dynamic capabilities and the subsequent reconfiguration of the available portfolio of resources and capabilities. Looking at the evidence collected by the authors, the business models resulting from the adoption of such technologies create intangible assets, such as reputation, trust, and bonding, that are sources of long-term financial and competitive benefits for international coffee supply chains, with blockchain technologies supporting the balance and distribution of value among coffee supply chain partners in industrialized and developing countries.

The following chapter illustrates the case of Socicana, authored by Kalaki, and Fava Neves; this case study describes how Socicana, an association of sugarcane growers, has sought to promote the sustainable development of its members. Presented at the IFAMA conference in 2021, this case is particularly interesting as it showcases the dynamics of an industry and an association that has fostered continuous improvement and developed a sustainable protocol for the inclusion of producers in international certifications, highlighting the relevance of not only the business model but also the entire ecosystem of business and institutional actors. It is an example of how associativism can be a driver for collective action and sustainable practices, and the author has developed this case as a teaching tool, serving as a perfect basis for class discussion.

The final chapter of this section is an interview conducted and discussed by Baghirova, Casprini, Fiorini, and Annosi with Sara Rajabli, founder of Buta Art & Sweets, a vibrant example of how social entrepreneurship is delivering additional value through the establishment of business models designed to pursue sustainable goals. Thus, the conversation in this chapter moves from a sustainable business model to a social business model, which – by defining social profit objectives and shareholders and emphasizing the context where the social business emerges – serves as a solution to local problems. This is particularly important in developing countries. Buta Art & Sweets has been funded by Ms. Rajabli with the objective of promoting the inclusion of disabled women in Azerbaijan. This young female social entrepreneur has developed a social business model integrating both economic and social values, thus successfully combining tradition, culture, and inclusion. What is particularly interesting is the contribution of these authors to our understanding of the processes related to "how" a social entrepreneur develops a social business model.

Using research into business-model innovation and sustainability innovations, the authors of these chapters all underpin the concept of sustainable value flows, describing the complexity of Sustainable and Social Business Models, as well as the role of sustainability and the tremendous opportunities offered by such designs.

## *The role of innovative technologies in sustainability*

Echoing the need for further analysis of the role of technologies for sustainability presented in Chapter 2 by Filippi and D'Angelo, this section, which comprises Chapter 7, aims to present the state of the art on sustainability and digitalization in agribusiness.

Smart Agriculture and 4.0 Technologies have brought several benefits to agri-food. Digital technologies have been introduced into the design, production, and sales processes, from robots to big-data analytics and artificial intelligence. Technology enables faster innovation and leads to seeking out new products, processes, modes of communication as well as business growth.

This chapter will leverage contributions focusing on the application of innovative technologies to implement sustainable practices and increase economic and environmental sustainability. To do so, Checchinato, Colapinto, Finotto, and Myshko have used a framework of analysis that relies on the three pillars of sustainability (economic, environmental, and social) in a holistic and not individual view, and adding the perspective of institutional analysis. In so doing, they have analyzed how innovative technologies enhance agricultural and agri-food sustainability, meant as a complex system of intertwined actors and stakeholders, with the three pillars acting as driving forces in innovation strategy choices. Thus, the authors highlight the importance of examining the factors and conditions behind the choice and application of particular innovations and digital strategies, recognizing the role of institutional actors for technological advancement and in order to enable the achievement of sustainable goals. The authors identify future research avenues, figuratively bringing everything full circle in relation to the previous chapters. Some of these future research avenues include the need to better understand the role of the supply chain and ecosystems, the need to uncover the dynamics within institutional environments, and technology diffusion and adoption choices.

## Conclusion

The time had come to provide a comprehensive analysis of what makes the agribusiness sector sustainable, advancing the most recent state-of-the-art knowledge on the drivers, barriers, approaches, strategic choices, business models, the nature of societal challenges, the variety of technological advancements, and the relevance of development goals.

The contributions collected in this book aim to advance this understanding, and, by offering a variety of theoretical and empirical approaches and evidence from diverse businesses in agri-food, we aim to start new conversations by providing suggestions for further avenues of research.

Let us conclude this introduction by thanking the colleagues that have supported our work with their precious contributions, and, in particular, Maria Jose Murcia, Maria Cristina Zagame, Viviane Filippi, Viviana D'Angelo, Filomena Buonocore, Davide de Gennaro, Concetta Metallo, Sabrina Pisano, Maria Jell-Ojobor, Michael Paul Kramer, Rafael Bordonal Kalaki, Marcos Fava Neves, Laman Baghirova, Elena Casprini, Niccolò Fiorini, Francesca Checchinato, Cinzia Colapinto, Vladi Finotto, and Alena Myshko.

## Note

1 Starik, M., & Rands, G. P. (1995). Weaving an integrated web: Multilevel and multisystem perspectives of ecologically sustainable organizations. *Academy of management Review*, 20(4), 908–935.

# Part I
# Theories, concepts, and definitions

# 1 State-of-the-art and conceptual issues

Agribusiness and sustainability

*Maria Carmela Annosi, Maria Jose Murcia, and Maria Cristina Zagame*

## Introduction

Agriculture is at a crossroads. While producers face mounting pressure to produce more food, at the same time, they face climate change, market volatility, pandemics, and shifting nutrition needs, in addition to the increasing physical resources' scarcity (Giovannucci et al., 2012). Furthermore, producers front on pressure to produce *sustainably*, entailing the adoption of behaviors geared toward minimizing environmental impact while maximizing social opportunities (Calicioglu et al., 2019).

According to the FAO 2021SOFA[1] report, fragile agriculture can affect many: it is estimated that 3 billion people cannot afford a healthy diet, and an additional 1 billion might add to this figure if a shock were to reduce their income by one-third. Poverty and hunger are, paradoxically, most evident among people in rural areas who earn a living from agriculture. Eradicating these issues requires measures to support productivity as well as the profitability of agriculture, linking farmers to markets. In addition, women in such contexts tend to experience greater barriers than men and suffer from unequal access to economic opportunities (Calicioglu et al., 2019). Hence, the enhanced resilience of agribusinesses is of paramount importance to ensuring food security, nutrition, livelihoods, and social inclusion for many.

The onset of sustainability represents an increase in the task environment complexity that agribusinesses deal with (Schneider et al., 2017). Firms are expected to expound greater accountability and comply with a new set of social norms and values (Lubin & Esty, 2010). Moreover, it has been suggested that sustainability has shifted societal perceptions of the nature of business in that its role now goes beyond production and commercialization, extending to engaging with tackling grand challenges, and even assuming roles traditionally considered under the public sector (Maak et al., 2016). Moreover, under the UN 2030 SDGs Agenda, business organizations in agriculture have been singled out as critical agents of change under the assumption that governments may take too much time to redress environmental and social ills (George et al., 2015; Howard-Grenville et al., 2014).

DOI: 10.4324/9781003223672-3

In this context, a steadfast interest has emerged in terms of agribusiness sustainability research being found in varied management domains, such as international business, marketing, organization theory, and strategy. Multiple research approaches have, in turn, led to a bewildering collection of findings, such that a coherent body has not yet emerged. Against this backdrop, we take stock of extant literature guided by the following research questions: (1) How is sustainability shaping the institutional environment in which agribusinesses operate? (2) How is sustainability permeating agribusinesses and their interorganizational contexts at the level of market and supply chains? (3) What are the main outcomes of the implementation of sustainability in the agribusiness context? (4) What are the relevant research avenues to further explore the implementation of sustainability in agriculture business organizations?

Our review findings provide a multilevel framework of agribusiness sustainability linking institutional changes as *antecedents;* organizational and value chain sustainability as *processes*; and the viability and contribution to sustainable development of business as *outcomes*. This effort aims to identify promising research avenues that may guide future research endeavors.

## Method for literature review

We conducted our review by selecting relevant literature in the field in an objective and reproducible manner and synthesizing results in a qualitative fashion (Fink, 2014). Our core search terms pertain to agribusiness and sustainability. Our working definition for agribusiness includes any business firm carrying out agriculture-related activities, including growing crops, raising animals, and harvesting fish and other animals from a farm, ranch, or their natural habitats (EPA, 2021[2]). In addition, we define sustainability as a firm's observable actions encompassing a broad set of stakeholder expectations, including environmental and social objectives (Aguinis & Glavas, 2012). We employed a two-pronged strategy – entailing sampling as well as coding and analysis – as described later.

*Sampling.* We gathered the state of the art of agribusiness and sustainability at the *organizational* level of analysis. In so doing, we focused on the body of work within mainstream management and organization studies (MOS) publications. We thus limited the search to the leading nine, high-impact MOS journals, following previous reviews (e.g., Hällgren et al., 2018; Locke & Golden-Biddle, 1997; Schnatterly et al., 2018), namely, Academy of Management Journal (AMJ), Academy of Management Review (AMR), Administrative Science Quarterly (ASQ), Journal of International Business Studies (JIBS), Journal of Management (JOM), Journal of Management Studies (JMS), Organization Science (Org Science), Organization Studies (Org Studies), and Strategic Management Journal (SMJ) (Bansal & Song, 2017).

We relied on a pre-defined selection algorithm for sample selection. The search was run using the Boolean phrase *"Results for [All agri\*] AND [All sustainab\*] within (Publication) Research Article"* using EBSCOhost and ProQuest databases to access our targeted journals. The algorithm considers the family of stemmed words (e.g., agriculture, agricultural, agribusiness) that were used as the search criteria in the titles, keywords, and abstracts of articles (excluding book reviews, replies, and introductions to special issues). Results covered all published research complying with the former criteria as of June 2021. After review of the abstracts and introduction section of original 591 search results, 64 articles were identified as having implications for either agribusiness or sustainability. We further excluded another 26 articles because they were not strictly within the intersection between agribusiness *and* sustainability.

The final sample thus yielded 38 relevant articles. Figure 1.1 depicts our search strategy. Figure 1.2 depicts the evolution of published articles per year.

*Coding and Analysis*. Data were analyzed using content analysis. This method reduces data and facilitates the analysis of a large quantum of text (Krippendorff, 2004). We used a formalized and inductively derived codebook for the coding

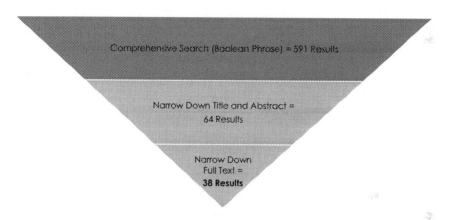

*Figure 1.1* Narrowing down the body of work

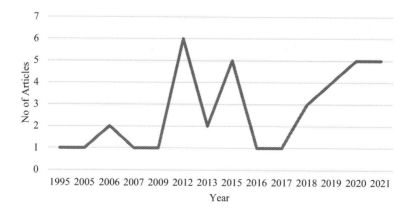

*Figure 1.2* Articles per year

process. To ensure plausibility and reliability, multiple rounds of coding were conducted with independent researchers. Differences were to be used as opportunities for clarifying or expanding the codebook. Upon reaching a consensual codebook, within-theme and between-theme comparisons were employed to identify emerging themes (Eisenhardt, 1989).

## Disciplinary, methodological, and contextual orientation of agribusiness sustainability research

*Disciplinary Orientation.* In-sample articles were published in nine leading management publications and four main disciplinary domains, as shown in Figure 1.3. Organizational theory – that is, concerned with the behavior of individuals or groups or subgroups, interacting with each other to perform activities intended toward accomplishing organizational goals – is, by far, the dominant disciplinary focus.

*Methodological Orientation.* In terms of the methodological approaches, the field is dominated by empirical papers (both quantitative and qualitative). Nonetheless, in-sample articles primarily employed qualitative or mixed methods inquiry (26 out of 38 articles), further reflecting the emerging nature of the field. In this vein, as shown in Figure 1.2, relevant articles exhibit recent steady growth as of 2017.

*Contextual Coverage.* Regarding geographic settings, unlike the broader management literature where research chiefly has a developed country focus (Aguinis et al., 2020), agribusiness and sustainability show a more balanced focus between Global North (Europe and North America: 18 articles) and Global South (Latin America and other developing countries: 13 articles) countries. Such an unprecedented representation of Global South countries as research settings may be explained by their relative abundance of natural resources and their commodity-based economies (Shapiro et al., 2018).

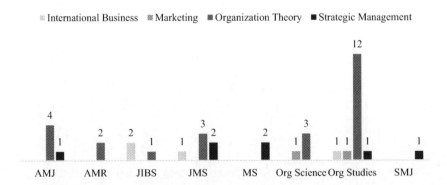

*Figure 1.3* Publications per journal and disciplinary orientation

## Theoretical underpinnings and major themes

During the systematic review process, we found that the theoretical framework of over one-third in-sample articles (n = 13) was based on neo-institutional theory (Scott, 1995). In most cases, it was not used on a stand-alone basis but in combination with other theories, and chiefly with stakeholder theory (Freeman, 1984). The former result is unsurprising since as agribusinesses are at the forefront of numerous environmental and social issues, they are increasingly looked upon by stakeholders to provide stewardship in addressing them through sustainability initiatives (Dauvergne & Lister, 2012).

Review results uncovered five emerging themes addressing the following phenomena: (1) coping with institutional change and legitimacy threats (n = 7; 19%); (2) organizational change in light of sustainability (n = 5; 13%); (3) engaging in sustainable value chains (n = 11; 29%); (4) viability of sustainable enterprise (n = 10; 26%); and (5) contributing to sustainable development (n=5; 13%).

We synthesize these various strands of conversation into a multilevel framework of agribusiness sustainability. Figure 1.4 depicts the organizing framework. The forthcoming sub-sections describe and integrate the findings of the literature around emerging themes.

### *Institutional change and legitimacy*

Our first theme is reflective of a broader phenomenon concerning the shifting paradigm defining agribusiness legitimacy, pertaining to how sector firms deal with demands to comply with sustainability as new social norm or "institution" affecting their ability to stand as competitive players and even survive (Bansal, 2005).

Specifically, agribusinesses operating in industries such as coffee, chocolate, and tea have been in the spotlight due to frequent social justice and

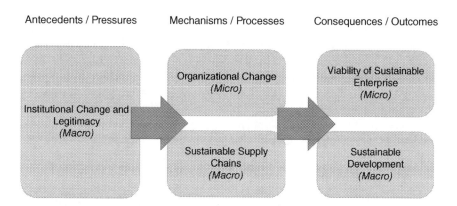

*Figure 1.4* Organizing framework

environmental transgressions (Richards et al., 2017). On the one hand, the exclusion of historically marginalized stakeholder groups like Indigenous peoples (George et al., 2016) compels agribusinesses to come up with an explicit understanding of Indigenous perceptions of justice. Whiteman (2009) shows that Indigenous peoples perceive situations as unjust when interactions, procedures, and decisions either are not reflective of their culture or result from contested power relations. In turn, when Indigenous peoples feel relations are unjust, social withdrawal and active resistance against businesses may arise.

On the other hand, agribusinesses have been subject to legitimacy threats related to ecological hazards. Kwon and Constantinides (2017) underscore the role of stakeholder group ideologies and the cognitive framings of ecological crises. Richards and colleagues (2017) find that firms relying on *"civic and green"* communication – exalting collective above individual values, and a harmonious relationship between humans and nature – versus *"domestic"* communication – exalting honoring traditions, personal ties, and family values – as a method of moral legitimization before external stakeholders are more prone to invest in sustainability certification.

Sustainability certifications are an attempt to show a firm's ethical standing that may potentially enhance a firm's legitimacy and avoid social withdrawal (Richards et al., 2017). Despite greater international convergence (Waddock, 2008), national institutional structures and political traditions around the world are important factors in explaining variance in how governments, NGOs, and the broader polity implement sustainability in different parts of the world (Matten & Moon, 2008).

Doh and Guay (2006) examined how differences in the institutional environments of the United States and Europe affected expectations about corporate responsibilities toward society concerning the regulation of genetically modified organisms (GMOs). They found that the relatively higher awareness of and support for sustainability in Europe (vis-à-vis the United States) created an environment that was more responsive to NGO influence in the GMO trade. In particular, Europe's greater resistance to GMO technology was related to three perceived environmental risks by NGOs, concerning (1) harm to non-target species, (2) genetic modification of native species, and (3) evolving resistance to protective features. In a similar vein, Voronov et al. (2013) investigated how agribusinesses seeking legitimacy within a global institutional framework manage the pressure to conform to international sustainability standards while also exploiting local distinctiveness. They show that conformity to and distinctiveness from global institutional norms do not represent two ends of the same continuum. Instead, in the case of Ontario fine wine production, conformity and distinctiveness jointly manifest as "glocalization," where global and local elements are combined in the pursuit of legitimacy.

More recently, Lee and colleagues (2017) have explored the complexity associated with attaining both legitimacy and distinctiveness as they examined how a standards-based certification organization balanced concerns related to legitimate organic foods (i.e., a new market category) while retaining a distinctive identity among members. Authors find that the pursuit of legitimacy involved a standards organization diluting the initial collective identity of the membership. However, by shifting the meaning of "organic" from the producer to the product, the organization was able to strengthen the categorical boundary and enhance its legitimacy (Lee et al., 2017).

The previous discussion suggests that other actors supporting agribusinesses, such as market intermediaries and regulators, are also subject to legitimacy threats. Hiatt and Park (2013) show how powerful stakeholders such as farmers' associations, big biotechnology corporations (e.g., Monsanto), and peer agencies (e.g., FDA in the United States) influence the rate of regulatory approval of GMO products. Authors find that whereas the influence of powerful stakeholders increased with greater *external* threats to legitimacy (e.g., if congressional electoral competitiveness is high and in the presence of GMO protests), the influence of peer agencies increased with *internal* threats to legitimacy (i.e., in the case of products from non-US firms, and if biotechnology product is novel).

## Organizational change

The second theme pertains to variations in organizational responses to emerging institutional demands. Findings point to a complex relationship among stakeholders' influence, the ambition of organizational goals, the structure of learning, and how that shapes the processes by which organizations engage with sustainability through, for instance, environmental management practices (Roome & Wijen, 2006).

Social movements have been deemed salient stakeholders that, through regular educative activities, may introduce new orders of worth to be used by consumers while shopping to evaluate agricultural products in terms of sustainability-related criteria, such as proximity, less packaging, local production, seasonality, and non-GM-fed (Dubuisson-Quellier, 2013). That said, the existence of new (sustainable) criteria for consumer choices may bring about valuable business opportunities and avenues for greater competitiveness.

In this connection, Valente (2012) finds that "sustaincentric" organizations – defined as firms equitably including interconnected social, ecological, and economic decision-making criteria – demonstrated a capacity for cognitive complexity and developing strong links with interconnected stakeholder groups, fostering sustainable competitive advantages. In particular, sustaincentric agricultural firms show (1) a prevalence of women as income earners resulting in access to education and healthcare; (2) a departure from industry norms of farmer exploitation and provision of fair margins, training, finance, and access to market; and (3) organic practices aimed at mending ecological issues (e.g., deforestation or biodiversity loss).

In turn, Lepoutre and Valente (2012) examined to what extent agribusinesses may become immune to and deviate from dominant institutional logics in the context of contradictory sustainability-related demands. Authors find that immunity emerges from decision-makers' cognitive maps connecting a deviating logic with future change. Hence, managerial cognition explains variance in non-conformity at the organizational level. More recently, notwithstanding, scholars are departing from traditional views where agribusinesses are generic catalysts of sustainability-related institutional demands to shed light on how specific biomaterial qualities of agricultural products may affect organizational efforts (Moser et al., 2021).

**Sustainable value chains**

Given increased expectations of social responsibility not only within organizational boundaries but also along multi-tiered agricultural supply chains, firms have responded by incorporating sustainability concerns into their management, toward standing as sustainable players and, in turn, participating in global value networks (Murcia et al., 2021). Schrempf-Stirling and Palazzo (2016) submit that, in the case of global buyers (chiefly, consumer product multinational firms), the debate shifted from focusing narrowly on "contract responsibility" for monitoring suppliers' social and environmental hazards, to "full producer responsibility," expanding responsibility to the whole chain regardless of contracting status.

In this context, also characterized by the absence of international hard law, voluntary standards have mushroomed to address sustainability demands, to the point where multiple social movements and industry-driven standards organizations are both competing and collaborating when it comes to governing global value chains (Reinecke et al., 2012). However, sustainability remains an ambiguous category, posing significant challenges for actors to collectively agree on its contents and desirable outcomes (Reinecke & Ansari, 2015b). Both incumbent businesses and challengers (e.g., NGOs) interact around sustainability practices such that both the meaning and practice of sustainability shift along this process and across different locations (Arnold & Loconto, 2020; Levy et al., 2016).

Recent research has focused on how proliferating sustainability standards may also foster the inclusion and active participation in agricultural supply chains, as well as the self-sufficiency of firms located in the developing world. Developing countries, characterized by commodity-rich economies, have not always been successful in translating such natural wealth into inclusive development (Rodríguez-Labajos et al., 2019). Moreover, Knight and colleagues (2007) find that a firm's country-of-origin – particularly, in the case of developing world firms – may lead them to face issues of confidence and trust in terms of integrity of local production, certification, and regulatory systems, such that they risk exclusion from value networks. Gammelgaard et al. (2020) argue that the underlying mechanisms explaining developing world firms' exploitation and exclusion pertain to local consequences being decoupled from global goals through governance gaps in both the horizontal and vertical dimensions of sustainability standards implementation, such that they should be integrated into a single framework of *"transglocal"* value chain governance.

Furthermore, a number of articles discuss the role of NGOs in facilitating both the adoption of global sustainability practices and the actual inclusion of farmers from low-income countries in global agricultural chains. Instead of following prescribed "imported" international standards, findings point to the relative superior effectiveness of approaches that emphasize local experimentation, livelihood and capacity-building, socio-environmental focus, and sensitivity toward historical relationships between the "foreigner" and the locals in order to address key uncertainties associated with locally novel sustainable agricultural practices (Claus et al., 2021; Dyck & Silvestre, 2019; McCarthy & Moon, 2018; McKague et al., 2015; van Wijk et al., 2020).

*Viability of sustainable enterprise*

The third emerging theme taps into the organizational performance implications of engaging with sustainability. In particular, as new (sustainability-related) institutional demands arise and consumer preferences change, it is worth examining how entrepreneurs make sense of and exploit sustainable agribusiness opportunities (Hiatt & Carlos, 2019). Research finds that the framing contests used by stakeholders may shape an entrepreneur's cognitive understanding of markets in ways that may enact different guidelines for market activity. In this connection, Negro and colleagues (2015) examined whether membership in a "sustainable" market category may operate as a signal for quality. In the context of sustainable viticulture, authors find that membership in a high-contrast category (i.e., "biodynamic") sends a stronger market signal relative to a low-contrast category (i.e., "organic") (Negro et al., 2015).

Moreover, it has been argued that an oppositional identity (i.e., membership in a sustainable market category), a sharply defined identity, is likely to face stigmatization (Siltaoja et al., 2020), and may potentially have to involve small-scale production and limits to organizational growth for such signaling to be "credible" and stable (Sikavica & Pozner, 2013). That said, the participation of established outsider organizations may help in scaling sustainable agricultural markets. In particular, a study by Hedberg and Lounsbury (2021) highlights the role of a cross-sector partnership in bridging local-sustainable and industrial food production logics. They find that such bridging was facilitated by cultural entrepreneurship that initially focused on communications that decoupled the values and practices associated with the local-sustainable food logic, and subsequently, reinfused community values by valorizing stories and activities that recoupled those values after logic conflict was diminished.

In a similar vein, several studies examined whether and when sustainable enterprise forms have a performance advantage over traditional agribusinesses. Boone and Özcan (2016) find that *focused* (vs. diversified) product-market engagement, combined with sufficient investment and careful planning, may render a lower failure rate for sustainable agribusinesses vis-à-vis corporations. In addition, careful planning combined with the adoption of sustainable agricultural practices (e.g., crop rotation) may yield superior results in terms of profitability and the individual welfare of farmers (Boyabatlı et al., 2019; Hu et al., 2019). More recently, Slade Shantz and colleagues (2020) zoomed in on the role of governance structures in mitigating conflict among organizational members that may lead to failure. Results suggest that formal hierarchical control structures lead to lower levels of collective psychological ownership, which, in turn, results in higher levels of conflict vis-à-vis flat control structures. However, these findings also suggest that the extent to which formal structures influence conflict can be contingent upon the presence of a strong informal hierarchy (e.g., age-based authority) that may diminish conflict (Slade Shantz et al., 2020).

Finally, along their developmental journey, sustainable enterprises may suffer from (present) resource constraints that may compromise their (future) long-term commitment to sustainable development. Kim et al. (2019) contend that previous studies have described the present as a "moment" in time, allowing managers to make intertemporal trade-offs for sustainable development. However, as producers do not see the future as a trade-off with the present and see duration in the present (a "long present"), they may be better placed to identify links among processes, such as resource flows (vs. stocks), inspiring incremental sustainability-oriented actions that may also alleviate resource shortages and enhance enterprise viability.

### *Contributing to sustainable development*

The final merging theme fundamentally acknowledges that agribusinesses play a vital role in reducing poverty and the insecurity of food production; at the same time, they need to become ever more conscious of natural limits to support their growth (Shrivastava, 1995). Moreover, agribusiness's impact on the natural environment is, at the time of this writing, no longer a vague concept, but it can rather be addressed via explicit measurement of planetary boundary processes (Whiteman et al., 2013).

The remaining articles encompassed in this theme focus on how business activities may be harnessed to ameliorate chronic poverty and broader forms of economic exploitation. Peredo and Chrisman (2006) present community-based entrepreneurship as a prospective holistic strategy for the sustainable alleviation of poverty, integrating economic, social, cultural, environmental, and political aspects of the community in question. Of recent, international business scholars have started to focus on the effects of forms of foreign direct investment and the launch of international agribusinesses in developing countries and their interplay with local and even community-level institutions.

Brandl and colleagues (2021) show how land acquisitions from multinational agribusinesses may increase rural poverty via the degradation of community strength (degree to which a community is interdependent and tight-knit). For their part, Parente et al. (2021) survey how local agribusinesses can maintain visibility and the salience of catch-up investments and initiatives subsequent to the entry and dominance of multinationals. Their findings underscore the critical roles of public sector organizations and public–private networks in technological catch-up. They find that, Embrapa, a public sector organization in Brazil forged partnerships to first develop absorptive capacity and innovation capabilities, and then build a diverse ecosystem to generate and disseminate catch-up outcomes to end users. Embrapa also developed critical knowledge and assets that, along with pursuing environmental sustainability and protecting national interests, remained salient after multinational companies entered the market (Parente et al., 2021).

## Sustainability and agribusiness: a future research agenda

The forthcoming discussion of our review results allowed us to identify promising research avenues in each of the categories highlighted in our theoretical framework.

*Institutional change and legitimacy.* Papers in this category report on the actions initiated by, more generically, single actors to gain legitimacy in the market and society. For instance, the work of Voronov et al. (2013) shows the selective compliance of actors in terms of global norms and the adaptation of these norms to local conditions as two non-mutually exclusive paths followed by actors to seek legitimation in the global context. However, the authors indicated the need for future research examining differences between adaptation to local norms and selective compliance to global norms.

In this connection, Lee et al. (2017) revealed the double-edged nature of legitimacy, presenting the path toward it as made up of a series of trade-offs to be addressed. In this vein, future research drawing on paradox theory (e.g., Smith & Lewis, 2011) may examine how firms can address the various tensions involved in legitimacy-seeking trajectories in new markets, including tensions between values and related logics. Also, future studies may also explore the role of standards organizations in the formation of new markets and successful legitimation.

The work by Whiteman (2009) underscores the importance of effective management of Indigenous stakeholder groups in gaining social license to operate in the natural resources sector. Whiteman (2009) contends that Indigenous cultures conceive justice in a broader fashion, weaving relations that operate in social, ecological, and spiritual spheres. This view can lead to raising new questions and studies: How do organizations interact and impact a variety of complex relations embedded in specific local ecologies? How can organizations restore and repair harmonious relations for themselves and with neighboring peoples?

Richards et al. (2017) discussed moral legitimization at the organizational level. They found that the dominant use of the "domestic world" is negatively related to the firm's investment in sustainability certifications. Based on this exploratory study, future research can investigate how such firms may still obtain moral legitimization and attract resources. Moreover, research may examine whether the co-existence of multiple worlds may create tensions within organizations and reveal the conditions under which they may achieve sustainability. Additional work may survey how investments in sustainability certifications relate to a firm's performance.

Kwon and Constantinides (2017) go in greater depth into the microfoundations of moral reasoning and how this may lead to polarized debates in the context of ecological crises. Being one of the first studies of its kind, future research may further explore how the narratives used by different stakeholders affect the trajectory of a crisis. Additional studies could also verify whether the nature of crisis can affect the way opposing stakeholders react and enact their course of action.

Lastly, Hiatt and Park (2013) also take a micro-foundational approach, studying regulatory agencies as social actors aiming to defend their legitimacy. Future research may explore the influence tactics enacted by third-party actors impacting regulatory decision-making. Table 1.1 summarizes our suggested research avenues.

*Organization change*. In this category, we have included papers illustrating the impact the natural environment and food materiality *per se* may have on the way firms get organized for food. Along with Moser et al. (2021), we submit to the need to devote more attention to not only the moral issues in food organizing but also the influence global food corporations have on the environment, as well as to the link between food production and consumption and climate change.

The work by Roome and Wijen (2006) lies precisely at the intersection between organizing food and the natural environment. Authors call for more research to enhance our understanding of the role of external agency when it

*Table 1.1* Future research avenues within "Institutional change and legitimacy"

| | |
|---|---|
| Research avenue 1 | Unpacking differences between adaptation to local norms and selective compliance to global norms |
| Research avenue 2 | Examining how firms may address the various tensions involved in legitimacy-seeking trajectories in new markets, including tensions between values and related logics using the paradox framework |
| Research avenue 3 | Analyzing the role of standards organizations in the formation of new markets and successful legitimation |
| Research avenue 4 | Investigating how organizations interact and impact a variety of complex relations embedded in specific local ecologies and how organizations restore and repair harmonious relations for themselves and with neighboring peoples |
| Research avenue 5 | Examining how firms relying on different narratives obtain moral legitimization in the public audience and attract resources. Verifying if the co-existence of narratives can create tensions in the organizations and exploring implications for sustainability and performance |
| Research avenue 6 | Exploring how the narratives used by different stakeholders, as well as the nature of a crisis, affect its trajectory |
| Research avenue 7 | Unpacking influence tactics enacted by third-party actors impacting regulatory decision-making |

comes to organizing food within firms. Additionally, new studies may explore the mediating effect of the organizational context expressed in terms of organizational ambitions, routines, networks, and the personal attributes of management. In a similar vein, Dubuisson-Quellier (2013) revealed how the centrality of food in people's lives can help sector firms in shaping new norms and values in the task environment in which firms operate. However, more research is required to better understand social evaluations of food toward inducing more pervasive social change.

Conversely, the work by Valente (2012) proposed an inward-looking approach, bringing up the concept of "sustaincentrism." This author argues for more new research developing tools to help businesses tackle complexities inherent in bridging various systems and stakeholders in the context of organizational decision-making. Table 1.2 summarizes the relevant research avenues related to this category.

*Sustainable supply chains.* This category comprises articles describing the challenges firms may face as they attempt to foster supply chain sustainability. A first challenge arises when trying to define the content and substance of sustainability in this context. Studies revealed the complexities involved when attempting "fair" product evaluations and prices that may account for sustainable production (Knight et al., 2007). A series of sensemaking mechanisms by which actors may reach consensus on what is "fair" and thus, ethical has been distilled (see Reinecke & Ansari, 2015a), but future research may develop a deeper understanding of the iterative nature of reflexive and interpretive work by social actors contextualizing and contingently modifying ethical evaluations on an ongoing basis. In addition, difficulties inherent to achieving a common definition of sustainability also manifest in the co-existence of businesses, social movements, and multiple industry-driven standards that compete over supply chain governance (Reinecke et al., 2012). Promising future research avenues pertain to getting to the bottom of the conditions that allow standards markets to work.

The study by Levy et al. (2016) reports on supply chain turbulence created by the presence of competing demands in the coffee sector: while civil society pushed for the adoption of sustainable production practices, mainstream coffee firms defended the status quo. Authors offered a process model of political corporate social responsibility showing how challengers and incumbents

*Table 1.2* Future research avenues within "Organization change"

| | |
|---|---|
| Research avenue 1 | *Investigating the role of external agency in the organizing of food within firms and the mediating effect of the organizational context* |
| Research avenue 2 | *Digging deeper into social evaluations to induce more pervasive change in the social order* |
| Research avenue 3 | *Developing theoretical frameworks and tools to help firms tackle and reduce the complexity of interconnecting various systems and stakeholders in decision-making* |

cooperated around sustainability practices, and how the practice and meaning of sustainability changed during the process. Future studies can further elaborate on the dynamics of NGO–business interaction in different sectors, allowing for a deeper examination of similarities and differences. Furthermore, current trends toward de-globalization in the context of the COVID-19 crisis and the resurgence of national economic priorities suggest potential government pushback against global standards as they would tend to prioritize domestic industries as national economies struggle to recover (Marques & Eberlein, 2020). Why and how national governments strategically engage with global sustainability standards remains largely unexplored. Future work may also extend the model to contexts where either firms only adopted ceremonial behaviors or challengers have succeeded in implementing substantive change.

The work by Gammelgaard et al. (2020) zooms into how local standards adoption may be dissociated from global goals due to both the horizontal and vertical governance gaps. Arnold and Loconto (2020), for their part, show how local producers in Ghana translate global standards into locally contingent networks. These studies showcase the importance of embracing agency and collective work. Furthermore, Claus et al. (2021) contend that standards adoption across institutionally distant contexts demands strategies enabling cultural detachment and assimilation that may foster respect for local meaning systems. In addition, studies by McKague et al. (2015), as well as Dyck and Silvestre (2019), highlight the relevance of intermediaries like NGOs that may conduct an adequate reading and interpretation of the characteristics of the context and may tackle local changes, such as gender inequality, more effectively (McCarthy & Moon, 2018). In this regard, future research may extend insights here offered to other high-distance translation contexts. Table 1.3 summarizes suggested research avenues.

*Viability of sustainable enterprise.* Papers in this category have collected information on external and internal drivers for sustainability-oriented firms to achieve sustainable positions in the market. The work by Hiatt and Carlos, (2019) calls for further studies to shed further light on the complex relationship

*Table 1.3* Research avenues within "Sustainable supply chains"

| | |
|---|---|
| *Research avenue 1* | Developing a deeper understanding of the iterative nature of reflexive and interpretive work by social actors contextualizing and contingently modifying ethical evaluations on an ongoing basis |
| *Research avenue 2* | Collecting more papers on the mechanisms allowing the co-existence of different standards markets and the conditions allowing them to work |
| *Research avenue 3* | Devoting more attention to the implementation of multiple standards with their consequent translation process enacted by local agents |
| *Research avenue 4* | Elaborating on the dynamic processes of NGO–business interaction in different sectors allowing for a deeper examination of similarities and differences |
| *Research avenue 5* | Examining how national governments strategically engage with global sustainability standards remains largely unexplored |

between the presence of competing stakeholders and organizational as well as market outcomes. Negro et al. (2015) and Siltaoja et al. (2020), for their part, called for more studies on the mechanisms underlying (dis)approval from different audiences in the market, and on how stigma may affect an agricultural category development. In this vein, Sikavica and Pozner (2013) as well as Hedberg and Lounsbury (2021) underscore the importance of cultural entrepreneurship to shape the social identities of businesses and promote their scaling-up. However, more research is required to work out the conditions under which institutional logics can be combined, hybridized, or adapted to favor the creation of new organizational forms and markets.

Some recent studies have offered an inward-looking perspective on how agribusinesses organize their internal structures, processes, and governance forms around sustainability to remain viable (Boone & Özcan, 2016; Boyabatlı et al., 2019; Hu et al., 2019). This opens up new opportunities for research since extant studies do not consider the influence of and connections with other business processes, such as resource flows, which might hold important implications for yield management and price and profitability fluctuations that have a tremendous impact on a firm's survival, as well as on extreme resource shortages at the macro-level.

Lastly, some studies focused on identifying viability conditions for cooperatives, a pervasive governance form among agricultural businesses (Boone & Özcan, 2016; Slade Shantz et al., 2020). Slade Shantz et al. (2020) highlighted the relative ability of cooperatives to reduce internal conflicts. Though reduced conflict is a relevant condition, this is only a very basic requisite for a firm's survival. Future research may devote more attention to identifying other structural elements that may foster the survival of cooperatives. In addition, based on Boone and Özcan (2016), forthcoming studies may compare cooperatives with corporations in terms of other performance measures. Table 1.4 summarizes suggested research avenues.

*Table 1.4* Research avenues within "Viability of sustainable enterprise"

| | |
|---|---|
| *Research avenue 1* | Shedding light on the complex relationship between the presence of competing stakeholders and organizational as well as market outcomes |
| *Research avenue 2* | Exploring the mechanisms underlying (dis)approval from different audiences in the market, and on how stigma may affect an agricultural category development |
| *Research avenue 3* | Working out the conditions in which institutional logics can be combined, hybridized, or adapted to favor the creation of new organizational forms and markets |
| *Research avenue 4* | Considering the influence of other business processes, such as resource flows, which might hold important implications for yield management, price and profitability fluctuations, as well as extreme resource shortages at the macro-level |
| *Research avenue 5* | Identifying other structural elements that may foster survival for cooperatives |
| *Research avenue 6* | Comparing cooperatives with corporations in terms of other performance measures |

Table 1.5 Research avenues within "Contribution to sustainable development"

| | |
|---|---|
| Research avenue 1 | Considering the ecological and systemic foundations for sustainability, drawing on natural sciences and the "planetary boundaries" framework as conducive tools to enhancing the identification of environmental impacts agricultural businesses have on boundary processes |
| Research avenue 2 | Offering novel perspectives on how natural resources and informal institutions interact to promote sustainable local development, also contributing to institutional theory more broadly |
| Research avenue 3 | Conducting interdisciplinary studies that may consider natural resources a constraint to strategic decision-making at both micro- and macro-levels |

*The contribution of agribusinesses to sustainable development.* The seminal work by Shrivastava (1995) brings forth both the ecological problems created by agricultural activities and the role of agribusinesses in achieving ecological sustainability. Similarly, Whiteman and colleagues (2013) stress the importance of future research considering the ecological and systemic foundations for sustainability, drawing on natural sciences and the "planetary boundaries" framework (Steffen et al., 2015), as conducive tools to enhancing the identification of environmental impacts agricultural businesses have on boundary processes beyond the three major threats concerning climate change, the global nitrogen cycle, and rate of biodiversity loss.

The works by Peredo and Chrisman (2006) and Brandl and colleagues (2021) explain how natural resources interact with local cultural and social capital as pillars to creating agricultural entrepreneurial ventures that may foster sustainable community development. These integrated approaches are, however, still embryonic. Future studies can, thus, validate the claims of earlier studies or offer novel perspectives on how natural resources and informal institutions interact to promote sustainable local development, also contributing to institutional theory more broadly. Similarly, Parente et al. (2021) call for more interdisciplinary research on sustainable development that may consider natural resources a constraint to strategic decision-making at both micro- and macro-levels. Table 1.5 summarizes suggested research avenues.

## Conclusion

We argue that the agribusiness sector showcases the multidimensionality of sustainability beyond its direct link to the exploitation of natural resources, to also encompass social concerns related to food security and nutrition, and dignified livelihoods for many. In this connection, recent studies have underscored the importance of placing the people at the center of managerial attention, not only as employees but also as members of the community agribusinesses operate in (e.g., Parente et al., 2021). Furthermore, the sector offers a unique entry point to analyzing how firms deal with contestation from social movements, challenging and broadening the conceptualization of sustainability, pushing for a more substantive contribution to sustainable development from the business world.

The proposed multilevel theoretical framework not only helps in synthesizing the literature that has grown in disparate directions, but also enhances our understanding of how sustainability permeates within-firms, between-firms and broader firms–environment relationships in the sector, suggesting that agribusinesses embracing sustainability may unleash positive systemic change. In this sense, the developed framework may serve as a conducive tool for sustainability studies addressing the peculiarities of agribusiness sector. Furthermore, it contributes to mainstreaming natural resources management to the center of research on wider socio-economic transformations toward sustainable development (George et al., 2015).

Despite efforts to rigorously synthesize the literature, we acknowledge that the scope of this review is limited to a specific sample of a broader body of literature. Nevertheless, we deliberately chose to limit sources to leading mainstream management journals since this can be considered validated knowledge and is likely to have the greatest impact in the field (Bansal & Song, 2017).

Finally, our proposed future research agenda reveals the need to better understand how business boundaries interact with different types of social structures and which are the mechanisms through which actors employ natural resources to reconfigure social structures to support sustainable development. Review results unveil new spaces for contribution with novel research studies that may shed further light on the complex relationship between business strategy and sustainability performance.

## Notes

1 Food and Agriculture Organization of the United Nations. (2021). *The state of food and agriculture 2021: Making agri-food systems more resilient to shocks and stresses.* www.fao.org/publications/sofa/sofa-2021/en/
2 www.epa.gov/regulatory-information-sector/agriculture-sectors-crop-naics-111-and-animal-naics-112

## References

Aguinis, H., & Glavas, A. (2012). What we know and don't know about corporate social responsibility a review and research agenda. *Journal of Management, 38*(4), 932–968.

Aguinis, H., Villamor, I., Lazzarini, S. G., Vassolo, R. S., Amorós, J. E., & Allen, D. G. (2020). Conducting management research in Latin America: Why and what's in it for you? *Journal of Management, 46*(5), 615–636.

Arnold, N., & Loconto, A. (2020). Serving magically perfect fruit globally: Local nesting in translating multiple standards. *Organization Studies, 42*(2), 327–349.

Bansal, P. (2005). Evolving sustainably: A longitudinal study of corporate sustainable development. *Strategic Management Journal, 26*(3), 197–218. https://doi.org/10.1002/smj.441

Bansal, P., & Song, H. C. (2017). Similar but not the same: Differentiating corporate sustainability from corporate responsibility. *Academy of Management Annals, 11*(1), 105–149.

Boone, C., & Özcan, S. (2016). Strategic choices at entry and relative survival advantage of cooperatives versus corporations in the US bio-ethanol industry, 1978–2015. *Journal of Management Studies*, *53*(7), 1113–1140.

Boyabatlı, O., Nasiry, J., & Zhou, Y. (2019). Crop planning in sustainable agriculture: Dynamic farmland allocation in the presence of crop rotation benefits. *Management Science*, *65*(5), 2060–2076.

Brandl, K., Moore, E., Meyer, C., & Doh, J. (2021). The impact of multinational enterprises on community informal institutions and rural poverty. *Journal of International Business Studies*, 1–20.

Calicioglu, O., Flammini, A., Bracco, S., Bellù, L., & Sims, R. (2019). The future challenges of food and agriculture: An integrated analysis of trends and solutions. *Sustainability*, *11*(1), 222.

Claus, L., Greenwood, R., & Mgoo, J. (2021). Institutional translation gone wrong: The case of villages for Africa in rural Tanzania. *Academy of Management Journal*, *64*(5), 1497–1526.

Dauvergne, P., & Lister, J. (2012). Big brand sustainability: Governance prospects and environmental limits. *Global Environmental Change*, *22*(1), 36–45.

Doh, J., & Guay, T. (2006). Corporate social responsibility, public policy, and NGO activism in Europe and the United States: An institutional-stakeholder perspective. *Journal of Management Studies*, *43*(1), 47–73.

Dubuisson-Quellier, S. (2013). A market mediation strategy: How social movements seek to change firms' practices by promoting new principles of product valuation. *Organization Studies*, *34*(5–6), 683–703.

Dyck, B., & Silvestre, B. S. (2019). A novel NGO approach to facilitate the adoption of sustainable innovations in low-income countries: Lessons from small-scale farms in Nicaragua. *Organization Studies*, *40*(3), 443–461.

Eisenhardt, K. M. (1989). Building theories from case study research. *Academy of Management Review*, *14*(4), 532–550.

EPA. (2021). https://www.epa.gov/regulatory-information-sector/agriculture-sectors-crop-naics-111-and-animal-naics-112

Fink, A. (2014). *Conducting research literature reviews: From the Internet to paper* (4th ed.). Thousand Oaks, CA: Sage Publications.

Freeman, R. (1984). *Strategic management: A stakeholder approach*. Boston: Pitman.

Gammelgaard, J., Haakonsson, S., & Just, S. N. (2020). Corporate scramble for Africa? Towards a postcolonial framework for transglocal development governance. *Organization Studies*, *41*(9), 1213–1233.

George, G., Howard-Grenville, J., Joshi, A., & Tihanyi, L. (2016). Understanding and tackling societal grand challenges through management research. *Academy of Management Journal*, *59*(6), 1880–1895.

George, G., Schillebeeckx, S., & Liak, T. (2015). The management of natural resources: An overview and research agenda. *Academy of Management Journal*, *58*(6), 1595–1613.

Giovannucci, D., Scherr, S. J., Nierenberg, D., Hebebrand, C., Shapiro, J., Milder, J., & Wheeler, K. (2012). Food and agriculture: The future of sustainability. In *The sustainable development in the 21st century (SD21) report for Rio+20*. New York: United Nations.

Hällgren, M., Rouleau, L., & De Rond, M. (2018). A matter of life or death: How extreme context research matters for management and organization studies. *Academy of Management Annals*, *12*(1), 111–153.

Hedberg, L. M., & Lounsbury, M. (2021). Not just small potatoes: Cultural entrepreneurship in the moralizing of markets. *Organization Science*, *32*(2), 433–454.

Hiatt, S. R., & Carlos, W. C. (2019). From farms to fuel tanks: Stakeholder framing contests and entrepreneurship in the emergent US biodiesel market. *Strategic Management Journal*, *40*(6), 865–893.

Hiatt, S. R., & Park, S. (2013). Lords of the harvest: Third-party influence and regulatory approval of genetically modified organisms. *Academy of Management Journal*, *56*(4), 923–944.

Howard-Grenville, J., Buckle, S. J., Hoskins, B. J., & George, G. (2014). Climate change and management. *Academy of Management Journal*, *57*(3), 615–623.

Hu, M., Liu, Y., & Wang, W. (2019). Socially beneficial rationality: The value of strategic farmers, social entrepreneurs, and for-profit firms in crop planting decisions. *Management Science*, *65*(8), 3654–3672.

Kim, A., Bansal, P., & Haugh, H. (2019). No time like the present: How a present time perspective can foster sustainable development. *Academy of Management Journal*, *62*(2), 607–634.

Knight, J. G., Holdsworth, D. K., & Mather, D. W. (2007). Country-of-origin and choice of food imports: An in-depth study of European distribution channel gatekeepers. *Journal of International Business Studies*, *38*(1), 107–125.

Krippendorff, K. (2004). *Content analysis: An introduction to its methodology* (2nd ed.). Thousand Oaks, CA: Sage Publications.

Kwon, W., & Constantinides, P. (2017). Ideology and moral reasoning: How wine was saved from the 19th century phylloxera epidemic. *Organization Studies*, *39*(8), 1031–1053.

Lee, B. H., Hiatt, S. R., & Lounsbury, M. (2017). Market mediators and the trade-offs of legitimacy-seeking behaviors in a nascent category. *Organization Science*, *28*(3), 447–470.

Lepoutre, J. M. W. N., & Valente, M. (2012). Fools breaking out: The role of symbolic and material immunity in explaining institutional nonconformity. *Academy of Management Journal*, *55*(2), 285–313.

Levy, D., Reinecke, J., & Manning, S. (2016). The political dynamics of sustainable coffee: Contested value regimes and the transformation of sustainability. *Journal of Management Studies*, *53*(3), 364–401.

Locke, K., & Golden-Biddle, K. (1997). Constructing opportunities for contribution: Structuring intertextual coherence and "problematizing" in organizational studies. *Academy of Management Journal*, *40*(5), 1023–1062.

Lubin, D., & Esty, D. (2010). The sustainability imperative. *Harvard Business Review*, *88*(5), 42–50.

Maak, T., Pless, N. M., & Voegtlin, C. (2016). Business statesman or shareholder advocate? CEO responsible leadership styles and the micro-foundations of political CSR. *Journal of Management Studies*, *53*(3), 463–493.

Marques, J. C., & Eberlein, B. (2020). Grounding transnational business governance: A political-strategic perspective on government responses in the global South. *Regulation & Governance*. https://doi.org/10.1111/rego.12356

Matten, D., & Moon, J. (2008). "Implicit" and "explicit" CSR: A conceptual framework for a comparative understanding of corporate social responsibility. *Academy of Management Review*, *33*(2), 404–424.

McCarthy, L., & Moon, J. (2018). Disrupting the gender institution: Consciousness-raising in the cocoa value chain. *Organization Studies*, *39*(9), 1153–1177.

McKague, K., Zietsma, C., & Oliver, C. (2015). Building the social structure of a market. *Organization Studies*, *36*(8), 1063–1093.

Moser, C., Reinecke, J., den Hond, F., Svejenova, S., & Croidieu, G. (2021). Biomateriality and organizing: Towards an organizational perspective on food. *Organization Studies*, *42*(2), 175–193.

Murcia, M. J., Panwar, R., & Tarzijan, J. (2021). Socially responsible firms outsource less. *Business & Society, 60*(6), 1507–1545.

Negro, G., Hannan, M. T., & Fassiotto, M. (2015). Category signaling and reputation. *Organization Science, 26*(2), 584–600.

Parente, R., Melo, M., Andrews, D., Kumaraswamy, A., & Vasconcelos, F. (2021). Public sector organizations and agricultural catch-up dilemma in emerging markets: The orchestrating role of Embrapa in Brazil. *Journal of International Business Studies, 52*(4), 646–670.

Peredo, A. M., & Chrisman, J. J. (2006). Toward a theory of community-based enterprise. *Academy of Management Review, 31*(2), 309–328.

Reinecke, J., & Ansari, S. (2015a). When times collide: Temporal brokerage at the intersection of markets and developments. *Academy of Management Journal, 58*(2), 618–648.

Reinecke, J., & Ansari, S. (2015b). What is a "fair" price? Ethics as sensemaking. *Organization Science, 26*(3), 867–888.

Reinecke, J., Manning, S., & von Hagen, O. (2012). The emergence of a standards market: Multiplicity of sustainability standards in the global coffee industry. *Organization Studies, 33*(5–6), 791–814.

Richards, M., Zellweger, T., & Gond, J. (2017). Maintaining moral legitimacy through worlds and words: An explanation of firms' investment in sustainability certification. *Journal of Management Studies, 54*(5), 676–710.

Rodríguez-Labajos, B., Yánez, I., Bond, P., Greyl, L., Munguti, S., Ojo, G. U., & Overbeek, W. (2019). Not so natural an alliance? Degrowth and environmental justice movements in the global South. *Ecological Economics, 157*, 175–184.

Roome, N., & Wijen, F. (2006). Stakeholder power and organizational learning in corporate environmental management. *Organization Studies, 27*(2), 235–263.

Schnatterly, K., Gangloff, K. A., & Tuschke, A. (2018). CEO Wrongdoing: A review of pressure, opportunity, and rationalization. *Journal of Management, 44*(6), 2405–2432.

Schneider, A., Wickert, C., & Marti, E. (2017). Reducing complexity by creating complexity: A systems theory perspective on how organizations respond to their environments. *Journal of Management Studies, 54*(2), 182–208.

Schrempf-Stirling, J., & Palazzo, G. (2016). Upstream corporate social responsibility: The evolution from contract responsibility to full producer responsibility. *Business & Society, 55*(4), 491–527.

Scott, W. (1995). *Institutions and organizations*. London: Sage Publications.

Shapiro, D., Hobdari, B., & Oh, C. H. (2018). Natural resources, multinational enterprises and sustainable development. *Journal of World Business, 53*(1), 1–14.

Shrivastava, P. (1995). The role of corporations in achieving ecological sustainability. *Academy of Management Review, 20*(4), 936–960.

Sikavica, K., & Pozner, J. E. (2013). Paradise sold: Resource partitioning and the organic movement in the US farming industry. *Organization Studies, 34*(5–6), 623–651.

Siltaoja, M., Lähdesmaki, M., Granqvist, N., Kurki, S., Puska, P., & Luomala, H. (2020). The dynamics of (de)stigmatization: Boundary construction in the nascent category of organic farming. *Organization Studies, 41*(7), 993–1018.

Slade Shantz, A. F., Kistruck, G. M., Pacheco, D. F., & Webb, J. W. (2020). How formal and informal hierarchies shape conflict within cooperatives: A field experiment in Ghana. *Academy of Management Journal, 63*(2), 503–529.

Smith, W. K., & Lewis, M. W. (2011). Toward a theory of paradox: A dynamic equilibrium model of organizing. *Academy of Management Review, 36*(2), 381–403.

Steffen, W., Richardson, K., Rockström, J., Cornell, S. E., Fetzer, I., Bennett, E. M., Biggs, R., Carpenter, S. R., De Vries, W., De Wit, C. A., & Folke, C. (2015). Planetary

boundaries: Guiding human development on a changing planet. *Science, 347*(6223), 1259855.
Valente, M. (2012). Theorizing firm adoption of sustaincentrism. *Organization Studies, 33*(4), 563–591.
van Wijk, J. J., van Wijk, J. J., Drost, S., & Stam, W. (2020). Challenges in building robust interventions in contexts of poverty: Insights from an NGO-driven multi-stakeholder network in Ethiopia. *Organization Studies, 41*(10), 1391–1415.
Voronov, M., De Clercq, D., & Hinings, C. R. (2013). Conformity and distinctiveness in a global institutional framework: The legitimation of Ontario fine wine. *Journal of Management Studies, 50*(4), 607–645.
Waddock, S. (2008). Building a new institutional infrastructure for corporate responsibility. *Academy of Management Perspectives, 22*(3), 87–108.
Whiteman, G. (2009). All my relations: Understanding perceptions of justice and conflict between companies and indigenous peoples. *Organization Studies, 30*(1), 101–120.
Whiteman, G, Walker, B., & Perego, P. (2013). Planetary boundaries: Ecological foundations for corporate sustainability. *Journal of Management Studies, 50*(2), 307–336.

# 2 The role of agribusiness in achieving sustainable development goals

Technologies, strategies, and ecosystems

*Viviane Filippi and Viviana D'Angelo*

## Introduction: the impact of agribusiness on the sustainable development goals (SDGs)

Public attention to the production, distribution, and consumption of food has increased over the last few decades, and agribusiness is in the spotlight due to the detrimental effects on the environment and human health (Luhmann and Theuvsen, 2016). An example of this is the use of chemicals and pesticides to increase farming productivity at the expense of rural ecosystems (Sharma et al., 2019). The pressure that environment, health, and animal rights advocates are putting on agribusiness is not expected to decrease (Edwards and Shultz, 2005) and requires concrete actions to tackle the growing concerns of the environmental and climate crises (Biró and Csete, 2021).

While there are several definitions of agribusiness, the origin of the term is attributed to Davis and Goldberg, who defined it as "multiple operations involving the manufacture and distribution of farm supplies and the storage, processing, and distribution of agricultural commodities" (Davis and Goldberg, 1957: 136). This definition has evolved over time, and food production has now turned into hyper-modern farming structure run by agro-industrial managers and owned by corporations (Ioris, 2018). However, there are differences between mature and emerging economies when it comes to the nature and characteristics of agribusinesses. In the former, agribusinesses consist of large- and medium-scale agricultural producers embedded in an integrated and mostly mechanized agro-industry. In the latter, the agribusiness sector mostly consists of small-scale producers adopting less sophisticated techniques and connected to the market and to other agents through less stable value chains (Wilkinson, 2009).

The increasing demographic pressure, the globalization of agri-food markets, and the financialization of production and consumption are leading to the worldwide adoption of intensive food production, processing, and distribution approaches, thanks to the diffusion of new technologies that also allow for an increase in productivity. This intensification of food production is associated with industrialized goods, standardized diets, and international commerce, which results in low-quality food, environmental disruption, and food

DOI: 10.4324/9781003223672-4

insecurity (Ioris, 2018). These facts – combined with growing malnutrition (stunting, underweight, overweight) and cancers, diabetes, and cardiovascular and respiratory diseases linked to nutrition – are making food one of the most serious threats to health.

In view of this negative impact, the food industry has been called to take part in the transformation of food systems aimed at implementing a transition toward more sustainable approaches in food production. The 2030 Agenda for Sustainable Development is officially to promote peace and development for people and the planet. The 17 sustainable development goals (SDGs), which are grounded on the previous Millennium Development Goals (MDGs), are the core of the agenda and contain a list of actions that need to be embraced at global scale by companies, institutions, and people from all the countries of the world. These goals recognize that ending poverty implies to work at the same time on improving health and education, reduce inequality, and spur economic growth while tackling climate change and the preservation of ecosystems (United Nations, 2015). Among the 17 SDGs, seven are strongly related to agribusiness heavily depending on agriculture performance, technological change, markets, institutions, climate change, and agricultural policies.

It appears evident that a business-as-usual approach to reform the agri-food system would create unavoidable trade-offs between one SDG and another (Nilsson et al., 2017), as exemplified by the potential trade-off between increased food production and the protection of ecosystems (Hosonuma et al., 2012). This is especially relevant for mass production, which intensively exploits natural resources (e.g., cropland expansion, water withdrawal for irrigation) to guarantee food security (SDG 2), but, at the same time, threatens biodiversity conservation (SDG 15), freshwater ecosystems (SDG 6), etc. Although these goals may appear to be at odds with each other, sustainable agricultural production is expected to improve environmental performance and to reconcile the existing trade-offs (Sharma et al., 2019). The solution includes the transformation of agribusinesses according to a consistent and unified approach that takes on all of the SDGs. This would allow for trade-offs to be mitigated and synergies among SDGs would be enhanced, thus making responsible consumption and production (SDG 12) not only one of the most critical challenges of our times for the agri-food sector (Hinson et al., 2019) but also the key solution to win this battle.

Extant research has explored the role of agribusiness in achieving the SDGs: reducing poverty and inequalities (Bhattacharyya et al., 2020); improving health and well-being (Paroda and Joshi, 2019); improving the condition of women (Bastian et al., 2018); and moderating resource depletion (Riedo et al., 2021; Tramberend et al., 2019) and climate change (Arora, 2019). However, the diversified nature of each of the SDGs (although they have the common goal of achieving a sustainable development) may require different enabling factors, strategic approaches, and policy initiatives. This has led previous research to focus on the impact of agribusiness on each single SDG, missing from providing a more holistic framework which considers the role of agribusiness to achieve the SDGs as whole. To fill this gap, the aim of this chapter is to provide a comprehensive overview of the potential role of agribusiness in achieving the SDGs. In particular, this chapter explores the role of agribusiness in achieving the SDGs focusing on the importance of agribusiness in fighting poverty (SDG 1) and improving health and well-being (SDG 3) through technological innovation, climate-smart agricultural solutions, genetic enhancement, geographical information system (GIS) technologies, and renewable energies (SDG 7). Specifically, we will analyze different impact areas of agribusiness on SDG. We will discuss the importance of agribusiness in empowering women in order to reduce inequalities and improve work conditions (SDGs 5 and 10). We will analyze the sustainability of current food consumption and production models in light of the increasing trends in natural resource use and greenhouse gas (GHG) emissions (SDGs 14 and 15). We will dissect the impact of climate change on agricultural productivity and the response of agribusiness and present the main tools to measure the sustainability of agricultural production through carbon footprint and life cycle assessment techniques (SDG 13). Furthermore, we will analyze the transformation of the food systems and the role of agribusiness to reach circular production and zero waste (SDG 12). Finally, we will provide some future directions for agribusiness in the framework of the SDGs.

## The importance of agriculture in fighting poverty and improving living conditions: technologies and innovative approaches

The goals of reducing poverty and hunger, and improving good health and well-being reflect the recent global interest in creating a better future, and the global acknowledgement that complete social and human development cannot be accomplished without reducing the number of people living in extreme poverty conditions. According to the United Nation's Food and Agriculture Organization (FAO), in 2019, more than 673 million people worldwide suffered from hunger and malnutrition (FAO, 2019). Also, while South and East Asia are going through a phase of great development, Sub-Saharan Africa still suffers from extremely high poverty levels (World Bank, 2021). This segment of the world's population represents the largest but poorest socio-economic group, defined by managerial literature as the "Bottom of Pyramid" (Prahalad, 2005), which is the portion of population of people living with less than $2 per day. In this regard, the distribution of income across the population assumes the shape of a pyramid and, as we move higher and higher up in income, we find fewer and fewer people having an increasing level of income (the top of the pyramid) and vice versa, and moving down in income we can find more and more people living in poor conditions. This unbalanced distribution of wealth across the world constitutes an obstacle to economic growth, although global income inequality has been increasingly being reduced in the past few years.

Hence, it is clear that poverty is still a serious problem for a large portion of the population, and, for this reason, the SDGs goals set by the United Nations need to prioritize reducing poverty and inequality.

The main cause of poverty in those countries where more than 673 million people worldwide have suffered from hunger and malnutrition is food scarcity and the lack of income sources. Therefore, it is clear that solving the problem of food represents the first action to undertake. Although global food systems would be able to satisfy the needs of the whole population, most of the world's population does not have enough purchasing power to access the food. Many people in rural areas fight a daily battle against hunger, poverty, and low productivity, hindering the agricultural development and a broader economic growth (FAO, 2019). The main causes of hunger and malnutrition include political instability, structural barriers, and lack of a solid institutional systems, which hinder the possibility to have stable working conditions and, therefore, generate stable income flow. What's more, the inability to face adverse climate conditions doesn't allow for a solid agricultural sector, which makes the food available, to flourish.

Therefore, in order to reduce poverty and to fight hunger and malnutrition, SDGs 1 and 2 were conceived to drive policymaking toward the development of suitable strategies to address these paramount challenges. In this regard, agriculture represents one of the most important drivers to achieve these goals, first and foremost because agriculture is the most important source of food, and second, because it represents the most important sector for the creation of jobs and employment in poor and rural areas.

### *The role of agriculture in fighting poverty*

In many developing countries, agriculture represents the most important production sector and the first source of income since the majority of the population lives in rural areas. Therefore, promoting agricultural development is a powerful means for poor people to escape from poverty and to improve their living conditions. Also, the prior experience of developed economies, which were dependent on the agricultural sector before they were developed, should be taken as an example (Kjeldsen-Kragh, 2007).

Agriculture plays a dominant role in the lives of those who live in rural areas; therefore, the policy strategies should leverage the agricultural sector to fight poverty in this sector (World Bank, 2021). Agriculture is at the base of economic activities in most African countries, and they tend to have a comparative advantage in the production of primary commodities (Rao, 2014). In addition, the effect of agricultural development on the GDP is stronger in rural as opposed to developed areas (Ligon and Sadoulet, 2007). However, sustainable agricultural development needs to be supported by technological innovation which allows for an increase in the efficiency and productivity of agricultural activities (Berthet et al., 2018; Global Sustainable Development

Report, 2019, UNCCD). Therefore, the role of agriculture in poor and rural countries requires the global development agenda to focus on promoting agribusiness sectors through technical innovation and knowledge sharing in order to increase land and labor productivity (Dorward et al., 2009).

The spread of agricultural innovation among rural areas has been slow, and most of the efforts to promote the adoption of new technologies have been unsuccessful, mainly due to the unfavorable institutional environments and the structural barriers characterizing these developing areas. Also, some important reasons behind the failure of the diffusion of innovation include the applications of traditional, Western-oriented approaches to fostering innovation. For example, traditional top-down approaches to the creation of local innovation systems have proven to be ineffective compared to more flexible and larger innovation ecosystems, which also include knowledge from various actors and stakeholders (Pamuk et al., 2015). Also, the role of microfinance has proven to play a critical role in fostering innovation in the agricultural sector. Microfinance, through microcredit, has been shown to encourage entrepreneurship among the poor studied in India (Banerjee and Duflo, 2009) and the Philippines (Karlan and Zinman, 2009). New forms of microfinance based on pooled savings have shown to be effective in improving the living conditions of about 4.6 million poor people in 54 countries in Africa, Asia, and Latin America (The Economist, 2011). Therefore, effective and sustainable policy initiatives must take into account these unique characteristics of rural, developing areas.

### *The role of technological innovation in agriculture*

Technological innovation in the agriculture sector plays a crucial role in fostering and improving agricultural techniques, especially in those countries characterized by harsh climate conditions that hamper agricultural production, that is, the arid and semi-arid regions in central Asia, the Middle East, and North Africa (Wada, 2014). The most important applications of technologies in agricultural sectors include technologies to treat soil and improve production or natural resource management practices, harvesting technologies, post-harvest treatments, and transport (Iannella et al., 2019; Ragasa, 2012).

Some of the latest technological advancements in farming have to do with the mechanization of farming (Steckel and White, 2012), drip irrigation, that is, a type of micro-irrigation system that minimizes evaporation and thus saves on water (Brinegar and Ward, 2009) and the use of genetically modified organisms (GMOs) (Barrows et al., 2014), which can better adapt to peculiar climate conditions, a frequent issue in the rural areas, and are conceived to reduce insecticide use, higher yields, minimum tillage, and lower production costs, benefitting productivity in the agriculture sector. Although the diffusion of GMOs has raised many concerns about the risks of assuming modified food, all crops developed using genetic engineering are subjected to extensive safety testing before being released for commercial use.

## The impact of agribusiness in fighting poverty: technological revolution, climate-smart agriculture, and genetic enhancement

Agriculture can contribute to sustainability and climate change adaptation through new management practices, such as in situ moisture conservation, mixed cropping, land treatments, sowing time, farm ponds, and through the application of soil-test-based nutrients, bioinoculants, biofertilizers, biopesticides, rhizobacteria, etc. (Bhattacharyya et al., 2020). In the last 30 years, the application of ecological principles to the management of sustainable farming has become more and more popular as a response to the need for preserving the ecosystems and addressing the reduction in yields due to extreme weather events (Altieri, 2018).

Also, as already mentioned, one-third to one-half of the earth's agricultural land suffers from erosion; as a consequence, there is the need to optimize the land use in different areas through technological application for slowing and reversing land degradation (Wani et al., 2016). Since the soil and oceans are the biggest carbon dioxide ($CO_2$) sinks, it is of paramount importance that agribusiness is engaged in the restoration of the soil and in increasing organic matter. Due to water scarcity and erratic precipitation, agribusinesses also play a central role in water management, improving water harvesting potential, developing micro-watersheds, and enhancing rainfed agriculture through scientific soil conservation plans (Paroda and Joshi, 2019). One of the most popular techniques to harvest, conserve, and utilize rainwater for crop production is watershed development. When agribusinesses adopt this type of intervention, they contribute to the replenishment of groundwater and the extension of base flow while storing water for domestic and productive uses throughout the year (Teshager et al., 2016). Water management can be paired with field-based technologies, such as contour cultivation, broadbed and furrow, conservation agriculture, field bunds, and vegetative bunds (Paroda and Joshi, 2019). Even more relevant for water saving is the adoption of micro-irrigation – via drip or sprinkler – which reduces water application, improves water use efficiency, and increases crop productivity.

A further element that is crucial for agriculture to achieve SDGs is the mechanization of agricultural activity. Many developing countries are launching farm-mechanization campaigns to increase access to machinery for small farms in order to offset prohibitive economies of scale and the high cost of ownership. The Indian government, for example, promoted the "custom hiring" of farm equipment through dedicated hubs to take on the shortage of agricultural labor and the lower productivity rates of non-mechanized agriculture (Paroda and Joshi, 2019). The adoption of farm mechanization can improve the efficient use of the inputs, enhancing the crop productivity and thus reducing the cost of production (Mehta et al., 2019). The main agricultural technologies which have been acknowledged to advance agricultural productivity, are the following: turbo seeders, rice transplanters, multi-purpose tractors for sugarcane, urea applicators using GPS, tractor-operated reaper binder, flail type fodder harvester-cum-chaffers, tractor-mounted root crop harvester-cum-elevators, etc. (Malhotra, 2017). In all these cases, machinery proved to be significantly more efficient, and the evidence collected was used to promote public–private partnerships for research and to develop not only precision and conservation agriculture but also cost-effective technologies for small-scale producers like smart tractors, unmanned aerial vehicles, and wireless technology (Paroda and Joshi, 2019; Kabir et al., 2020).

All these new technologies and climate-smart and climate-resilient practices have great potential in terms of achieving SDGs, but they will fail to do so if agribusinesses will not be made aware of their benefits in increasing productivity, reducing costs, and addressing the challenges of climate change (Venkatramanan and Shah, 2019). The advantages are numerous and include a more stable crop production, a more complete diet, and integration of different sectors such as horticulture, fodder, and fishery sectors. Also, the environment can benefit from them greatly in the form of reduced climate risk and GHG emissions, improved carbon balance, and a preserved ecosystem through sustainable soil, water, and crop residue management (Wani et al., 2016).

## *The role of frugal innovation in democratizing agricultural innovation*

The harsh condition characterizing rural areas in terms of environmental and institutional constraints may be an obstacle to the diffusion of traditional forms of innovation. The traditional approaches to innovation are expressed as an imperative to adhere to the universally accepted techno-economic frontier that aims for continuous forward advancement (Bell and Pavitt, 1993). However, besides the traditional idea of innovation, a second approach is emerged: the concept of frugal innovation. Frugal innovation refers to the process of being innovative by removing the "frills" from product design while at the same time preserving or even improving functionality (Weyrauch and Herstatt, 2017). The idea is to start from constrained conditions to turn such constraints into a source of innovative solutions in order to tackle problems, according to the idea of "doing more with less" (Prabhu, 2017). The result of frugal innovations is simplified alternatives of existing products (or services), whose architecture may be different from the "standard" ones because based on a different design and different technologies, often downgraded ones. Thanks to the unique features of such an approach, the results of frugal innovation meet the condition of the rural areas as it is centered around overcoming the types of constraints that characterize those areas (Zeschky et al., 2014).

The frugal innovation approach has shown to be very successful in the agricultural sector (Musona, 2021). For example, it has been applied to developing cheap digital sensors to monitor real-time information on the status of the soil and other problems, solving the issue of many countries in Africa that were facing severe soil fertility depletion challenges due to soil degradation (Drechsel et al., 2001). Soil-sensing technology complies with all of the requirements of the frugal innovation approach: it is cheap, accurate, simple, and fast, and it is supported by an SMS service that provides information about the status of the soil and how eventually solves the issues. Also, it has significantly improved the smallholder farming activities, which, in turn, lead to an improvement in the crop yield.

Wastewater treatment systems are also an important field of application for frugal innovation approaches in agribusiness (Molina-Maturano et al., 2020). The success of frugal innovation in such areas stems from the lack of structured wastewater treatment systems and the role of wastewater in agriculture, as it may be (and typically is) used to irrigate crops, but if wastewater undergoes some form of treatment, this may cause issues for public health. A "frugal" wastewater treatment system – based on an innovative natural system that purifies water through the use of microorganisms, aquatic plants, and worms – was created in Mexico by two young entrepreneurs. Such innovation is easy and cheap to implement, and it is beneficial for irrigation systems in agriculture, overcoming the lack of infrastructure dedicated to wastewater treatment and allowing to reuse water that would be otherwise wasted.

Another successful application of frugal innovation is a peculiar form of solar-powered pump to abstract and convey water to the fields, developed and implemented in one of the driest parts of southern Africa (Duker et al., 2020). The technology allows for treating shallow aquifers in ephemeral rivers and irrigating the fields; it has also been shown to significantly improve the working conditions in agriculture and livelihoods.

Last but not least, frugal innovation has proven to be successful also for the development of a machine able to convert biomass into gas, which is an efficient way to recycle bio-waste resulting from agricultural activities (Pansera and Sarkar, 2016). The technology draws on "gasification technology" that allows for producing gas from bio-waste through a simple architecture and is built with easily available materials.

## The role of agribusiness in empowering women: reducing inequalities and improving work conditions

The role of agribusiness in fostering gender equality (SDG 5) has a particular echo in the rural areas of the developing countries, where agribusiness represents the most important sectors and where the women are more likely to be employed in the workforce. In fact, almost around 30% of women are employed globally in agriculture, with only 2.6% in high-income countries against 9.5% in upper-middle-income countries (United Nations, 2018). Those women play a key role within their households and communities, contributing to agriculture and rural enterprises and being one main fuel of local economies. However, women from rural areas face a variety of unequal conditions that result in severe gender disparities and human-rights violations. For example, women are often recruited for jobs that are viewed as low skilled and easily accomplished, such as working on sorting and selecting flowers, while men are more likely to be hired in positions viewed as higher skilled (Tallontire et al., 2005).

However, agriculture still represents an important source of jobs for women in rural areas, which helps promote gender equality and access to resources and economic opportunities. This would also result in a greater independent financial life, lowering the dependence on their husbands (Tsiboe et al., 2018). In this sense, the women's entrepreneurship initiatives in agriculture have proven to be effective in empowering women (Aggarwal and Johal, 2021), which, in turn, fosters agricultural and economic development and better human conditions. This is also due to the low-intensity skills required by agricultural activities, which mostly include duties and tasks that have been passed down through the generations.

However, women face severely unequal conditions in agricultural activities, not only due to their lower productivity because of physical limitations (Doss, 2018) but also due to the different accesses to input and resources (Croppenstedt et al., 2013), such as technological innovation (Ragasa, 2012), education on knowledge and skills to use such new technologies (Lubwama, 2011), lack of mobility and access to transport (Mahapa and Mashiri, 2010), lower education levels that can compromise their understanding, and therefore adoption of new technology (Ogunlana, 2004).

## Natural resource depletion and greenhouse gas emissions pose questions about the sustainability of current food consumption and production models

Food production has evolved over time in response to accelerated human population growth and changing lifestyle (Kopittke et al., 2019). Indeed, global human population is projected to reach 9.8 billion by the year 2050 (UN, 2017). Accordingly, in order to achieve global food security, food production must increase by 70% between 2005 and 2050 (Noel, 2015) and this requires an active modification of natural production systems to guarantee sustenance that finds in intensification and agricultural biotechnologies examples of this transformation (Middendorf et al., 2013).

Although this approach to production is more common in mature economies, also emerging countries went through transformation of their agricultural production systems aimed at strengthening their agro-industrial apparatus (Magdoff et al., 2000). This is what happened during the green revolution following World War II, when policies promoted by international actors in emerging countries fostered rapid production growth to implement an intense agro-export strategy which turn out to be detrimental to the environment and not conducive to sustainable development (Shiva, 2000; Wolf, 2007). This strategy was reiterated by the free-trade agreements of the following decades, which promoted economic liberalization via deregulation and unsustainable production approaches that eventually led to land degradation and reduced productivity (Magdoff et al., 2000). The agricultural techniques introduced with mass production posed sustainability threats to ecosystems due to excessive specialization, mono-cropping, synthetic fertilizers, and other chemical pesticides. These processes made food production more vulnerable to disease due to the reduction in genetic diversity (Foster, 2009; Altieri, 2004). These challenges coupled with other factors, such as the declining size of land holdings, deteriorating natural resources, climate change, increasing input prices, unstable markets, declining factor productivity, and diminished income (Paroda and Joshi, 2019), amplified the scale of the problem. In the rest of this chapter, we will discuss the nexus among agribusiness and evolving economic systems, agricultural techniques, natural resources, biotechnologies, and the main threats to health and ecosystems.

## *Agribusiness and the increasing pressure on natural resources*

Current projections show that by 2050, the world population will reach 10 billion people and more than 50% of additional food will be needed as compared to 2010. With the current production model, detrimental consequences on the environment due to land degradation, excessive water use, deforestation, pollution of ecosystems, and chemical overuse appear unavoidable (Sharma et al., 2021). In fact, the increasing population, resource-intensive consumption patterns, and fast growing demand in emerging economies are jeopardizing land, water, and other natural resources (Tramberend et al., 2019). In order to meet this additional food demand, global cropland will have to produce around 60% more output and an additional 70% of meat and dairy products by 2050 (Alexandratos and Bruinsma, 2012).

Land scarcity has resulted in agricultural intensification through the increase in cropping intensity and the adoption of new techniques to achieve higher yields (Lambin and Meyfroidt, 2011). Intensification strategies imply mechanization, more intense irrigation, agro-chemical inputs such as enhanced seed varieties, fertilizers, and pest-management practices (Garnett et al., 2013). Intensification is often associated with soil damage due to land-usage practices and ignorance of soil conservation methods to mitigate erosion, maintain fertility, avoid degradation, and minimize pollution, for example, avoid overgrazing, promote conservation tillage, integrated pest management, rotation, etc. (van Leeuwen et al., 2019; Assefa and Hans-Rudolf, 2016).

Nearly, a quarter of ice-free land areas have gone through degradation, and the increasing surface of cultivated land caused loss of soil and nutrients (Howden, 2019). Land degradation refers to a temporary or permanent decline in ecosystem function and productivity potential of existing fertile lands (Eswaran et al., 2019). Soil deterioration reduces the productivity of croplands, pastures, woodland, and forests, and is also associated with biodiversity loss, disruption of ecological processes, and declining ecosystem resilience due to the gradual impoverishment of land (Singh, 2018). Indeed, increasing land degradation is intensifying the problem of desertification and polluting coastal areas. One of the main obstacles to achieving SDGs 1 and 2 is the environmental consequence of land degradation, which is posing questions about the sustainability of intensive agriculture (Sharma et al., 2021).

However, land degradation is not the only threat to the integrity of ecosystems. Deforestation is another factor reducing biodiversity and contributing to increasing levels of greenhouse gas (GHG) emissions, due to the role of the forest in absorbing carbon dioxide. Forests and trees absorb carbon dioxide from the atmosphere as they grow, and then they convert it into carbon and store it in their branches, leaves, trunks, roots, and the soil. When forests are cleared or burned for logging or cultivation purposes, the stored carbon is released into the atmosphere in the form of carbon dioxide, thus no longer serving as carbon sinks. The deforestation of tropical forest contributes to about 20% of annual GHG, of which 53% was derived from timber harvest, 30% from wood fuel harvest, and 17% from forest fires (Pearson et al., 2017).

In 2010, the largest global source of freshwater withdrawal was agriculture, which accounted for about 70% of water use for the irrigation of cultivated land (one-fifth of global land) (Portmann et al., 2010). In addition, excessive usage of pesticides impoverished the water quality due to the contamination of ground and surface water. Being a limited resource, in arid and semi-arid regions in central Asia, the Middle East, and North Africa, the lack of water is increasingly a concern and jeopardizes food security and economic development (Wada et al., 2011; Taylor et al., 2013). The impact of the agri-industry on environmental degradation is even more visible in mature economies where rapid economic growth led to natural resource depletion and risks to human health. Nevertheless, emerging countries are not immune from this trend, hence the need for a global agenda to prioritize environmental preservation and to achieve sustainable development goals by 2030 (Merchant, 2016).

## *The role of agriculture in GHG emissions*

The recent GHG emission trend has reached a historical peak and is expected to hit 416.3 ppm in 2021 (Betts, 2021). Agriculture contributes to a significant share of GHG emissions, but, at the same time, it acts as a $CO_2$ sink thus leading to dual opposing effects on climate change. During crop growth, $CO_2$ is released by plant and soil respiration, thus contributing to GHG emissions (Cole et al., 1997; Gokmenoglu et al., 2019). The intergovernmental panel on climate change (IPCC) has reported that *"agriculture and other land-use changes accounted for about 23% of net anthropogenic global GHG emissions during the period of 2007–2016, comprising $CO_2$ (13%), methane (44%), and nitrogen oxide (81%)."* In the agricultural sector, GHG emissions are associated not only to fossil fuels used for machinery and process heating but also to the enteric fermentation of domestic animals and the storage of livestock manure in animal breeding (Al-Mansour and Jejcic, 2017). In addition, emissions are produced by agricultural land use through fertilization, the rinsing of nitrogen compounds in water, the decomposition of crop residues, and processing of organic soil, just to name a few (Al-Mansour and Jejcic, 2017). With the continuous increase in the world population and rising food demand, forests, wetlands, and grasslands have been converted into areas for agricultural production, which resulted in increased GHG emissions due to the rise of intensive farming. In response to population growth, crop and livestock productions are expected to become the primary sources of emissions (Mbow et al., 2019), and the share of indirect GHG emissions generated by electricity consumption and district heating for the agricultural sector will keep growing.

It appears evident that agriculture and the environment are strongly intertwined as the agricultural sector considerably contributes to GHG emissions (Frank et al., 2017; Zurek et al., 2020). The combination of all these factors is expected to drive up food-related GHG emissions to the point that almost half of the total emissions required to keep global warming under 2 °C by 2050 will derive from agriculture (Sharma et al., 2021). Pursuing conventional agriculture approaches represents a considerable hazard to environmental health (Bongaarts, 2019) because these emissions can hinder the effectiveness of the global warming reduction strategy and measures to mitigate climate change (Shahzad et al., 2021; Springmann et al., 2017).

### Climate change, ecosystems, and agricultural productivity

Climate change is a constant, cyclical process on earth, but, in the last century, the pace of this variation has been accelerating, and its effects have been altering the earth's ecosystems. Due to anthropogenic activities and the GHG emissions in the atmosphere, the average temperature of the planet has risen by 0.9 °C since the nineteenth century (Sharma et al., 2021) and 15 billion tons of fertile soil have been lost every year to the point that a quarter of the world's land has been marked as degraded (Arora, 2019).

Climate change, imbalanced ecosystems, and intensive agricultural practices have increased the carbon footprint of food systems and induced unpredictable climatic patterns, which have resulted in negative outcomes for agricultural productivity and health (Gomez-Zavaglia et al., 2020). More specifically, extreme climatic conditions reduce the productivity of crops by causing nutrient stagnation and salt accumulation in soil, which become dry, unhealthy, and finally infertile. The result is that barren lands become non-arable and are eventually abandoned with consequent economic losses and social issues. In 2018, the World Food Programme revealed that the increase in crop yield per hectare is significantly slower compared to the population growth (Arora, 2019). Based on data published by the Food and Agriculture Organization in 2016, if GHG emissions and climate change trends continue on the current trajectory, the yields of major cereal crops will drastically decline by 2100. In this scenario of reduced production and increasing food prices, it will be extremely difficult to address the nutritional needs of a growing population. The adoption of intensive agricultural practices, including the increased use of agro-chemicals and irrigation, is a common coping strategy, which has already shown all of its limitations. As a matter of fact, intensification further aggravates the situation with a greater release of GHGs, water withdrawal rate above natural regeneration capacity, groundwater pollution, and the eventual loss of soil fertility (Riedo et al., 2021).

## Carbon footprint, life cycle assessment techniques, and other tools to measure agribusiness sustainability

Over the years, several tools, audit instruments, footprint calculators, and methodologies have been developed to perform a quantitative analysis of agricultural consumption, GHG emissions, and natural resource use. These tools are intended to support agri-entrepreneurs and policymakers with effective evaluations of the environmental impact and use of natural resources (e.g., Farm Carbon Toolkit, Agrecalc, Cool Farm Tool) (De Simone et al., 2020; Al-Mansour and Jejcic, 2017). These methodologies primarily aim to calculate the GHG emissions of economic agents, including agribusinesses, and to define the ecological footprint for the use of land, water, energy, and other natural resources (Galli et al., 2011). In order to understand complex supply chains and evaluate resource use, consumption-based accounting and footprint analysis are used to estimate environmental or social impacts vis-à-vis defined sustainability goals in production and consumption (Hoekstra and Wiedmann, 2014; Wiedmann and Lenzen, 2018; O'Neill et al., 2018). Indeed, governments, businesses, and consumers are expected to resort more and more to footprints to evaluate their resource dependencies (Moran et al., 2013).

A carbon footprint is a quantitative measurement used to indicate the level of natural resources eroded by humans. It presents the total amount of $CO_2$ and other GHGs emitted over the full life cycle of a process or product (BSI, 2008). Therefore, footprints have the potential to estimate to what extent human activities affect global sustainability (Hoekstra, 2008; Power, 2009). Consequently, it become an important environmental protection indicator (Wiedmann and Minx, 2008) for monitoring agricultural production and assessing its sustainability and efficiency. In order to calculate the carbon footprint of agricultural products, the evaluator should conduct a detailed analysis of the total input energy required for the realization of intermediary products and final outputs (Bailey et al., 2003). Future strategies to calculate ecological footprints will apply remote sensing and satellite imaging to develop predictions of agro-ecosystems, corrective measures, and preparedness strategies to face extreme events such as water scarcity, heat waves, floods, and so on (Bruckner et al., 2015). Having obtained a carbon-footprint assessment, an agribusiness may decide to use the evidence from the study to develop a sustainability strategy. Taking as an example the livestock sector, producers can reduce emissions by improving soil health, fertilizer use, and manure storage and handling. Overall animal performance can be improved also by looking at genetics, feed efficiency, growth rates, fertility, and disease control (Bajan and Mrówczyńska-Kamińska, 2020). Regardless of the sector, every farm can cut emissions by reducing energy requirements associated with heating and ventilation through renewable energy sources (Sharma et al., 2021).

# How food systems should be reformed to achieve sustainability and become instrumental for climate action

As defined by FAO, "*a food system is the ensemble of actors and their interlinked value-adding activities involved in the production, aggregation, processing, distribution, consumption, and disposal of food products that originate from agriculture, forestry, or fisheries*" (FAO, 2018). This systemic approach includes the broader economic, societal, and natural environments in which food production is embedded. The food system is made up of subsystems (e.g., farming, waste management, input supply), and it is connected to neighboring systems like the health system, ecological systems, the energy system, and so on (Therond et al., 2017). The interaction with neighboring systems is motivated by the plurality of dimensions covered by food production, which affects human health, depletes natural resources, and alters the overall order of the ecosystems. In this systemic representation of food production and consumption, agribusiness is in a central position because of its ability to influence related systems either positively or negatively. This influence is not limited to food production; on the contrary, it extends to marketing, consumption behavior, nutrition, etc. (Van Berkum et al., 2018).

## *The role of agribusiness in the food system: a holistic versus an atomistic view*

In a context of rapid population growth leading to urbanization and of increasing levels of wealth associated with new consumption patterns, as well as climate change and natural resource depletion, the conceptualization of food production has had to be reconsidered accordingly (Hajer et al., 2016). Many of the issues and challenges connected to food production are complex problems with solutions that are controversial and span across broad boundaries. In fact, these challenges result from interactions across different scales, due to the increasingly globalized nature of food systems. Due to this high degree of complexity, public and private stakeholders at local, national, regional, and global levels should undertake integrated and coordinated actions. In response to this need, the food systems approach was developed and adopted as a holistic way of conceiving food production as a complex system of factors whose causes and effects mutually reinforce. This system is not confined to one single sector, subsystem, or discipline. On the contrary, each aspect is interpreted as the result of an intricate web of interlinked elements (Therond et al., 2017). As such, the food systems approach was adopted to overcome the limitations of more traditional approaches based on sectors and individual value chains, which adopt a narrowly defined focus or an atomistic style limited to subsystems (Van Berkum et al., 2018).

A transformational systemic change is considered the best way to address the challenges discussed so far, and the food systems approach offers the framework to evaluate all the relevant causal variables and the social, environmental, and economic effects of the solutions. The scope of action is not limited to agriculture; on the contrary, it also includes trade policy, health, environmental regulation, gender norms, education, transport, infrastructure, and so on (Caron et al., 2018).

### Transition to sustainable food systems

As has already been discussed, agriculture, food processing, transportation, and related activities absorb energy, impoverish the land, deplete water resources, generate GHG emissions, and have a number of other negative side effects that should be addressed. For this reason, the concept of the food system was reinterpreted in order to account for sustainability (Pierce-Quinonez, 2012). As defined by FAO, *"a sustainable food system is a system that offers food security and nutrition in such a way that the economic, social, and environmental bases to generate food security and nutrition also for future generations are not compromised"* (FAO, 2018). Such a system is the foundation for the "Agenda 2030" being profitable throughout, providing benefits for society and having a positive or neutral impact on the natural environment. In consideration of the increasing vulnerability of global food system and the negative effects on natural resources and ecosystems, the agri-food system should be reformed to become more productive, efficient, inclusive, environmentally sustainable, climate neutral, health-driven, and business friendly (Koc, 2016). These complex and systemic challenges require the combination of interconnected actions at local, national, regional, and global levels. There is no silver bullet for resolving these issues, but it has become clear that no action alone is expected to succeed. A better understanding of the interaction among food system components is critical to ensure the minimization of their negative effects and the maximization of their positive contributions. The need for a multi-pronged approach to the creation of sustainable global food systems has stirred up a great debate among practitioners (Hurni et al., 2015). The "Growing Better Report" from the Food and Land Use Coalition has identified ten crosscutting reforms to transform food and land use and has highlighted the actors that should be responsible for the transition (Pharo and Oppenheim, 2019). These reforms cover a number of different aspects including healthy diets, productive and regenerative agriculture, protecting and restoring nature, healthy and productive oceans, diversifying protein supply, reducing food loss and waste, harnessing the digital revolution, increasing rural livelihoods, and addressing gender and demographic issues.

### Agri-enterprises, circular production, zero waste, and other sustainability paradigms

The unsustainability of the current linear production models, based on the take-make-waste paradigm, has been proved in many ways, and the urgency to embrace circular, closed-loop approaches in production cannot be ignored (Schroeder et al., 2019). Such production approaches can be encompassed under the broader spectrum of a circular economy, which is a systemic approach where the waste generated by production and consumption processes becomes the input, generating a closed loop that mimics the living systems of the environment. Unfortunately, this is not without challenges as the benefits and profitability of circular economies are difficult to measure, and the social and environmental externalities are not included in GDP and prices. In fact, negative externalities deriving from overuse of natural resources, polluting production practices, non-recyclable waste, and so on are not estimated and, therefore, are not factored into the environmental sustainability estimates of food production (Esposito et al., 2020). In addition, many enterprises have to do an upfront investment without any public financial support to shift to circular productions. This is highly discouraging for agri-enterprises, which, although they have been showing a growing interest in such practices, still pursue short-term objectives, unlike the circular economy, which is based on a long-term value creation model. Despite all of these challenges, the benefits of circular production are unquestionable and policymakers understood the importance of developing and adopting methodologies that account for the negative externalities of the agricultural sector, translating them into actual costs (i.e., quantification of pollution, hazardous waste, natural resource overuse) (Schroeder et al., 2019; Sijtsema et al., 2020; Zarbà et al., 2021).

Agri-enterprises and small-scale food producers willing to embrace sustainability should reform not only their production, distribution, marketing, and sales processes (Reardon and Zilberman, 2019) but also their attitudes and methods in relation to food safety, animal and human health, food loss and waste, increased energy-intensity, etc. One particularly significant issue has to do with the production of high-calorie and food items with low nutritional value associated with the industrialization of food supply chains that have proven to be one of the main causes of noncommunicable diseases (NCDs) (Paroda and Joshi, 2019). Agribusinesses should redesign their product portfolios keeping the human and planetary health diet in mind. This requires a number of interventions including the development of true cost accounting to estimate environmental system services and the adoption of standards to certify that supply chains do not contribute to deforestation and that land use is kept below a sustainable level. Agri-entrepreneurs supported by dedicated institutional authorities can play an important role in using innovative financing tools to invest in emerging technologies and use procurement as an instrument to reconceive the supply chains and make them more resilient (Lipper et al., 2021). Lastly, agribusinesses could join public–private–philanthropic partnerships to drive change by raising a new generation of young farmer entrepreneurs receptive to digital innovation to drive productivity, climate-smart technologies, and renewable energies. Pharo and Oppenheim (2019) provided model-based evidence showing that the SDGs and the Paris Agreement targets will be beyond reach if food and land use systems remain on their current trajectory. This is a clear call to action not limited to a single class of stakeholders; conversely, the international community should provide data, guidance, and multilateral fora to coordinate actions. In order to promote this revolution, policymakers should adopt a holistic outlook to facilitate multi-stakeholder collaboration and policy coordination at different levels (Termeer et al., 2018). In this regard, the food systems approach is a valuable tool to identify synergies and facilitate coordination (Van Berkum et al., 2018). The pathways toward food system transformation are multifaceted and require interventions on many fronts including the transition to circular production, waste reduction, global health policies, consumer behavior change, access to credit, research, new technologies, etc. (Schwoob et al., 2019).

## *The agri-food industry toward sustainability: agricultural research, GIS technologies, and renewable energies*

Agricultural research can significantly contribute to agricultural growth, sustainable food production, and in accomplishing the SDGs. This contribution is mediated by a wide range of technologies for conservation of natural resources, efficiency in resource use, modernization of input/output markets, farm support services, and so on (Huber, 2000; Hajer et al., 2016). Agricultural research investments have led to the development of a number of enhanced crop varieties, improved agronomic practices, and knowledge throughout a given value chain. Precision agriculture and on-farm renewable energy production are already a reality in mature countries where they offer tangible help to farmers in optimizing input, reducing maintenance costs, simplifying farm management, and increasing productivity and profits. In emerging countries, digital agriculture is taking its first steps, but most agribusinesses remain anchored to traditional farming practices due to low capital for investments, lack of public incentives, and limited human capital. In these countries, technologies are usually promoted by international development investors in partnership with national public institutions to reach extension agents and farmer organizations. However, a new generation of agri-entrepreneurs is promoting the adoption of technologically advanced solutions in emerging countries as well, thus marking a turnaround in the accumulation of technological assets (Aker, 2011; Hinson et al., 2019).

Many new biotechnologies were made available to agribusinesses, including biofortified crops, high-yielding nutrient-rich hybrids, and self-pollinated crops with a wider gene pool and higher level phenotyping (Paroda and Joshi, 2019). In addition, farmers were taught better agronomic practices for crop diversification toward high-value crops, watershed development techniques, and many other natural resources management approaches and practices to improve yield and, ultimately, income (Reardon and Zilberman, 2019). Agricultural research is also an entry point to promote farm mechanization through the manufacturing of equipment for land preparation, seeding, plant protection, harvesting, and so on. In emerging countries, the construction of machinery goes hand in hand with the establishment of custom hiring centers to promote shared use and knowledge exchange at the level of farmers' organizations (Paroda and Koshi, 2019).

One field where the technological revolution led to breakthrough innovations, increasing the income of farmers, and efficiency is ICT (Information and Communications Technology). Among the broad array of ICT technologies, the diffusion of mobile telephone connectivity is an innovation, which has radically changed rural agribusinesses, in both mature and emerging countries (Singh et al., 2017). Smartphones and other portable devices have been used to create a localized information flow when it comes to weather, real-time commodity prices, crop cultivation, and technical advice through automatic text alerts. Thus, different types of information and digital content were disseminated among farmers via SMS and mobile apps to help them make better planting, harvesting, and selling decisions (Aker, 2011).

In mature countries and, more frequently, in emerging countries as well, geographical information system (GIS) and other digital technologies are reforming precision agriculture by means of ICT and cloud computing to manage crops and fields in a safer, easier, more efficient, and profitable way (Dunaieva et al., 2018). Digital agriculture can provide significant benefits to both agribusinesses and the environment. It improves efficiency by reducing the consumption of water, fertilizer, and other types of input, and decreases chemical runoff into local groundwater, and rivers with a smaller negative impact on ecosystems (Pierce and Clay, 2007). Agricultural technologies, such as GIS, GPS, satellite imagery, drones, farming software, and datasets, make agribusinesses cost-effective, smart, and sustainable (Holloway and Mengersen, 2018; Kumar et al., 2021). The application of geospatial technology in agriculture consists of the use of satellites, aircraft, drones, and sensors to produce images and then connect them with maps and other types of non-visual data. As a result, farmers are able to map topography, soil type, precipitation, temperature, fertilization, crop yields, health status, and so on (Radoglou-Grammatikis et al., 2020; Kumar et al., 2017; Bansod and Debnath, 2017). The sensors are able to provide imagery in various spectra allowing spectral indices, such as the normalized difference vegetation index (NDVI), the modified soil-adjusted vegetation index (MSAVI), the canopy chlorophyll content index (CCCI), and the Normalized Difference RedEdge (NDRE) for vegetation, nutrients, and nitrogen observation. For more accurate insecticide application and data collection, drones support farmers in defining crop biomass, plant height, weed proliferation, insect invasion, and water saturation without the risks of direct exposure to chemicals and with high-resolution images (Kitonsa and Kruglikov, 2018). This information is processed through GPS-based applications to monitor and control flooding, erosion, drought, insect invasions, pests, crop, and livestock health. Software and technologies, such as convolutional neural networks (ConvNets or CNNs), radial basis function network (RBFN), perceptron, and the combination of Universal Soil Loss Equation (USLE), GIS and remote sensing, are some of the key crop-monitoring innovations of the digital agriculture revolution (Dunaieva et al., 2018). Crop-monitoring apps were developed to simplify field observation through digital field maps, satellite monitoring, and scouting solutions to collect weather data, inspect fields, and make records in the app. This way, the apps generate reliable information on the fly, narrow the scope of interventions, and speed up reaction time. As a result, farmers can make predictions about crop yields; optimize the application of fertilizers, pesticides, and irrigation; and prevent frost or heat damage, thanks to accurate data. The most advanced agribusiness techniques could even equip seeding machines, intelligent irrigation systems, driverless harvesters, and weed-remover robots with sensors or connect them to an integral GIS system (Kumar and Babu, 2016).

Another leverage to make agribusiness more sustainable and effective is through renewable energies, which are now safer and more reliable than fossil fuels (Sharma et al., 2021; Doğan et al., 2021; Wang et al., 2021). In recent years, the consumption of energy coming from renewable sources grew by more than 10% with an average increase that only in the past decade exceeded 10% on an annual basis (Rapier, 2020). If this pace is maintained, the world has a greater chance of achieving the necessary transition from fossil fuels to clean and sustainable energy (US Briefing, 2013). Renewable energies reduce GHG emissions, improve energy efficiency (Gou et al., 2021), reduce environmental degradation, and advance sustainable economic growth (Ahmad and Tahar, 2014; Bekun et al., 2019; Güney, 2019).

It has become evident that climate change, global warming, and ecosystem preservation can find a valuable ally in the adoption of innovation and new technologies. However, they are of no use in the absence of skilled human capital to adopt them (Sharma et al., 2021; Nathaniel et al., 2021). In order to foster technological innovation and spur knowledge integration, human capital should be trained to acquire technical knowledge and awareness of the actions to handle the existing food system challenges. In fact, skilled manpower is essential for adapting to the ongoing and upcoming climate risks, increase resource efficiency and sustainable behaviors (Chankrajang and Muttarak, 2017), and to produce and consume environmentally sustainable food without prejudice for the economic growth of the primary sector (Nyla Saleem and Shujah-ur-Rahman, 2019).

## Conclusion: future directions for agribusiness in the framework of the SDGs

This chapter reviews and explores how agribusiness contributes to the achievement of the SDGs, providing a comprehensive view of the technologies, ecosystems, and strategies that may affect the SDGs promoted by the United Nations. We have explored some of the leverages of sustainable development in agriculture from the perspective of the agri-food industry. We have dealt with the challenges, obstacles, and opportunities and emphasized the key role of agribusiness on the path toward sustainability without sparing criticism of the current production system. Nevertheless, we also acknowledged the great potential of food producers in leveraging technology, innovation, and high-level knowledge to create a better future for the agri-food sector and the planet. In conclusion, we would like to draw the reader's attention to some of the key areas of intervention to maximize the catalytic role of agribusiness in the transformation of food systems, in both emerging and more mature countries.

As discussed, research in biotechnologies, digital agriculture, and renewable energies favors the achievement of key SDGs such as affordable and clean energy (SDG 7), sustainable cities and communities (SDG 11), and climate action (SDG 13). In addition, their positive impact on yields and natural resource conservation contributes also to eradicating poverty (SDG 1) and hunger (SDG 2), and promoting health and well-being (SDG 3). They can also help to counterbalance the impact of chemical pesticides, combat natural resource depletion, and increase carbon storage, thus enabling the achievement of other SDGs such as clean water, and sanitation (SDG 6), responsible consumption and production (SDG 12), and life on land (SDG 15) (United Nations, 2019). However, the agri-food system reform has to face a number of challenges including poverty persistence, rapid urbanization, natural resource degradation, and the impact of climate change on agriculture (Koc, 2016). The magnitude of the endeavor and the complexity of each of these challenges imply that appropriate conditions need to be created for the achievement of the SDGs.

The pace of climate action and the improvement of natural resource management systems are other key conditions to achieving the SDGs due to the adverse effects that climate change and resource depletion exert on agricultural performance (Nerini et al., 2019). As climate change unleashes its negative effects, efforts have to be made to mainstream climate and agriculture-related education and to improve climate-smart agriculture (Rao et al., 2018). The adoption of eco-friendly and climate-resilient technologies, such as new crop varieties with higher tolerance to drought, submergence, salinity, and aerobic stresses, was a very good starting point, but the development and adoption of climate-smart solutions should be more widespread (McCarthy et al., 2018). Furthermore, land conservation should be systematized, thanks to context-specific land-use plans, which allow for improving soil health through conservation agriculture, need-based use of nutrients, and organic-matter recycling (Bonfante et al., 2020). These plans should promote conservation-agriculture technologies and decision-support systems based on soil test results. Also, more efficient water management and micro-irrigation techniques should become central to building resilience in agriculture (Praharaj et al., 2018).

As discussed earlier in this chapter, policy reforms and interventions are key to reorganizing food systems and as part of the ongoing debate on how to redesign the system of farm subsidies and an incentive mechanism to support the income of farmers (Schipanski et al., 2016). This relates also to the policy discussion on the creation and protection of social-safety-net programs for farmers and other agri-food industry actors, who experience obstacles to the physical and economic access to resources, especially in emerging countries (Hoddinott et al., 2012; Awal et al., 2013; Adimassu and Kessler, 2015). Ad hoc policy measures to enhance the income of rural households and to address the negative spillover of rural-urban migration are an integral part of this reform (De Brauw et al., 2014). In addition, governments should broaden the scope of their agricultural strategy engaging all the most important agri-industry stakeholders and creating an enabling institutional environment to develop the agribusiness sector (Hinson et al., 2019). In order to do so, governments of low- and middle-income countries should give impetus to investments in infrastructures, introduce land leasing reforms, and promote the adoption of crop insurance products and institutional loans which do not use land as collateral. Furthermore, they should promote a favorable legal environment for contract farming, which is a valuable tool for spurring the transition from subsistence farming to commercial agriculture through contracts between small-scale producers and buyers that define prices and minimum quality standards. Lastly, emerging countries could foster the adoption of collective hiring of costly equipment in order to reduce the production costs incurred by small-scale producers, who are then able to access modern machinery through the shared-renting mechanism (Rao et al., 2018; Paroda and Joshi, 2019).

The food industry in emerging countries also requires the strengthening of agri-marketing systems to improve the linkages between farmers and markets; promote online and offline retail chains of agricultural commodities (Paroda and Joshi, 2019); and develop warehousing, cold chains, and food-processing facilities managed collectively. The need to develop agri-food systems services for the pre- and post-production phases is more urgent in emerging countries, where food processing and value addition are often defective (Trienekens, 2011). On the contrary, improving price monitoring and forecasting of major food commodities require the attention of policymakers almost everywhere in the world to inform selling decisions and waste reduction during storage, transportation, and consumption (Iizumi and Kim, 2019).

Governments should also acknowledge the central role of agriculture in the global economy, thus increasing research efforts (Fuglie et al., 2019). In emerging countries, a suitable budget allocation for research has been estimated at no less than 1% of the agricultural GDP (Mink, 2016). Unfortunately, only a few countries have reached this goal; therefore, it should be a priority also in future political agenda (Stads and Beintema, 2017). In more mature economies, very good results have been achieved through public–private partnerships, which are a good vehicle to create effective incentive mechanisms, de-risking the private action. This approach should be out scaled and promoted also in emerging countries to allow agribusiness to take the lead (Spielman et al., 2010; Smyth et al., 2021). The composition of the research portfolio requires a continuous re-prioritization to address fast-changing global, regional, and national needs. So far, experience showed that participatory "bottom-up" approaches involving farmers achieved better results in the development of technologies for food diversification and in breeding biofortified crops, high-yielding and high-nutrient crop varieties (Fuglie and Toole, 2014).

A shift toward a more holistic farming system is demanded also for the uptake of biotechnologies, ICT, GIS, and good agronomic practices, just to name a few. In order to make good use of available knowledge and technologies, countries should build multi-sectoral technology transfers to connect civil society and scientific community, strengthening input delivery, developing market linkage mechanisms, and updating farmers on technology advancements (Reddy et al., 2017; Patra and Samal, 2018). Agribusiness should play a key role in technology targeting and farm mechanization in order to accelerate the total factor productivity of crops, livestock, horticulture, fisheries, and other productions to increase competitiveness and take full advantage of globalization of agriculture (Rao et al., 2018).

In order to build the conditions for sustainable consumption and production, economic actors should possess the relevant information and awareness (SDG 12). However, baseline data for several of the SDG targets are missing, and agriculture is no exception. For this reason, strengthening data collection is another condition for achieving the SDGs through the creation of convergence and coordination mechanisms at all levels. In fact, the impact of these interconnected goals can be appreciated only through an interdisciplinary and interentity approach mediated by data and updated information (Tramberend et al., 2019). Since agriculture is still the largest economic sector in most low-income countries, the strategies to achieve the SDGs should acknowledge the importance of understanding and measuring the interlinkages among the numerous factors involved in food consumption and production (De Schutter, 2017).

All in all, our analysis has shown that the global population should remember the importance and the role that agriculture has played in the development of human prosperity over time, and it should leverage agribusiness to face the big challenges underpinned by the SDGs in order to build a more sustainable world for future generations.

## References

Adimassu, Z., and Kessler, A. (2015). Impact of the productive safety net program on farmers' investments in sustainable land management in the Central Rift Valley of Ethiopia. *Environmental Development*, 16, 54–62.

Aggarwal, M., and Johal, R. K. (2021). Rural women entrepreneurship: a systematic literature review and beyond. *World Journal of Science, Technology and Sustainable Development*, 18(4), 373–392.

Ahmad, S., and Tahar, R. M. (2014). Selection of renewable energy sources for sustainable development of electricity generation system using analytic hierarchy process: a case of Malaysia. *Renewable Energy*, 63, 458–466.

Aker, J. C. (2011). Dial "A" for agriculture: a review of information and communication technologies for agricultural extension in developing countries. *Agricultural Economics*, 42(6), 631–647.

Alexandratos, N., and Bruinsma, J. (2012). *World agriculture towards 2030/50: the 2012 revision, ESA work paper 12-03*. Rome: UN Food Agriculture Organization (FAO).

Al-Mansour, F., and Jejcic, V. (2017). A model calculation of the carbon footprint of agricultural products: the case of Slovenia. *Energy*, 136, 7–15.

Altieri, M. A. (2004). Linking ecologists and traditional farmers in the search for sustainable agriculture. *Frontiers in Ecology and the Environment*, 2(1), 35–42.

Altieri, M. A. (2018). *Agroecology: the science of sustainable agriculture*. Boca Raton: CRC Press.

Arora, N. K. (2019). Impact of climate change on agriculture production and its sustainable solutions. *Environmental Sustainability*, 2(2), 95–96.

Assefa, E., and Hans-Rudolf, B. (2016). Farmers' perception of land degradation and traditional knowledge in Southern Ethiopia – resilience and stability. *Land Degradation and Development*, 27(6), 1552–1561.

Awal, M. A., Rashid, M. H. A., Islam, A. F. M. T., and Imam, M. F. (2013). *Adapting social safety net programs to climate change shocks: issues and options for Bangladesh*. Mymensingh: Bangladesh Agricultural University.

Bailey, A. P., Basford, W. D., Penlington, N., Park, J. R., Keatinge, J. D. H., Rehman, T., and Yates, C. M. (2003). A comparison of energy use in conventional and integrated arable farming systems in the UK. *Agriculture, Ecosystems and Environment*, 97(1–3), 241–253.

Bajan, B., and Mrówczyńska-Kamińska, A. (2020). Carbon footprint and environmental performance of agribusiness production in selected countries around the world. *Journal of Cleaner Production*, 276, 123389.

Banerjee, A. V., and Duflo, E. (2009). The experimental approach to development economics. *Annual Reviews of Economics*, 1, 151–178. https://doi.org/10.1146/ANNUREV.ECONOMICS.050708.143235

Bansod, B. K., and Debnath, S. K. (2017). Prashant Kumar, Praveen K. Thakur. *Environmental Monitoring Assessment*, 189, 1–24.

Barrows, G., Sexton, S., and Zilberman, D. (2014). Agricultural biotechnology: the promise and prospects of genetically modified crops. *Journal of Economic Perspectives*, 28(1), 99–120. https://doi.org/10.1257/JEP.28.1.99

Bastian, B. L., Sidani, Y. M., and El Amine, Y. (2018). Women entrepreneurship in the middle East and North Africa: a review of knowledge areas and research gaps. *Gender in Management: An International Journal*, 33(1), 14–29. https://doi.org/10.1108/GM-07-2016-0141

Bekun, F. V., Alola, A. A., and Sarkodie, S. A. (2019). Toward a sustainable environment: nexus between $CO_2$ emissions, resource rent, renewable and non-renewable energy in 16-EU countries. *Science of the Total Environment*, 657, 1023–1029.

Bell, M., and Pavitt, K. (1993). Technological accumulation and industrial growth: contrasts between developed and developing countries. *Industrial and Corporate Change*, 2. https://doi.org/10.1093/icc/2.2.157

Berthet, E. T., Hickey, G. M., and Klerkx, L. (2018). Opening design and innovation processes in agriculture: insights from design and management sciences and future directions. *Agricultural Systems*, 165, 111–115. https://doi.org/10.1016/J.AGSY.2018.06.004

Betts, R. (2021). Met office: atmospheric $CO_2$ now hitting 50% higher than pre-industrial levels. *Carbon Brief*. https://www.carbonbrief.org/met-office-atmospheric-co2-now-hitting-50-higher-than-pre-industrial-levels

Bhattacharyya, P., Pathak, H., and Pal, S. (2020). Dimensions of climate-smart agriculture. In *Climate smart agriculture*, pp. 33–39. Singapore: Springer.

Biró, K., and Csete, M. S. (2021). Corporate social responsibility in agribusiness: climate-related empirical findings from Hungary. *Environment, Development and Sustainability*, 23(4), 5674–5694.

Bonfante, A., Basile, A., and Bouma, J. (2020). Targeting the soil quality and soil health concepts when aiming for the United Nations sustainable development goals and the EU green deal. *Soil*, 6(2), 453–466.

Bongaarts, J. (2019). *IPBES 2019: summary for policymakers of the global assessment report on biodiversity and ecosystem services of the intergovernmental science-policy platform on biodiversity and ecosystem services.* https://ipbes.net/sites/default/files/inline/files/ipbes_global_assessment_report_summary_for_policymakers.pdf

Brinegar, H. R., and Ward, F. A. (2009). Basin impacts of irrigation water conservation policy. *Ecological Economics*, 69(2), 414–426. https://doi.org/10.1016/J.ECOLECON.2009.07.020

Bruckner, M., Fischer, G., Tramberend, S., and Giljum, S. (2015). Measuring telecouplings in the global land system: a review and comparative evaluation of land footprint accounting methods. *Ecological Economics*, 114, 11–21.

BSI. (2008). *Guide to PAS 2050: how to assess the carbon footprint of goods and services.* https://aggie-horticulture.tamu.edu/faculty/hall/publications/PAS2050_Guide.pdf

Caron, P., de Loma-Osorio, G. F., Nabarro, D., Hainzelin, E., Guillou, M., Andersen, I., Arnold, T., Astralaga, M., Beukeboom, M., Bickersteth, S., Bwalya, M., and Verburg, G. (2018). Food systems for sustainable development: proposals for a profound four-part transformation. *Agronomy for Sustainable Development*, 38(4), 1–12.

Chankrajang, T., and Muttarak, R. (2017). Green returns to education: does schooling contribute to pro-environmental behaviours? Evidence from Thailand. *Ecological Economics*, 131, 434–448.

Cole, C. V., Duxbury, J., Freney, J., Heinemeyer, O., Minami, K., Mosier, A., Paustian, K., Rosenberg, N., Sampson, N., Sauerbeck, D., and Zhao, Q. (1997). Global estimates of potential mitigation of greenhouse gas emissions by agriculture. *Nutrient Cycling in Agroecosystems*, 49(1), 221–228.

Croppenstedt, A., Goldstein, M., and Rosas, N. (2013). Gender and agriculture: inefficiencies, segregation, and low productivity traps. *The World Bank Research Observer*, 28(1), 79–109. https://doi.org/10.1093/WBRO/LKS024

Davis, J., and Goldberg, R. (1957). *A concept of agribusiness*, pp. 1–136. Boston, MA: Alpine Press.

De Brauw, A., Mueller, V., and Lee, H. L. (2014). The role of rural–urban migration in the structural transformation of Sub-Saharan Africa. *World Development*, 63, 33–42.

De Schutter, O. (2017). The political economy of food systems reform. *European Review of Agricultural Economics*, 44(4), 705–731.

De Simone, W., Iannella, M., D'Alessandro, P., and Biondi, M. (2020). Assessing influence in biofuel production and ecosystem services when environmental changes affect plant – pest relationships. *GCB Bioenergy*, 12(10), 864–877.

Doğan, B., Driha, O. M., Balsalobre Lorente, D., and Shahzad, U. (2021). The mitigating effects of economic complexity and renewable energy on carbon emissions in developed countries. *Sustainable Development*, 29(1), 1–12.

Dorward, A., Anderson, S., Bernal, Y. N., Vera, E. S., Rushton, J., Pattison, J., and Paz, R. (2009). Hanging in, stepping up and stepping out: livelihood aspirations and strategies of the poor. *Development in Practice*, 19(2), 240–247. https://doi.org/10.1080/09614520802689535

Doss, C. R. (2018). Women and agricultural productivity: reframing the issues. *Development Policy Review*, 36(1), 35–50. https://doi.org/10.1111/DPR.12243

Drechsel, P., Gyiele, L., and Kunze, D. (2001). Population density, soil nutrient depletion, and economic growth in sub-Saharan Africa. *Ecological Economics*, 38(2), 251–258.

Duker, A., Cambaza, C., Saveca, P., Ponguane, S., Mawoyo, T. A., Hulshof, M., Nkomo, L., Hussey, S., Van den Pol, B., Vuik, R., Stigter, T., and van der Zaag, P. (2020). Using nature-based water storage for smallholder irrigated agriculture in African drylands: lessons from frugal innovation pilots in Mozambique and Zimbabwe. *Environmental Science and Policy*, 107, 1–6. https://doi.org/10.1016/J.ENVSCI.2020.02.010

Dunaieva, I., Mirschel, W., Popovych, V., Pashtetsky, V., Golovastova, E., Vecherkov, V., Melnichuk, A., Terleev, V., Nikonorov, A., Ginevsky, R., Lazarev, V., and Topaj, A. (2018, December). GIS services for agriculture monitoring and forecasting: development concept. In *Energy management of municipal transportation facilities and transport*, pp. 236–246. Cham: Springer.

The Economist. (2011). Helping the poor to save small wonder. *The Economist*.

Edwards, M. R., & Shultz, C. J. (2005). Reframing agribusiness: moving from farm to market centric. *Journal of Agribusiness*, 23(345-2016-15095), 57–73.

Esposito, B., Sessa, M. R., Sica, D., and Malandrino, O. (2020). Towards circular economy in the agri-food sector: a systematic literature review. *Sustainability*, 12(18), 7401.

Eswaran, H., Lal, R., and Reich, P. F. (2019). Land degradation: an overview. *Response to Land Degradation*, 20–35.

FAO. (2019). *The state of food and agriculture 2019*. Rome: FAO.

FAO. (2018). *Sustainable food systems concept and framework*. Rome: FAO.

Foster, J. B. (2009). *The ecological revolution*. New York: Monthly Review Press.

Frank, S., Havlík, P., Soussana, J. F., Levesque, A., Valin, H., Wollenberg, E., Obersteiner, M. et al. (2017). Reducing greenhouse gas emissions in agriculture without compromising food security? *Environmental Research Letters*, 12(10), 105004.

Fuglie, K. O., Gautam, M., Goyal, A., and Maloney, W. F. (2019). *Harvesting prosperity: technology and productivity growth in agriculture*. Washington, DC: World Bank Publications.

Fuglie, K. O., and Toole, A. A. (2014). The evolving institutional structure of public and private agricultural research. *American Journal of Agricultural Economics*, 96(3), 862–883.

Galli, A., Wiedmann, T. O., Ercin, E., Knoblauch, D., Ewing, B. R., and Giljum, S. (2011). *Integrating ecological, carbon and water footprint: defining the footprint family and its application in tracking human pressure on the planet*. Open-EU. https://research.utwente.nl/en/publications/integrating-ecological-carbon-and-water-footprint-into-a-footprin/fingerprints/

Garnett, T., Appleby, M. C., Balmford, A., Bateman, I. J., Benton, T. G., Bloomer, P., and Godfray, H. C. J. (2013). Sustainable intensification in agriculture: premises and policies. *Science*, 341(6141), 33–34.

Global Sustainable Development Report. (2019). *The future is now – science for achieving sustainable development*. UNCCD.

Gokmenoglu, K. K., Taspinar, N., and Kaakeh, M. (2019). Agriculture-induced environmental Kuznets curve: the case of China. *Environmental Science and Pollution Research*, 26(36), 37137–37151.

Gomez-Zavaglia, A., Mejuto, J. C., and Simal-Gandara, J. (2020). Mitigation of emerging implications of climate change on food production systems. *Food Research International*, 134, 109256.

Güney, T. (2019). Renewable energy, non-renewable energy and sustainable development. *International Journal of Sustainable Development and World Ecology*, 26(5), 389–397.

Guo, J., Zhou, Y., Ali, S., Shahzad, U., and Cui, L. (2021). Exploring the role of green innovation and investment in energy for environmental quality: an empirical appraisal from provincial data of China. *Journal of Environmental Management*, 292, 112779.

Hajer, M. A., Westhoek, H., Ingram, J., Van Berkum, S., and Özay, L. (2016). Food systems and natural resources. United Nations Environmental Programme. https://www.mdpi.com/2071-1050/14/13/7739/pdf

Hinson, R., Lensink, R., and Mueller, A. (2019). Transforming agribusiness in developing countries: SDGs and the role of FinTech. *Current Opinion in Environmental Sustainability*, 41, 1–9.

Hoddinott, J., Berhane, G., Gilligan, D. O., Kumar, N., and Seyoum Taffesse, A. (2012). The impact of Ethiopia's productive safety net programme and related transfers on agricultural productivity. *Journal of African Economies*, 21(5), 761–786.

Hoekstra, A. Y. (2008). *Water neutral: reducing and offsetting the impacts of water footprints: business water footprint accounting Hoekstr*. Value of Water Research Report Series No. 28. Delft, The Netherlands: UNESCO-IHE. www.waterfootprint.org34

Hoekstra, A. Y., and Wiedmann, T. O. (2014). Humanity's unsustainable environmental footprint. *Science*, 344(6188), 1114–1117.

Holloway, J., and Mengersen, K. (2018). Statistical machine learning methods and remote sensing for sustainable development goals: a review. *Remote Sensing*, 10(9), 1365.

Hosonuma, N., Herold, M., De Sy, V., De Fries, R. S., Brockhaus, M., Verchot, L., and Romijn, E. (2012). An assessment of deforestation and forest degradation drivers in developing countries. *Environmental Research Letters*, 7(4), 044009.

Howden, M. (2019). UN climate change report: land clearing and farming contribute a third of the world's greenhouse gases. *The Conversation*, 8.

Huber, J. (2000). Towards industrial ecology: sustainable development as a concept of ecological modernization. *Journal of Environmental Policy and Planning*, 2(4), 269–285.

Hurni, H., Giger, M., Liniger, H., Studer, R. M., Messerli, P., Portner, B., Breu, T. et al. (2015). Soils, agriculture and food security: the interplay between ecosystem functioning and human well-being. *Current Opinion in Environmental Sustainability*, 15, 25–34.

Iannella, M., De Simone, W., D'Alessandro, P., Console, G., and Biondi, M. (2019). Investigating the current and future co-occurrence of *Ambrosia artemisiifolia* and *Ophraella communa* in Europe through ecological modelling and remote sensing data analysis. *International Journal of Environmental Research and Public Health*, 16(18), 3416.

Iizumi, T., and Kim, W. (2019). Recent improvements to global seasonal crop forecasting and related research. In *Adaptation to climate change in agriculture*, pp. 97–110. Singapore: Springer.

Ioris, A. A. (2018). The politics of agribusiness and the business of sustainability. *Sustainability*, 10(5), 1648.

Kabir, M. S., Salam, M. U., Islam, A. K. M. S., Sarkar, M. A. R., Mamun, M. A. A., Rahman, M. C., Rahman, N. M. F. et al. (2020). Doubling rice productivity in Bangladesh: a way to achieving SDG 2 and moving forward. *Bangladesh Rice Journal*, 24(2), 1–47.

Karlan, D., and Zinman, J. (2009). Observing unobservables: identifying information asymmetries with a consumer credit field experiment. *Econometrica*, 77(6), 1993–2008. https://doi.org/10.3982/ECTA5781

Kitonsa, H., and Kruglikov, S. V. (2018). Significance of drone technology for achievement of the United Nations sustainable development goals. *R-Economy*, 4(3), 115–120.

Kjeldsen-Kragh, S. (2007). *The role of agriculture in economic development: the lessons of history*. Copenhagen: Business School Press.

Koc, M. (2016). Sustainability: a tool for food system reform? In *Imagining sustainable food systems*, pp. 37–46. London: Routledge.

Kopittke, P. M., Menzies, N. W., Wang, P., McKenna, B. A., and Lombi, E. (2019). Soil and the intensification of agriculture for global food security. *Environment International*, 132, 105078.

Kumar, A., Pramanik, M., Chaudhary, S., and Negi, M. S. (2021). Land evaluation for sustainable development of Himalayan agriculture using RS-GIS in conjunction with analytic hierarchy process and frequency ratio. *Journal of the Saudi Society of Agricultural Sciences*, 20(1), 1–17.

Kumar, P., Thakur, P. K., Bansod, B. K., and Debnath, S. K. (2017). Multi-criteria evaluation of hydro-geological and anthropogenic parameters for the groundwater vulnerability assessment. *Environmental Monitoring and Assessment*, 189(11), 1–24.

Kumar, S. K., and Babu, S. D. B. (2016). A web GIS based decision support system for agriculture crop monitoring system-A case study from part of Medak district. *Journal of Remote Sensing and GIS*, 5(177), 2.

Lambin, E. F., and Meyfroidt, P. (2011). Global land use change, economic globalization, and the looming land scarcity. *Proceedings of the National Academy of Sciences*, 108(9), 3465–3472.

Ligon, E., and Sadoulet, E. (2007). *Estimating the effects of aggregate agricultural growth on the distribution of expenditures, background paper for the world development report 2008*. https://openknowledge.worldbank.org/handle/10986/9096

Lipper, L., Cavatassi, R., Symons, R., Gordes, A., and Page, O. (2021). Financing adaptation for resilient livelihoods under food system transformation: the role of multilateral development banks. *Food Security*, 1–16.

Lubwama, F. (2011). *Can labor saving technologies help rural women in Uganda? The case of the manual forage chopper for smallholder dairy farmers*. ICWES 15: The 15th International Conference for Women Engineers and Scientists. https://www.slideshare.net/EngineersAustralia/icwes15-can-labour-saving-technologies-help-rural-women-in-uganda-the-case-of-the-manual-forage-chopper-for-smallholder-dairy-farms-presented-by-florence-b-lubwama-kiyimba-national-agricultural-research-organization-uganda

Luhmann, H., and Theuvsen, L. (2016). Corporate social responsibility in agribusiness: literature review and future research directions. *Journal of Agricultural and Environmental Ethics*, 29(4), 673–696.

Magdoff, F., Foster, J. B., and Buttel, F. H. (Eds.). (2000). *Hungry for profit: The agribusiness threat to farmers, food, and the environment*. New York: New York University Press.

Mahapa, S. M., and Mashiri, M. (2010). Social exclusion and rural transport: gender aspects of a road improvement project in Tshitwe, Northern Province. *Development Southern Africa*, 18(3), 365–376. https://doi.org/10.1080/03768350120070026

Malhotra, S. K. (2017). Horticultural crops and climate change: a review. *The Indian Journal of Agricultural Sciences*, 87(1), 12–22. https://epubs.icar.org.in/index.php/IJAgS/article/view/67138

Mbow, C., Rosenzweig, C., Barioni, L. G., Benton, T. G., Herrero, M., Krishnapillai, M., Xu, Y. et al. (2019). Climate change and land. Chapter 5: food security. IPCC Special Report Global Warming of 1.5°C, pp. 1–200. https://www.ipcc.ch/srccl/cite-report/

McCarthy, N., Lipper, L., and Zilberman, D. (2018). Economics of climate smart agriculture: an overview. *Climate Smart Agriculture*, 31–47.

Mehta, C. R., Chandel, N. S., Jena, P. C., and Jha, A. (2019). Indian agriculture counting on farm mechanization. *Agricultural Mechanization in Asia, Africa and Latin America*, 50(1), 84–89.

Merchant, A. (2016). Climate change challenges: catalyst for sustainable development. *Climate Change in the Bay of Bengal Region*, 111.

Middendorf, G., Skladany, M., Ransom, E., and Busch, L. (2013). New agricultural biotechnologies: the struggle for democratic choice. In Counihan, Carole M. (Ed.), *Food in the USA*, pp. 383–394. London: Routledge.

Mink, S. D. (2016). *Findings across agricultural public expenditure reviews in African countries*, vol. 1522. Washington, DC: International Food Policy Research Institute.

Molina-Maturano, J., Bucher, J., and Speelman, S. (2020). Understanding and evaluating the sustainability of frugal water innovations in México: an exploratory case study. *Journal of Cleaner Production*, 274, 122692. https://doi.org/10.1016/J.JCLEPRO.2020.122692

Moran, D. D., Lenzen, M., Kanemoto, K., and Geschke, A. (2013). Does ecologically unequal exchange occur? *Ecological Economics*, 89, 177–186.

Musona, J. (2021). New business models for frugal innovation: experience from an enterprise supporting sustainable smallholder agriculture in Kenya. *Frugal Innovation and Its Implementation: Leveraging Constraints to Drive Innovations on a Global Scale*, 165. https://doi.org/10.1007/978-3-030-67119-8_8

Nathaniel, S. P., Yalçiner, K., and Bekun, F. V. (2021). Assessing the environmental sustainability corridor: linking natural resources, renewable energy, human capital, and ecological footprint in BRICS. *Resources Policy*, 70, 101924.

Nerini, F. F., Sovacool, B., Hughes, N., Cozzi, L., Cosgrave, E., Howells, M., Milligan, B. et al. (2019). Connecting climate action with other sustainable development goals. *Nature Sustainability*, 2(8), 674–680.

Nilsson, A., Bergquist, M., and Schultz, W. P. (2017). Spillover effects in environmental behaviors, across time and context: a review and research agenda. *Environmental Education Research*, 23(4), 573–589. https://doi.org/10.1080/13504622.2016.1250148

Noel, S. (2015). *Economics of land degradation initiative: report for policy and decision makers_ Reaping economic and environmental benefits from sustainable land management*. Bonn, Germany: ELD Initiative and Deutsche Gesellschaft für Internationale Zusammenarbeit (GIZ) GmbH.

Ogunlana, E. A. (2004). The technology adoption behavior of women farmers: the case of alley farming in Nigeria. *Renewable Agriculture and Food*, 19(1), 57–65.

O'Neill, D. W., Fanning, A. L., Lamb, W. F., and Steinberger, J. K. (2018). A good life for all within planetary boundaries. *Nature Sustainability*, 1(2), 88–95.

Pamuk, H., Bulte, E., Adekunle, A., and Diagne, A. (2015). Decentralised innovation systems and poverty reduction: experimental evidence from Central Africa. *European Review of Agricultural Economics*, 42(1), 99–127. https://doi.org/10.1093/ERAE/JBU007

Pansera, M., and Sarkar, S. (2016). Crafting sustainable development solutions: frugal innovations of grassroots entrepreneurs. *Sustainability (Switzerland)*, 8(1), 1–51. https://doi.org/10.3390/su8010051

Paroda, R. S., and Joshi, P. K. (2019). Sustainable development goals: role of agriculture. In Chaturvedi, S., James, T., Saha, S., and Shaw, P. (Eds.), *2030 agenda and India: moving from quantity to quality. South Asia economic and policy studies*. Singapore: Springer.

Patra, S., and Samal, P. (2018). Integrated farming system in India: a holistic approach to magnify the economic status of innovative farmers. *Journal of Pharmacognosy and Phytochemistry*, 7(3), 3632–3636.

Pearson, T. R., Brown, S., Murray, L., and Sidman, G. (2017). Greenhouse gas emissions from tropical forest degradation: an underestimated source. *Carbon Balance and Management*, 12(1), 1–11.

Pharo, P., and Oppenheim, J. (2019). *Growing better: ten critical transitions to transform food and land use*. https://www.foodandlandusecoalition.org/wp-content/uploads/2019/09/FOLU-GrowingBetter-GlobalReport.pdf

Pierce, F. J., and Clay, D. E. (Eds.). (2007). *GIS applications in agriculture*, vol. 1. New York: CRC Press.

Pierce-Quinonez, M. (2012). *Are we planning for sustainable food systems? An evaluation of the goals and vision of food system assessments and their usefulness to planning* (Doctoral dissertation), Tufts University, Boston.

Portmann, F. T., Siebert, S., and Döll, P. (2010). MIRCA2000 – global monthly irrigated and rainfed crop areas around the year 2000: a new high-resolution data set for agricultural and hydrological modeling. *Global Biogeochemical Cycles*, 24(1).

Power, W. (2009). *Life cycle management: how business uses it to decrease footprint, create opportunities and make value chains more sustainable.* Washington, DC: United Nations Environment Programme and Society of Environmental Toxicology and Chemistry Europe.

Prabhu, J. (2017). Frugal innovation: doing more with less for more. *Philosophical Transactions of the Royal Society A: Mathematical, Physical and Engineering Sciences.* https://doi.org/10.1098/rsta.2016.0372

Prahalad, C. K. (2005). *The fortune at the bottom of the pyramid.* New Delhi: Wharton School Pub.

Praharaj, C. S., Singh, U., Singh, S. S., and Kumar, N. (2018). Tactical water management in field crops: the key to resource conservation. *Current Science*, 115(7), 1262–1269.

Radoglou-Grammatikis, P., Sarigiannidis, P., Lagkas, T., and Moscholios, I. (2020). A compilation of UAV applications for precision agriculture. *Computer Networks*, 172, 107148.

Ragasa, C. (2012). *Gender and institutional dimensions of agricultural technology adoption: a review of literature and synthesis of 35 case studies.* International Association of Agricultural Economists (IAAE) Triennial Conference, Brazil.

Rao, B. C. (2014). Alleviating poverty in the twenty-first century through frugal innovations. *Challenge*, 57(3), 40–59. https://doi.org/10.2753/0577-5132570302

Rao, N. C., Bathla, S., Kumar, A., and Jha, G. K. (2018). Agriculture and sustainable development goals: an overview and issues. *Agricultural Economics Research Review*, 31, 1–7.

Rapier, R. (2020). Renewable energy growth continues at a blistering pace. *Forbes*.

Reardon, T., Lu, L., and Zilberman, D. (2019). Links among innovation, food system transformation, and technology adoption, with implications for food policy: overview of a special issue. *Food Policy*, 83, 285–288.

Reddy, Y. R., Sastry, N. S. R., Varma, C. G., and Rao, K. S. (2017). Nutritional security: holistic animal farming approach for livelihood security and sustainability. *Indian Journal of Animal Production and Management*, 33(3–4), 112–119.

Riedo, J., Wettstein, F. E., Rösch, A., Herzog, C., Banerjee, S., Büchi, L., and van der Heijden, M. G. (2021). Widespread occurrence of pesticides in organically managed agricultural soils – the ghost of a conventional agricultural past? *Environmental Science and Technology*, 55(5), 2919–2928.

Saleem, N., and Shujah-ur-Rahman, J. Z. (2019). The impact of human capital and biocapacity on environment: environmental quality measure through ecological footprint and greenhouse gases. *Journal of Pollution Effects & Control*, 7(237), 10–35248.

Schipanski, M. E., MacDonald, G. K., Rosenzweig, S., Chappell, M. J., Bennett, E. M., Kerr, R. B., Schnarr, C. et al. (2016). Realizing resilient food systems. *BioScience*, 66(7), 600–610.

Schroeder, P., Anggraeni, K., and Weber, U. (2019). The relevance of circular economy practices to the sustainable development goals. *Journal of Industrial Ecology*, 23(1), 77–95.

Schwoob, M. H., Timmer, P., Andersson, M., and Treyer, S. (2019). Agricultural transformation pathways toward the SDGs. In *Agriculture and food systems to 2050: global trends, challenges and opportunities*, pp. 417–436. Rome: FAO.

Shahzad, U., Fareed, Z., Shahzad, F., and Shahzad, K. (2021). Investigating the nexus between economic complexity, energy consumption and ecological footprint for the United States: new insights from quantile methods. *Journal of Cleaner Production*, 279, 123806.

Sharma, A., Kumar, V., Shahzad, B., Tanveer, M., Sidhu, G. P. S., Handa, N., and Thukral, A. K. (2019). Worldwide pesticide usage and its impacts on ecosystem. *SN Applied Sciences*, 1(11), 1–16.

Sharma, G. D., Shah, M. I., Shahzad, U., Jain, M., and Chopra, R. (2021). Exploring the nexus between agriculture and greenhouse gas emissions in BIMSTEC region: the role of renewable energy and human capital as moderators. *Journal of Environmental Management*, 297, 113316.

Shiva, V. (2000). North-South conflicts in intellectual property rights. *Peace Review*, 12(4), 501–508.

Sijtsema, S. J., Fogliano, V., and Hageman, M. (2020). Tool to support citizen participation and multidisciplinarity in food innovation: circular food design. *Frontiers in Sustainable Food Systems*, 4.

Singh, S. (2018). Reforming agricultural markets in India. *Economic and Political Weekly*, 53(51), 15–18.

Singh, S., Ahlawat, S., and Sanwal, S. (2017). Role of ICT in agriculture: policy implications. *Oriental Journal of Computer Science and Technology*, 10(3), 691–697.

Smyth, S. J., Webb, S. R., and Phillips, P. W. (2021). The role of public-private partnerships in improving global food security. *Global Food Security*, 31, 100588.

Spielman, D. J., Hartwich, F., and Grebmer, K. (2010). Public–private partnerships and developing-country agriculture: evidence from the international agricultural research system. *Public Administration and Development*, 30(4), 261–276.

Springmann, M., Mason-D'Croz, D., Robinson, S., Wiebe, K., Godfray, H. C. J., Rayner, M., and Scarborough, P. (2017). Mitigation potential and global health impacts from emissions pricing of food commodities. *Nature Climate Change*, 7(1), 69–74.

Stads, G. J., and Beintema, N. M. (2017). *A comprehensive overview of investments and human resource capacity in African agricultural research*. https://www.researchgate.net/publication/241485007_Diversity_in_Agricultural_Research_Resources_in_the_Asia-Pacific_Region

Steckel, R. H., and White, W. J. (2012). *Engines of growth: farm tractors and twentieth-century U.S. economic welfare*. NBER Working Papers, 17879. https://www.nber.org/system/files/working_papers/w17879/w17879.pdf

Tallontire, A., Dolan, C., Smith, S., and Barrientos, S. (2005). Reaching the marginalised? Gender value chains and ethical trade in African horticulture. *Development in Practice*, 15(3–4), 559–571. https://doi.org/10.1080/09614520500075771

Taylor, R. G., Scanlon, B., Döll, P., Rodell, M., Van Beek, R., Wada, Y., and Treidel, H. (2013). Ground water and climate change. *Nature Climate Change*, 3(4), 322–329.

Termeer, C. J., Drimie, S., Ingram, J., Pereira, L., and Whittingham, M. J. (2018). A diagnostic framework for food system governance arrangements: the case of South Africa. *NJAS-Wageningen Journal of Life Sciences*, 84, 85–93.

Teshager, A. D., Gassman, P. W., Schoof, J. T., and Secchi, S. (2016). Assessment of impacts of agricultural and climate change scenarios on watershed water quantity and quality, and crop production. *Hydrology and Earth System Sciences*, 20(8), 3325–3342.

Therond, O., Duru, M., Roger-Estrade, J., and Richard, G. (2017). A new analytical framework of farming system and agriculture model diversities: a review. *Agronomy for Sustainable Development*, 37(3), 1–24.

Tramberend, S., Fischer, G., Bruckner, M., and van Velthuizen, H. (2019). Our common cropland: quantifying global agricultural land use from a consumption perspective. *Ecological Economics*, 157, 332–341.

Trienekens, J. H. (2011). Agricultural value chains in developing countries: a framework for analysis. *International Food and Agribusiness Management Review*, 14(2), 51–83.

Tsiboe, F., Zereyesus, Y. A., Popp, J. S., and Osei, E. (2018). The effect of women's empowerment in agriculture on household nutrition and food poverty in Northern Ghana.

*Social Indicators Research*, 138, 89–108. https://doi.org/10.1007/S11205-017-1659-4/TABLES/5

United Nations. (2015). Transforming our world: the 2030 agenda for sustainable development. *United Nations*, 41. https://sustainabledevelopment.un.org/post2015/transformingourworld

United Nations. (2017). World population prospects: The 2017 revision, key findings and advance tables. *Working Paper No. ESA/P/WP/248*, United Nations, New York, NY. https://population.un.org/wpp/publications/files/wpp2017_keyfindings.pdf

United Nations. (2018). Challenges and opportunities in achieving gender equality and the empowerment of rural women and girls. In *Women 2000: gender equality, development and peace for the twenty-first century*. New York: United Nations.

United Nations. (2019). *Global conference on strengthening synergies*. Copenhagen, Denmark: United Nations.

US Briefing. (2013). *International energy outlook 2013*, 506–507. US Energy Information Administration. https://www.scirp.org/(S(i43dyn45te-exjx455qlt3d2q))/reference/referencespapers.aspx?referenceid=3190760

Van Berkum, S., Dengerink, J., and Ruben, R. (2018). *The food systems approach: sustainable solutions for a sufficient supply of healthy food*. No. 2018-064. Wageningen Economic Research. https://www.mdpi.com/2071-1050/14/15/9716/pdf

van Leeuwen, C. C., Cammeraat, E. L., de Vente, J., and Boix-Fayos, C. (2019). The evolution of soil conservation policies targeting land abandonment and soil erosion in Spain: a review. *Land Use Policy*, 83, 174–186.

Venkatramanan, V., and Shah, S. (2019). Climate smart agriculture technologies for environmental management: the intersection of sustainability, resilience, wellbeing and development. In *Sustainable green technologies for environmental management*, pp. 29–51. Singapore: Springer.

Wada, Y. (2014). Sustainability of global water use: past reconstruction and future projections. *Environmental Research Letters*, 9(10), 104003.

Wada, Y., Van Beek, L. P. H., and Bierkens, M. F. (2011). Modelling global water stress of the recent past: on the relative importance of trends in water demand and climate variability. *Hydrology and Earth System Sciences*, 15(12), 3785–3808.

Wang, Z., Jebli, M. B., Madaleno, M., Doğan, B., and Shahzad, U. (2021). Does export product quality and renewable energy induce carbon dioxide emissions: evidence from leading complex and renewable energy economies. *Renewable Energy*, 171, 360–370.

Wani, S. P., Chander, G., Sahrawat, K. L., Pal, D. K., Pathak, P., Pardhasaradhi, G., and Kamadi, P. J. (2016). Sustainable use of natural resources for crop intensification and better livelihoods in the rainfed semi-arid tropics of central India. *NJAS-Wageningen Journal of Life Science*, 78, 13–19, September.

Weyrauch, T., and Herstatt, C. (2017). What is frugal innovation? Three defining criteria. *Journal of Frugal Innovation*, 2(1), 1. https://doi.org/10.1186/s40669-016-0005-y

Wiedmann, T., and Lenzen, M. (2018). Environmental and social footprints of international trade. *Nature Geoscience*, 11(5), 314–321.

Wiedmann, T., and Minx, J. (2008). A definition of 'carbon footprint'. *Ecological Economics Research Trends*, 1, 1–11.

Wilkinson, J. (2009). The globalization of agribusiness and developing world food systems. *Monthly Review*, 61(4), 38.

Wolf, B. (2007). The monopolization of biodiversity: terminator bioscience and the criminalization of the harvest. *Theory and Science*, 9(3).

World Bank. (2021). *The world bank annual report 2021: from crisis to green, resilient, and inclusive recovery*. Washington, DC: World Bank.

Zarbà, C., Chinnici, G., La Via, G., Bracco, S., Pecorino, B., and D'Amico, M. (2021). Regulatory elements on the circular economy: driving into the agri-food system. *Sustainability*, 13(15), 8350.

Zeschky, M., Winterhalter, S., and Gassmann, O. (2014). *"Resource – constrained innovation": classification and implications for multinational firms*. The XXV ISPIM Conference – Innovation for Sustainable Economy and Society, June. https://www.alexandria.unisg.ch/232147/1/ZeschkyWinterhalterGassmann_ISPIM2014_final.pdf

Zurek, M., Hebinck, A., and Selomane, O. (2020). *Food and agriculture systems foresight study: implications for climate change and the environment-synthesis*. https://www.researchgate.net/publication/348499397_Looking_across_diverse_food_system_futures_Implications_for_climate_change_and_the_environment

# 3 The sustainability disclosure on gender equality

Insights from Italian agri-food listed companies

*Filomena Buonocore, Davide de Gennaro, Concetta Metallo, and Sabrina Pisano*

## Introduction

A very interesting attempt to support sustainable development is represented by the 2030 Agenda for Sustainable Development. It is a set of goals for people, the environment, and economic growth which are mainly based on 17 Sustainable Development Goals (SDGs), framed within a broader program of action consisting of 169 sub-goals. This is a series of initiatives, signed on September 25, 2015, by the governments of the 193 UN member countries and approved by the UN General Assembly, that focus on the environmental, economic, social, and institutional spheres and should be implemented by 2030. The 17 Goals (see Figure 3.1) are a set of important development issues that aim to end poverty, combat inequality, address climate change, and build peaceful societies that respect human rights by taking into account the three dimensions of sustainable development – economic, social, and environmental – in a balanced manner (Sachs, 2012).

Among the SDGs, the issue of gender equality takes on considerable importance: other than SDG 5, which is precisely focused on reducing violence and discrimination against women in all areas and of all types, at least 11 of the 17 SDGs refer to gender-related issues (Doss et al., 2018). Work, time, health, power, money, knowledge, and violence are the macro-areas of study on which even the United Nations Universal Declaration of Human Rights focuses in order to ensure a standard of equality within all countries of the European Union (Pascall & Lewis, 2004; Walby, 2004).

This study focuses specifically on gender equality in agri-food businesses, since women being involved and having the chance to make decisions in the agricultural sector is an important source of sustainability (Farnworth et al., 2020), although it is a topic that has been treated in a confusing and sloppy manner in previous studies (Doss et al., 2018). Indeed, agribusiness is a source of development – from all points of view, starting with human and social development and ending with economic development; it is a sector and an activity that can guarantee poverty reduction, especially in the ability to produce and

DOI: 10.4324/9781003223672-5

| #  | **Description of the SDG** |
|----|---|
| 1  | End poverty in all its forms everywhere |
| 2  | End hunger, achieve food security and improved nutrition, and promote sustainable agriculture |
| 3  | Ensure healthy lives and promote well-being for all at all ages |
| 4  | Ensure inclusive and equitable quality education and promote lifelong learning opportunities for all |
| 5  | Achieve gender equality and empower all women and girls |
| 6  | Ensure availability and sustainable management of water and sanitation for all |
| 7  | Ensure access to affordable, reliable, sustainable, and modern energy for all |
| 8  | Promote sustained, inclusive and sustainable economic growth, full and productive employment, and decent work for all |
| 9  | Build resilient infrastructure, promote inclusive and sustainable industrialization, and foster innovation |
| 10 | Reduce inequality within and among countries |
| 11 | Make cities and human settlements inclusive, safe, resilient, and sustainable |
| 12 | Ensure sustainable consumption and production patterns |
| 13 | Take urgent action to combat climate change and its impacts |
| 14 | Conserve and sustainably use the oceans, seas, and marine resources for sustainable development |
| 15 | Protect, restore, and promote sustainable use of terrestrial ecosystems, sustainably manage forests, combat desertification, and halt and reverse land degradation and halt biodiversity loss |
| 16 | Promote peaceful and inclusive societies for sustainable development, provide access to justice for all, and build effective, accountable, and inclusive institutions at all levels |
| 17 | Strengthen the means of implementation and revitalize the global partnership for sustainable development |

*Figure 3.1* Sustainable development goals (SDGs)

Source: https://sdgs.un.org/2030agenda

supply food. In this sense, women play a critical role although this topic, as well as the study of gender equality, is underestimated in literature (Anderson & Sriram, 2019; Giroud & Huaman, 2019). In fact, although pro-gender equality initiatives have proliferated in recent years, the situation is still not acceptable (Collins, 2018; Polar et al., 2021) and women face pervasive difficulties when it comes to emancipating themselves in agribusinesses (Malapit, 2019).

Gender equality is a critical issue that needs further input, especially in this specific economic sector, in light of the SDGs. This chapter aims to investigate sustainability disclosure initiatives in terms of gender equality. Through sustainability reporting prepared by companies, it is in fact possible to identify a series of actions (or omissions) by organizations so that the state of the art can be valued. In particular, the focus is on listed Italian companies in the agricultural and food sector. Focusing on this chapter on gender equality in a context such as Italy can help to understand how much the cultural context can influence these issues and what gender strategies are adopted (Acosta et al., 2021). Implications for theory and practice will be discussed.

## Gender equality and SDGs in agri-food

Women today still live in a condition of strong discrimination in all areas, from the social sphere to the workplace, and in all geographical contexts in different ways and intensities (World Health Organization, 2020), although small improvements in this regard can be appreciated (European Union, 2017).

Assuring women's equality contributes to the development of sustainable economies that benefit society and humankind (Farnworth et al., 2020), also providing and ensuring a peaceful environment (Cortright et al., 2017; Pathania, 2017). Specifically, one of the goals of the SDGs is to demonize and attempt to end all situations in which women experience discriminatory situations or suffer violence, whether in the world of work or in the private and emotional view (Leach, 2016). The SDGs include the progressive elimination of all abusive practices such as, but not limited to, arranged marriages, child brides, and female genital mutilation, and at the same time they enhance women's empowerment in politics, economics, and public life (Miotto et al., 2019).

The SDGs are therefore geared toward improving the status of women, and this certainly also concerns the agricultural sector (Giroud & Huaman, 2019). Gender differences also exist in agriculture, partly because this is traditionally considered a male sector (Doss, 2014). Women actually make up a very substantial number of agricultural workers (Agarwal, 2018; FAO, 2014), and these numbers are growing steadily in virtually every geographic context in the world (Agarwal, 2014). What these data hide is that the hierarchical level and type of work performed are still markedly hierarchically, professionally, and prestigiously different in the agricultural sector (Cross & Bagilhole, 2002).

Some statistics highlight a very high number of women working in the agricultural sector with informal contracts or without being paid (ILO, 2018). Women in agribusiness are characterized by low or no pay, experiencing job uncertainty, instability, and an inability to make a career (Giroud & Huaman, 2019). Women's salaries in the agricultural sector are significantly lower than those of men (in Africa, the gap is from 15% to 60%, Shimeles et al., 2018) but not only that, but their employment contracts are also less stable and more precarious (Oduol et al., 2017). In addition, women generally do not hold top positions on farms, so they are underrepresented in top management and have no opportunity to take part in strategic decisions (Shimeles et al., 2018). Moreover, there is a further problem in terms of the ability to balance the private and working life. This is a critical issue found not only in agriculture but also in all economic sectors. However, in this sector, it is accentuated; surveys have highlighted how women farmers, when considering the hours worked for professional and family activities, have a longer working day than not only farmers but also those employed in other sectors (see Jean & Karbowski, 2020).

There are still obstacles and challenges to affirming the status of women in this particular sector, and in order to overcome these, a renewed political–institutional commitment is needed (Huyer, 2016; Quisumbing et al., 2014). One example is barriers to entry for women in accessing land, as land tenure rules in some countries exclude women (Barrientos, 2019; FAO, 2018). There are numerous statistics that show how, generally, women do not succeed in becoming landowners, also and above all because of (written and unwritten) norms, stereotypes, and social expectations (Agarwal & Bina, 1994). There is also a problem of unequal access to the most profitable crops (Quisumbing et al., 2014) but, first and foremost, of unequal access to services, markets, and market information (UNIDO, 2013), for example, less access to credit to open new businesses and less established marketing infrastructure (World Bank, 2009).

Thus, gaps between men and women in career and salary opportunities remain wide. However, regulations for greater transparency and disclosure about social, as well as environmental, issues can help reduce them. In some countries, it is already mandatory to provide information on matters like differences in pay or employment opportunities, such as in Australia (since 2012), the United Kingdom (since 2017), as well as Ontario (Canada), and California (from January 2021, but not in the rest of the United States). In the Eurozone, Directive 2014/95/EU is the reference decree in this sense.

## Gender equality in sustainability disclosures

Sustainability disclosures have become important components of corporate reporting for promoting accountability and transparency. Sustainability reports published by organizations about their economic, environmental, and social performance help improve dialog with their stakeholders. Thus, people, whether they are partners, suppliers, or even customers of the organizations, want to be informed of an organization's conduct and on how it contributes to the objectives of sustainable development (Ordonez-Ponce & Khare, 2021; Spallini et al., 2021). As a consequence, in recent years there has been a proliferation of sustainability reports (e.g., Schreck & Raithel, 2018), and research has begun to focus on aspects such as actions that support social or environmental sustainability, and especially how organizations measure and sponsor these data (Spallini et al., 2021).

One of the most commonly recognized ways to promote and report on sustainability-related actions is through the use of the global reporting initiative (GRI) standards. The GRI framework consists of guidelines on how to report on the following topics: environmental sustainability, such as environmental impact, resource and waste management, and production; economic sustainability, meaning market presence, indirect economic impacts, and anti-corruption initiatives; and social sustainability, in terms of work conditions, human rights, gender equality, diversity, and health and safety (e.g., Levy et al., 2010; Roca & Searcy, 2012; Skouloudis et al., 2009).

The GRI framework represents a structured and schematic way to talk about sustainability that follows certain benchmark standards (Miles, 2011). Moreover, GRI offers "a guide for business action on the SDGs . . . to assist companies in maximizing their contribution to the SDGs" (GRI, 2015). In fact, GRI offers numerous reporting recommendations for SDGs at a target level, for improving the link between SDGs and the GRI standards (GRI, 2021). Through the GRI framework, organizations can implement the SDGs into business strategy and can report externally on actions implemented that may have an impact on sustainability at all levels (García-Sànchez et al., 2020; Ivic et al., 2021). The GRI standards can be directly linked to the SDGs (e.g., Bebbington & Unerman, 2018; Calabrese et al., 2021; Michalczuk & Konarzewska, 2018) and support organizations in disclosing the effect of their actions on the SDGs (e.g., Calabrese et al., 2021; Tsalis et al., 2020). However, few studies in the literature have focused on the relationship between SDGs and sustainability reporting (Diaz-Sarachaga, 2021). Some scholars proposed a framework for evaluating the information disclosure in corporate sustainability reports to analyze the alignment with the SDGs (Brown et al., 2009), showing that the GRI is a useful measurement tool to operationalize the SDGs (Calabrese et al., 2021; Ordonez-Ponce & Khare, 2021; Tsalis et al., 2020).

With reference to disclosure in terms of gender equality, this is usually included in sustainability's social dimension (Kuhlman & Farrington, 2010) and thus highlighted in corporate reports (Miles, 2011). The importance of gender diversity for organizations generally can be identified in a series of annual reports that organizations are required to prepare (Singh & Pandey, 2019); in particular, thanks to GRI indicators, it is possible to understand the direction in which we are going with regard to gender issues (Oliveira et al., 2018). For example, Vuontisjärvi (2006) pointed out that stakeholders are interested in having information on the employment of minorities or women, equal opportunities, work–life balance, or diversity topics. In particular, Grosser et al. (2008) highlighted how investors perceive an organization's engagement in terms of diversity and gender equality issues as an indicator "of the quality of the management and leadership of the company." However, studies focusing on sustainability disclosure showed that gender equality is an issue that has remained under-researched and often overlooked or handled superficially (Grosser & Moon 2005, 2008, 2019; Maj, 2018; Oliveira et al., 2018).

Given the importance of the topic and the attention it captures from a range of different actors and stakeholders, the literature reports many studies on gender dynamics in organizations and how they are reported externally (e.g., Alvarez, 2015; Chapple & Humphrey, 2014; Ehnert et al., 2016; Furlotti et al., 2019; García-Sánchez et al., 2020; Gazzola et al., 2016; Issa & Fang, 2019; Nath et al., 2013; Pisano & Alvino, 2015). Many of these studies use GRI guidelines to examine sustainability reporting practices related to human resources, but these studies have not specifically addressed gender equality reporting (Grosser & Moon, 2019). Very little research has analyzed the gender equality policies and practices disclosed by organizations in their annual reports (e.g., Benschop & Meihuizen, 2002; Grosser & Moon, 2005, 2008; Maji, 2019; Singh & Pandey, 2019), and fewer still are the scholars that have analyzed the degree of disclosure about gender equality through the sustainability report, with reference to GRI standards linked to SDG 5 (e.g., da Rocha Garcia et al.,

2021; Kocollari et al., 2021). For example, Miotto et al. (2019) analyzed gender equality practices in sustainable reports from business schools, focusing on SDG 5. Meanwhile, da Rocha Garcia et al. (2021) looked to see if sustainability reports of Brazilian companies were in line with GRI standards, adopting greater disclosure of gender equality.

Despite the importance of social sustainability disclosure, much research has shown that, for the agricultural industry, these practices are neglected, highlighting the need for greater transparency for operators in the sector (e.g., Bellantuono et al., 2018). Literature agrees that gender equity should play a key role in the sustainability and the development of the agricultural sector, also suggesting specific metrics and indicators, studying this phenomenon in different geographical and social contexts (Dekeyser et al., 2018; Ruiz-Almeida & Rivera-Ferre, 2019) and showing that greater transparency and accountability improve profitability for agri-food organizations (e.g., Conca et al., 2021). However, there's still limited attention within the agricultural sector when it comes to the disclosure of gender equality.

## A study of listed agri-food companies in Italy

### Sample and data source

This study puts all agri-food companies listed in Italy as of December 31, 2021, under a magnifying glass, since they had drawn up sustainability reports according to Directive 2014/95/EU. Table 3.1 reports the size, measured using the sales in 2020, for each sampled company. The size of the companies analyzed varies from a minimum value of € 80.4 (B.F.) to a maximum of €.1.772.0 (Campari).

Most of these companies have their registered offices in Northern Italy; only one company (La Doria) has its registered office in Southern Italy. However, all companies analyzed have different manufacturing facilities around various Italian regions (except for Valsoia) and operate in different countries around the world. The attention to sustainability is demonstrated also by the presence of a specific section dedicated to sustainability issues on the website of five out of six companies (B.F., Campari, La Doria, Orsero, Valsoia).

The reporting fiscal baseline year that was used in this study is 2020.

Table 3.1 The sample

| Company | Registered office | Sales (€/000000) |
|---|---|---|
| B.F. | Ferrara | 80.4 |
| Campari | Milano | 1,772.0 |
| La Doria | Angri | 848.1 |
| Newlat Food | Reggio Emilia | 516.9 |
| Orsero | Albenga | 1,041.5 |
| Valsoia | Bologna | 83.5 |

## Research method

Disclosure in terms of gender equality was measured using content analysis (Krippendorff, 2013). To select the information that companies had to release, this study referred to the GRI disclosures contained in the GRI standards (2016) linked to SDG 5 (see Table 3.2).

Table 3.2 GRI standards on social and employee matters linked to the targets of SDG 5 on gender equality

| Targets of SDG 5 | GRI standard | GRI disclosure |
| --- | --- | --- |
| **5.1 End all forms of discrimination against all women and girls everywhere** | GRI 202: Market Presence | Disclosure 202–1 Ratios of standard entry level wage by gender compared to local minimum wage |
| | GRI 401: Employment | Disclosure 401–1 New employee hires and employee turnover |
| | | Disclosure 401–3 Parental leave |
| | GRI 404: Training and Education | Disclosure 404–1 Average hours of training per year per employee |
| | | Disclosure 404–3 Percentage of employees receiving regular performance and career development reviews |
| | GRI 405: Diversity and Equal Opportunity | Disclosure 405–1 Diversity of governance bodies and employees |
| | | Disclosure 405–2 Ratio of basic salary and remuneration of women to men |
| | GRI 406: Non-discrimination | Disclosure 406–1 Incidents of discrimination and corrective actions taken |
| **5.2 Eliminate all forms of violence against all women and girls in the public and private spheres, including trafficking and sexual and other types of exploitation** | GRI 408: Child Labor | Disclosure 408–1 Operations and suppliers at significant risk for incidents of child labor |
| | GRI 409: Forced or Compulsory Labor | Disclosure 409–1 Operations and suppliers at significant risk for incidents of forced or compulsory labor |
| | GRI 414: Supplier Social Assessment | Disclosure 414–1 New suppliers that were screened using social criteria |
| | | Disclosure 414–2 Negative social impacts in the supply chain and actions taken |

| Targets of SDG 5 | GRI standard | GRI disclosure |
|---|---|---|
| **5.4 Recognize and value unpaid care and domestic work through the provision of public services, infrastructure and social protection policies, and the promotion of shared responsibility within the household and the family as nationally appropriate** | GRI 203: Indirect Economic Impacts<br><br>GRI 401: Employment | Disclosure 203–1 Infrastructure investments and services supported<br><br>Disclosure 401–2 Benefits provided to full-time employees that are not provided to temporary or part-time employees<br><br>Disclosure 401–3 Parental leave |
| **5.5 Ensure women's full and effective participation and equal opportunities for leadership at all levels of decision-making in political, economic, and public life** | GRI 102: General disclosures<br><br><br><br>GRI 405: Diversity and Equal Opportunity | Disclosure 102–22 Composition of the highest governance bodies and its committee<br><br>Disclosure 102–24 Nominating and selecting the highest governance body<br><br>Disclosure 405–1 Diversity of governance bodies and employees |

Once the GRI disclosure items were selected, the sustainability report of each sampled company was investigated, and data were gathered for each item.

A score of 1 was assigned to each GRI disclosure released. The level of disclosure about gender equality was computed by counting the number of GRI disclosures provided.

$$\textit{Disclosure on gender equality}_i = \sum_{n=0}^{k} \textit{GRI disclosure}_{in}$$

The disclosure about gender equality of company i is equal to the sum of GRI disclosures provided by the company i.

Two associate professors conducted the analysis. To control for intercoder reliability, Krippendorff's alpha was computed, which gave a 93% result.

### Results

Table 3.3 shows the disclosure about gender equality provided by the listed Italian agri-food companies investigated.

The last two columns indicate the quantity of organizations, in both absolute and relative values, which provided information on the specific GRI disclosure

72  Filomena Buonocore et al.

Table 3.3 The human resource disclosure released by Italian listed agri-food companies

| Targets of SDG 5 | GRI standard | GRI disclosure | Number of companies | % of companies |
|---|---|---|---|---|
| 5.1 | GRI 202: Market Presence | Disclosure 202–1 | 1 | 16% |
|  | GRI 401: Employment | Disclosure 401–1 | 6 | 100% |
|  |  | Disclosure 401–3 | 0 | 0% |
|  | GRI 404: Training and Education | Disclosure 404–1 | 6 | 100% |
|  |  | Disclosure 404–3 | 1 | 16% |
|  | GRI 405: Diversity and Equal Opportunity | Disclosure 405–1 | 6 | 100% |
|  |  | Disclosure 405–2 | 3 | 50% |
|  | GRI 406: Non-discrimination | Disclosure 406–1 | 4 | 66% |
| 5.2 | GRI 408: Child Labor | Disclosure 408–1 | 2 | 33% |
|  | GRI 409: Forced or Compulsory Labor | Disclosure 409–1 | 2 | 33% |
|  | GRI 414: Supplier Social Assessment | Disclosure 414–1 | 4 | 66% |
|  |  | Disclosure 414–2 | 1 | 16% |
| 5.4 | GRI 203: Indirect Economic Impacts | Disclosure 203–1 | 0 | 0% |
|  | GRI 401: Employment | Disclosure 401–2 | 1 | 16% |
|  |  | Disclosure 401–3 | 0 | 0% |
| 5.5 | GRI 102: General disclosures | Disclosure 102–22 | 1 | 16% |
|  |  | Disclosure 102–24 | 1 | 16% |
|  | GRI 405: Diversity and Equal Opportunity | Disclosure 405–1 | 5 | 100% |

identified in column 3. Most information is released pertaining to targets 5.1, 5.2, and 5.5; fewer data are disclosed pertaining to target 5.4. This means that all companies investigated contribute to all the SDG 5 targets recognized; however, they do not provide information on all the items identified by the GRI standards linked to this SDG. On average, the level of disclosure about gender equality is low: the average number of companies providing data on all GRI disclosures is 2.5.

More specifically and with reference to target 5.1, all companies provided information on GRI disclosure 401–1, 404–1, and 405–1, by describing newly hired employees and employee turnover by demographic characteristics, such as the average hours of employee training[1]. Most companies released data on GRI disclosure 405–2 (Campari, La Doria, Newlat Food) and 406–1 (B.F., La Doria, Newlat Food, Orsero), mainly describing and highlighting possible gender-based wage differentials[2]. Only Newlat Food gave information on GRI disclosure 404–3, and only Campari released data on GRI disclosure 202–1. Finally, no companies released data on GRI disclosure 401–3 on parental leave.

With respect to target 5.2, the majority of companies (Campari, La Doria, Newlat Food, Orsero) released data on GRI disclosure 414–1, and this suggests that there is a focus on the sustainability aspect with reference to supply. In addition, Campari and Orsero provided data on GRI disclosure 408–1 and 409–1 about child and compulsory labor, and only La Doria disclosed information on GRI disclosure 414–2.

*Table 3.4* The companies' rank

| Company | Quantity of disclosure about gender equality |
|---|---|
| Campari | 9 |
| La Doria | 9 |
| Newlat Food | 8 |
| Orsero | 8 |
| Valsoia | 6 |
| B.F. | 5 |

Moving on to target 5.4, none of the companies released data on both GRI disclosure 203–1, related to infrastructure, and 401–3, having to do with parental leave. Only La Doria disclosed information on GRI disclosure 401–2, and this is a relevant indicator with reference to the types of contracts through which workers are incardinated.

Finally, with respect to target 5.5, all companies provided information on GRI disclosure 405–1, as reported for target 5.1, and only Valsoia disclosed data on GRI disclosure 102–22 and 102–24 on the top management's characteristics.

Table 3.4 ranks the analyzed companies according to the quantity of disclosure about gender equality.

Campari and La Doria are the companies that received the highest scores. However, Newlat Food and Orsero were close behind. Valsoia and B.F. saw the lowest values.

Table 3.5 reports the quality of the disclosure about gender equality. More specifically, this study investigates three dimensions of quality (Beattie et al., 2004; Pisano & Alvino, 2015), that is, nature, type, and time orientation. Column 2 exclusively reports the GRI disclosures for which at least one company released information. Each cell shows the percentage of companies that provided information on the specific GRI disclosure indicated in column 2, respecting the quality attribute reported in columns 3–9.

With respect to nature, for some GRI disclosures (e.g., 202–1 or 401–2) all companies exclusively reported qualitative data, and for others (e.g., 404–3 or 414–2) they exclusively disclosed quantitative information. It probably depends on the specific type of information to provide. For other GRI disclosures, companies released both quantitative and qualitative information. With respect to GRI disclosure 404–1, for example, all companies released quantitative data on the average hours of employee training and, except for Valsoia, thoroughly described, in a narrative manner, the training programs carried out. With regard to GRI disclosure 405–2, all companies provided both quantitative data and a detailed description of (any) gender wage differences.

Moving on to the type dimension, all the information released was non-financial, except for the GRI disclosure 404–1, for which one company (Campari) also added data on the costs sustained for employee training.

74  *Filomena Buonocore et al.*

*Table 3.5* The quality of disclosure about gender equality released by listed Italian agri-food companies

| Targets of SDG 5 | GRI disclosure | Nature | | Type | | Time orientation | | |
|---|---|---|---|---|---|---|---|---|
| | | Qualitative | Quantitative | Financial | Non-financial | Historical | Present | Forward-looking |
| 5.1 | Disclosure 202–1 | 100% | 0% | 0% | 100% | 0% | 100% | 0% |
| | Disclosure 401–1 | 16% | 100% | 0% | 100% | 100% | 100% | 0% |
| | Disclosure 404–1 | 83% | 100% | 16% | 100% | 100% | 100% | 33% |
| | Disclosure 404–3 | 0% | 100% | 0% | 100% | 100% | 100% | 0% |
| | Disclosure 405–1 | 66% | 100% | 0% | 100% | 100% | 100% | 0% |
| | Disclosure 405–2 | 100% | 100% | 0% | 100% | 100% | 100% | 0% |
| | Disclosure 406–1 | 100% | 25% | 0% | 100% | 25% | 100% | 0% |
| 5.2 | Disclosure 408–1 | 100% | 0% | 0% | 100% | 0% | 100% | 0% |
| | Disclosure 409–1 | 100% | 0% | 0% | 100% | 0% | 100% | 0% |
| | Disclosure 414–1 | 75% | 25% | 0% | 100% | 0% | 100% | 0% |
| | Disclosure 414–2 | 0% | 100% | 0% | 100% | 100% | 100% | 0% |
| 5.4 | Disclosure 401–2 | 100% | 0% | 0% | 100% | 0% | 100% | 0% |
| 5.5 | Disclosure 102–22 | 100% | 0% | 0% | 100% | 0% | 100% | 0% |
| | Disclosure 102–24 | 100% | 0% | 0% | 100% | 0% | 100% | 0% |
| | Disclosure 405–1 | 66% | 100% | 0% | 100% | 100% | 100% | 0% |

Finally, with respect to the time orientation dimension, for all GRI disclosures companies provided information concerning the year to which the sustainability report refers. In addition, for most GRI disclosures companies also reported the data for the previous year. Exclusively for disclosure 404–1, two companies (La Doria and Orsero) described the training programs that will be carried out next year, providing forward-looking information.

## Emerging drivers for gender reporting in the Italian agri-food sector

Findings from the study reveal a low level of disclosure about gender equality, although the increasing requirement for gender equity in agri-food companies by food sovereignty (Ruiz-Almeida & Rivera-Ferre, 2019). While these are interesting insights, they do not differ particularly from the literature on the topic in revealing that almost all companies provided data on gender issues in workforce profile and training (e.g., Kocollari et al., 2021), little information on gender equality in career development (e.g., Grosser & Moon, 2008) and no or little data on SDG targets 5.2 and 5.4 (Oliveira et al., 2018; Singh & Pandey, 2019). All companies referred to the GRI standards, making their sustainability reports more comparable. Therefore, the issuing of GRI standards enhanced the quality of the information released, overlapping the limits of the findings of previous studies revealing non-comparable reports (e.g., Grosser & Moon, 2008; Vuontisjärvi, 2006).

Companies mainly release sustainability reports to communicate that their activities are consistent with social values, in order to obtain legitimacy and support from stakeholders (De Villiers & Marques, 2016). The release of gender equality information, in fact, reflects the company vision of equal opportunities policies (Lee & Parpart, 2018), improving financial performance of agri-food companies (Conca et al., 2021). In this sense, the release of data on gender equality by bigger companies required by a number of national and international amendments will further encourage the implementation of an integrated approach to equal opportunities (Kocollari et al., 2021).

### *Practical implications*

Organizations play an important role in achieving gender equality. In general, organizations should promote policies and practices for gender equality so as to facilitate the reconciliation of family, work, and private life, and again, provide fair pay and encourage the participation of all actors in decision-making processes.

In terms of participation, organizations can come up with a social responsibility policy to create mechanisms capable of averting the risk of discrimination, violence, and harassment, establish measures to increase female representation in the company, collaborate with other entities, and invest in initiatives that promote SDG #5.

Typically, in industries related to engineering or information technology, there is a higher percentage of men, while in areas related to education and health, there is a higher percentage of women. Thus, issues related to gender roles are of particular importance. Organizations can set medium- or long-term goals and attempt to reduce this disparity and take it into account in hiring processes. Organizations can also encourage men and women to have equal time off for parenting responsibilities.

In terms of cultural identity, companies can hire women from the most vulnerable social groups and offer education and job training opportunities; and also, this is the right opportunity for organizations to stand up as "champions of justice" in promoting gender equality in all contexts, from the advertising of their products to the treatment of staff in the company.

## Notes

1 However, it is important to note that, with respect to GRI disclosure 401–1, some companies (B.F., La Doria, Orsero) only described the turnover, without providing information on the new employee hired, and Valsoia did not provide the breakdown of both the new employee hired and the turnover by gender. With regard to GRI disclosure 404–1, La Doria and Valsoia did not provide the breakdown of the average hours of training programs, as opposed to Valsoia which details its activities.
2 With reference to GRI disclosure 406–1, all the companies providing this information reported to not be aware of episodes of discrimination occurred during the year.

## References

Acosta, M., van Wessel, M., van Bommel, S., & Feindt, P. H. (2021). Examining the promise of 'the local' for improving gender equality in agriculture and climate change adaptation. *Third World Quarterly*, *42*(6), 1135–1156. https://doi.org/10.1080/01436597.2021.1882845

Agarwal, B. (2014). Food sovereignty, food security and democratic choice: Critical contradictions, difficult conciliations. *Journal of Peasant Studies*, *41*(6), 1247–1268. https://doi.org/10.1080/03066150.2013.876996

Agarwal, B. (2018). Gender equality, food security and the sustainable development goals. *Current Opinion in Environmental Sustainability*, *34*, 26–32. https://doi.org/10.1016/j.cosust.2018.07.002

Agarwal, B., & Bina, A. (1994). *A field of one's own: Gender and land rights in South Asia* (No. 58). Cambridge University Press.

Alvarez, A. (2015). Corporate response to human resource disclosure recommendations. *Social Responsibility Journal*, *11*(2), 306–323. https://doi.org/10.1108/SRJ-06-2013-0076

Anderson, S., & Sriram, V. (2019). Moving beyond Sisyphus in agriculture R&D to be climate smart and not gender blind. *Frontiers in Sustainable Food Systems*, *3*, 84. https://doi.org/10.3389/fsufs.2019.00084

Barrientos, S. (2019). *Gender and work in global value chains: Capturing the gains*. Cambridge University Press.

Beattie, V., McInnes, B., & Fearnley, S. (2004). A methodology for analyzing and evaluating narratives in annual reports: A comprehensive descriptive profile and metrics for disclosure quality attributes. In *Accounting forum* (Vol. 28, No. 3, pp. 205–236). Elsevier. https://doi.org/10.1016/j.accfor.2004.07.001

Bebbington, J., & Unerman, J. (2018). Achieving the United Nations sustainable development goals: An enabling role for accounting research. *Accounting, Auditing & Accountability Journal*, *31*(1), 2–24. https://doi.org/10.1108/AAAJ-05-2017-2929

Bellantuono, N., Pontrandolfo, P., & Scozzi, B. (2018). Guiding materiality analysis for sustainability reporting: The case of agri-food sector. *International Journal of Technology, Policy and Management*, *18*(4), 336–359. https://doi.org/10.1504/IJTPM.2018.096181

Benschop, Y., & Meihuizen, H. E. (2002). Keeping up gendered appearances: Representations of gender in financial annual reports. *Accounting, Organizations and Society*, *27*(7), 611–636. https://doi.org/10.1016/S0361-3682(01)00049-6

Brown, H. S., de Jong, M., & Levy, D. L. (2009). Building institutions based on information disclosure: Lessons from GRI's sustainability reporting. *Journal of Cleaner Production*, *17*(6), 571–580. https://doi.org/10.1016/j.jclepro.2008.12.009

Calabrese, A., Costa, R., Gastaldi, M., Ghiron, N. L., & Montalvan, R. A. V. (2021). Implications for sustainable development goals: A framework to assess company disclosure in sustainability reporting. *Journal of Cleaner Production*, *319*, 128624. https://doi.org/10.1016/j.jclepro.2021.128624

Chapple, L., & Humphrey, J. E. (2014). Does board gender diversity have a financial impact? Evidence using stock portfolio performance. *Journal of Business Ethics*, *122*(4), 709–723. https://doi.org/10.1007/s10551-013-1785-0

Collins, A. (2018). Saying all the right things? Gendered discourse in climate-smart agriculture. *The Journal of Peasant Studies*, *45*(1), 175–191. https://doi.org/10.1080/03066150.2017.1377187

Conca, L., Manta, F., Morrone, D., & Toma, P. (2021). The impact of direct environmental, social, and governance reporting: Empirical evidence in European-listed companies in the agri--food sector. *Business Strategy and the Environment*, *30*(2), 1080–1093. https://doi.org/10.1002/bse.2672

Cortright, D., Seyle, C., & Wall, K. (2017). *Governance for peace: How inclusive, participatory and accountable institutions promote peace and prosperity*. Cambridge University Press.

Cross, S., & Bagilhole, B. (2002). Girls' jobs for the boys? Men, masculinity and non-traditional occupations. *Gender, Work & Organization*, *9*(2), 204–226. https://doi.org/10.1111/1468-0432.00156

da Rocha Garcia, E. A., Araújo, I. A., & Albuquerque Filho, A. R. (2021). Level of social disclosure of Brazilian companies regarding the sustainable development objectives of United Nations (UN). *Contextus: Revista Contemporânea de Economia e Gestão*, *19*, 217–231.

Dekeyser, K., Korsten, L., & Fioramonti, L. (2018). Food sovereignty: Shifting debates on democratic food governance. *Food Security*, *10*(1), 223–233. https://doi.org/10.1007/s12571-017-0763-2

De Villiers, C., & Marques, A. (2016). Corporate social responsibility, country-level predispositions, and the consequences of choosing a level of disclosure. *Accounting and Business Research*, *46*(2), 167–195. https://doi.org/10.1080/00014788.2015.1039476

Diaz-Sarachaga, J. M. (2021). Shortcomings in reporting contributions towards the sustainable development goals. *Corporate Social Responsibility and Environmental Management*, *28*(4), 1299–1312. https://doi.org/10.1002/csr.2129

Doss, C. (2014). Data needs for gender analysis in agriculture. In *Gender in agriculture* (pp. 55–68). Springer. https://doi.org/10.1007/978-94-017-8616-4_3

Doss, C., Meinzen-Dick, R., Quisumbing, A., & Theis, S. (2018). Women in agriculture: Four myths. *Global Food Security*, *16*, 69–74. http://dx.doi.org/10.1016/j.gfs.2017.10.001

Ehnert, I., Parsa, S., Roper, I., Wagner, M., & Muller-Camen, M. (2016). Reporting on sustainability and HRM: A comparative study of sustainability reporting practices by the world's largest companies. *The International Journal of Human Resource Management*, 27(1), 88–108. https://doi.org/10.1080/09585192.2015.1024157

European Union. (2017). *Sustainable development in the European Union: Monitoring report on progress towards the SDGs in an EU context*. European Union.

FAO. (2014). *State of food and agriculture, women in agriculture: Closing the gender gap in development*. Food & Agriculture Organization.

FAO. (2018). *Empowering rural women, powering agriculture*. Food & Agriculture Organization.

Farnworth, C. R., Badstue, L., Williams, G. J., Tegbaru, A., & Gaya, H. I. M. (2020). Unequal partners: associations between power, agency and benefits among women and men maize farmers in Nigeria. *Gender, Technology and Development*, 24(3), 271–296. https://doi.org/10.1080/09718524.2020.1794607

Furlotti, K., Mazza, T., Tibiletti, V., & Triani, S. (2019). Women in top positions on boards of directors: Gender policies disclosed in Italian sustainability reporting. *Corporate Social Responsibility and Environmental Management*, 26(1), 57–70. https://doi.org/10.1002/csr.1657

García-Sánchez, I. M., Oliveira, M. C., & Martínez-Ferrero, J. (2020). Female directors and gender issues reporting: The impact of stakeholder engagement at country level. *Corporate Social Responsibility and Environmental Management*, 27(1), 369–382. https://doi.org/10.1002/csr.1811

García-Sánchez, I. M., Rodríguez-Ariza, L., Aibar-Guzmán, B., & Aibar-Guzmán, C. (2020). Do institutional investors drive corporate transparency regarding business contribution to the sustainable development goals? *Business Strategy and the Environment*, 29(5), 2019–2036. https://doi.org/10.1002/bse.2485

Gazzola, P., Sepashvili, E., & Pezzetti, R. (2016). CSR as a mean to promote gender equality. *Economia Aziendale Online*, 7(1), 95–99. https://doi.org/10.6092/2038-5498/7.1.95-99

Giroud, A., & Huaman, J. S. (2019). Investment in agriculture and gender equality in developing countries. *Transnational Corporations*, 26(3), 89–113.

GRI. (2015). *SDG compass: The guide for business action on the SGD's*. Global Reporting Initiative. https://sdgcompass.org/wp-content/uploads/2015/12/019104_SDG_Compass_Guide_2015.pdf

GRI. (2021). *Linking the SDGs and the GRI standards*. Global Reporting Initiative. www.globalreporting.org/public-policy-partnerships/sustainable-development/integrating-sdgs-into-sustainability-reporting/

Grosser, K., & Moon, J. (2005). Gender mainstreaming and corporate social responsibility: Reporting workplace issues. *Journal of Business Ethics*, 62(4), 327–340. https://doi.org/10.1007/s10551-005-5334-3

Grosser, K., & Moon, J. (2008). Developments in company reporting on workplace gender equality?: A corporate social responsibility perspective. In *Accounting forum* (Vol. 32, No. 3, pp. 179–198). Elsevier. https://doi.org/10.1016/j.accfor.2008.01.004

Grosser, K., & Moon, J. (2019). CSR and feminist organization studies: Towards an integrated theorization for the analysis of gender issues. *Journal of Business Ethics*, 155(2), 321–342. https://doi.org/10.1007/s10551-017-3510-x

Grosser, K., Moon, J., & Adams, C. (2008). *Equal opportunity for women in the workplace: A study of corporate disclosure*. ACCA.

Huyer, S. (2016). Closing the gender gap in agriculture. *Gender, Technology and Development*, 20(2), 105–116. https://doi.org/10.1177/0971852416643872

ILO. (2018). *Women and men in the informal economy: A statistical picture*. International Labour Office.

Issa, A., & Fang, H. X. (2019). The impact of board gender diversity on corporate social responsibility in the Arab Gulf states. *Gender in Management*, *34*(7), 577–605. https://doi.org/10.1108/GM-07-2018-0087

Ivic, A., Saviolidis, N. M., & Johannsdottir, L. (2021). Drivers of sustainability practices and contributions to sustainable development evident in sustainability reports of European mining companies. *Discover Sustainability*, *2*(1), 1–20. https://doi.org/10.1007/s43621-021-00025-y

Jean, M., & Karbowski, E. (2020). *Working women, the backbone of family farms*. Michigan State University Extension.

Kocollari U., Addabbo, T., & Girardi, A. (2021). Measuring progress on SDG 5: Insights from private companies to research performing organizations. In *4th international conference on gender research ICGR 2021* (pp. 148–155). Academic Conferences International Limited Reading.

Krippendorff, K. (2013). *Content analysis: An introduction to its methodology*. Sage Publications.

Kuhlman, T., & Farrington, J. (2010). What is sustainability? *Sustainability*, *2*(11), 3436–3448. https://doi.org/10.3390/su2113436

Leach, M. (2016). *Gender equality and sustainable development*. Routledge.

Lee, J., & Parpart, J. L. (2018). Constructing gender identity through masculinity in CSR reports: The South Korean case. *Business Ethics: A European Review*, *27*(4), 309–323. https://doi.org/10.1111/beer.12191

Levy, D. L., Szejnwald Brown, H., & De Jong, M. (2010). The contested politics of corporate governance: The case of the global reporting initiative. *Business & Society*, *49*(1), 88–115. https://doi.org/10.1177/0007650309345420

Maj, J. (2018). Embedding diversity in sustainability reporting. *Sustainability*, *10*(7), 2487. https://doi.org/10.3390/su10072487

Maji, S. G. (2019). Disclosure pattern of labour practices and decent work and its impact on corporate financial performance: Evidence from Asia. *Global Business Review*. https://doi.org/10.1177/0972150919876523

Malapit, H. J. (2019). Women in agriculture and the implications for nutrition. *Agriculture for Improved Nutrition: Seizing the Momentum*, 58–67.

Michalczuk, G., & Konarzewska, U. (2018). The use of GRI standards in reporting on actions being taken by companies for sustainable development. *Optimum: Economic Studies*, *4*(94), 72–86. https://doi.org/10.15290/oes.2018.04.94.07

Miles, K. (2011). Embedding gender in sustainability reports. *Sustainability Accounting, Management and Policy Journal*, *2*(1), 139–146. https://doi.org/10.1108/20408021111162164

Miotto, G., Polo López, M., & Rom Rodríguez, J. (2019). Gender equality and UN sustainable development goals: Priorities and correlations in the top business schools' communication and legitimation strategies. *Sustainability*, *11*(2), 302. https://doi.org/10.3390/su11020302

Nath, L., Holder-Webb, L., & Cohen, J. (2013). Will women lead the way? Differences in demand for corporate social responsibility information for investment decisions. *Journal of Business Ethics*, *118*(1), 85–102. https://doi.org/10.1007/s10551-012-1573-2

Oduol, J. B. A., Mithöfer, D., Place, F., Nang'ole, E., Olwande, J., Kirimi, L., & Mathenge, M. (2017). Women's participation in high value agricultural commodity chains in Kenya: Strategies for closing the gender gap. *Journal of Rural Studies*, *50*, 228–239. https://doi.org/10.1016/j.jrurstud.2017.01.005

Oliveira, M. C., Júnior, M. S. R., de Oliveira Lima, S. H., & De Freitas, G. A. (2018). The influence of the characteristics of the national business system in the disclosure of gender-related corporate social responsibility practices. *Administrative Sciences*, *8*(2), 14. https://doi.org/10.3390/admsci8020014

Ordonez-Ponce, E., & Khare, A. (2021). GRI 300 as a measurement tool for the United Nations sustainable development goals: Assessing the impact of car makers on sustainability. *Journal of Environmental Planning and Management*, *64*(1), 47–75. https://doi.org/10.1080/09640568.2020.1746906

Pascall, G., & Lewis, J. (2004). Emerging gender regimes and policies for gender equality in a wider Europe. *Journal of Social Policy*, *33*(3), 373–394. https://doi.org/10.1017/S004727940400772X

Pathania, S. K. (2017). Sustainable development goal: Gender equality for women's empowerment and human rights. *International Journal of Research*, *5*(4), 72–82. https://doi.org/10.29121/granthaalayah.v5.i4.2017.1797

Pisano, S., & Alvino, F. (2015). New European Union's requirements and IFRS practice statement "management commentary": Does MD&A disclosure quality affect analysts' forecasts. *Journal of Modern Accounting and Auditing*, *11*(6), 283–301. https://doi.org/10.17265/1548-6583/2015.06.001

Polar, V., Mohan, R. R., McDougall, C., Teeken, B., Mulema, A. A., Marimo, P., & Yila, J. O. (2021). Examining choice to advance gender equality in breeding research. *Advancing Gender Equality Through Agricultural and Environmental Research: Past, Present, and Future*, 77.

Quisumbing, A. R., Meinzen-Dick, R., Raney, T. L., Croppenstedt, A., Behrman, J. A., & Peterman, A. (2014). *Gender in agriculture* (p. 444). Springer.

Roca, L. C., & Searcy, C. (2012). An analysis of indicators disclosed in corporate sustainability reports. *Journal of Cleaner Production*, *20*(1), 103–118. https://doi.org/10.1016/j.jclepro.2011.08.002

Ruiz-Almeida, A., & Rivera-Ferre, M. G. (2019). Internationally-based indicators to measure agri-food systems sustainability using food sovereignty as a conceptual framework. *Food Security*, *11*(6), 1321–1337. https://doi.org/10.1007/s12571-019-00964-5

Sachs, J. D. (2012). From millennium development goals to sustainable development goals. *The Lancet*, *379*(9832), 2206–2211. https://doi.org/10.1016/S0140-6736(12)60685-0

Schreck, P., & Raithel, S. (2018). Corporate social performance, firm size, and organizational visibility: Distinct and joint effects on voluntary sustainability reporting. *Business & Society*, *57*(4), 742–778. https://doi.org/10.1177/0007650315613120

Shimeles, A., Verdier-Chouchane, A., & Boly, A. (2018). *Building a resilient and sustainable agriculture in Sub-Saharan Africa*. Palgrave Macmillan. https://doi.org/10.1007/978-3-319-76222-7

Singh, S., & Pandey, M. (2019). Women-friendly policies disclosure by companies in India. *Equality, Diversity and Inclusion: An International Journal*, *38*(8), 857–869. https://doi.org/10.1108/EDI-12-2017-0291

Skouloudis, A., Evangelinos, K., & Kourmousis, F. (2009). Development of an evaluation methodology for triple bottom line reports using international standards on reporting. *Environmental Management*, *44*(2), 298–311. https://doi.org/10.1007%2Fs00267-009-9305-9

Spallini, S., Milone, V., Nisio, A., & Romanazzi, P. (2021). The dimension of sustainability: A comparative analysis of broadness of information in Italian companies. *Sustainability*, *13*(3), 1457. https://doi.org/10.3390/su13031457

Tsalis, T. A., Malamateniou, K. E., Koulouriotis, D., & Nikolaou, I. E. (2020). New challenges for corporate sustainability reporting: United Nations' 2030 agenda for sustainable development and the sustainable development goals. *Corporate Social Responsibility and Environmental Management, 27*(4), 1617–1629. https://doi.org/10.1002/csr.1910

UNIDO. (2013). *Converting commodities into products: The role of women in least developed countries (LDCs)*. United Nations Industrial Development Organization.

Vuontisjärvi, T. (2006). Corporate social reporting in the European context and human resource disclosures: An analysis of Finnish companies. *Journal of Business Ethics, 69*(4), 331–354. https://doi.org/10.1007/s10551-006-9094-5

Walby, S. (2004). The European Union and gender equality: Emergent varieties of gender regime. *Social Politics: International Studies in Gender, State & Society, 11*(1), 4–29. https://doi.org/10.1093/sp/jxh024

World Bank. (2009). *Gender in agriculture sourcebook*. World Bank.

World Health Organization. (2020). *HRP annual report 2019*. WHO.

# Part II
# The role of business models and ecosystems

# 4 Inclusive value creation in the coffee industry

A framework of blockchain-enabled dynamic capabilities for sustainable international supply chain transformation

*Maria Jell-Ojobor and Michael Paul Kramer*

## Introduction

In recent years, when making purchasing decisions, coffee market customers have become interested in knowing more about the source of coffee cherries and beans and how they are processed in their countries of origin. Embracing the "from farm to fork" concept introduced by the European Food Safety Authority (EFSA) to trace food throughout the entire supply chain, these customers are best served by a business model in which the supply chain relationship between coffee producers and farmers becomes shorter, more direct, and more inclusive. Sustainable business models of international coffee supply chains integrate organic, fair, and green practices to address the pillars of economic, social, and environmental responsibility.

While sustainable business models and practices can lead to a positive brand reputation and increase the customer's willingness to pay premium prices, they are also more complex than traditional methods. The dominant trade relationships in coffee supply chains occur with farmers in developing countries, characterized by economic, political, institutional, cultural, and geographic distances. These factors pose challenges to the implementation and monitoring of sustainable practices (Kshetri, 2021). Furthermore, cause-conscious stakeholders and the spread of information in globally connected markets increase the constant pressure to enhance sustainable practices in these distant countries.

The challenging conditions of international coffee supply chains call for business model innovations that will ensure a company's financial performance and competitive advantage in the long run. Digital transformations of supply chains are important sources of value creation (Amit & Zott, 2001; Schlecht, Schneider, & Buchwald, 2021) for sustainable business models. Blockchain technology has evolved as a novel way to restructure traditional supply chain relationships in the coffee industry. While the use of blockchain technology to organize and manage business relationships is only in its infancy, research has shown its great potential for efficiency and differentiation, especially for sustainable business models in the agri-food industry (Aldrighetti,

DOI: 10.4324/9781003223672-7

Canavari, & Hingley, 2021; Cole, Stevenson, & Aitken, 2019; Feng et al., 2020; Hald & Kinra, 2019; Rocha, de Oliveira, & Talamini, 2021; Saberi et al., 2019). To use blockchain technology effectively, we need to develop a rigorous framework to guide its implementation in sustainable supply chains (Queiroz, Telles, & Bonilla, 2019; Wang, Han, & Beynon-Davies, 2019).

Our study presents a theoretical framework of blockchain-transformed business models of sustainable coffee supply chains. On the basis of the dynamic capabilities of resource-based theory, we explain how the proactive strategy of international coffee brands to invest in the complementary asset (Barney & Mackey, 2005; Teece, 1986) of blockchain technology helps them release dynamic capabilities (e.g., Eisenhardt & Martin, 2000; Teece, 2007; Teece, Pisano, & Shuen, 1997) that they can then use to reconfigure their existing resources and capabilities to meet the challenges of dynamic markets (Beske, 2012; Hong, Zhang, & Ding, 2018; Santa-Maria, Vermeulen, & Baumgartner, 2021). Thus, blockchain-transformed business models create intangible assets, such as reputation, trust, and bonding, that are sources of long-term financial and competitive benefits for international coffee supply chains.

Our study helps explain the long-term competitiveness of sustainable coffee supply chains with regard to their economic, social, and environmental responsibility (Hong, Zhang, & Ding, 2018; Saberi et al., 2019). Building on the dynamic capabilities of strategic supply chain management (Hitt, Xu, & Carnes, 2016), we maintain that the adoption of blockchain technology helps create the novel resources and capabilities necessary for sustainable practices (Schilke, Hu, & Helfat, 2018). Our framework responds to the call for more theoretical explanations about the use of blockchain technology in sustainable supply chains (Queiroz et al., 2019; Wang, Han, & Beynon-Davies, 2019). Ultimately, our study shows that blockchain-transformed business models help balance the distribution of value among coffee supply chain partners in industrialized, developing, and emerging countries (Cole et al., 2019; Kshetri, 2021; Wang, Han, & Beynon-Davies, 2019).

**Sustainable supply chains**

Sustainable development should meet "the needs of the present without compromising the ability of future generations to meet their own needs" (World Commission on Environment and Development, 1987). Grounded in the concept of the triple bottom line (Elkington, 1994), stakeholders such as governments, society, and businesses must collaborate on the three interdependent dimensions of economic growth (profit), environmental improvement (planet), and social equity (people), without compromising the ability to meet the needs of future generations (Dyllick & Hockerts, 2002). Therefore, when coordinating the processes of marketing, manufacturing, information systems, purchasing, and logistics, sustainable supply chain management considers all three dimensions of sustainable development – economic, social, and environmental – that stakeholders demand (Seuring & Müller, 2008).

Emphasizing the businesses' responsibility for the social dimension, the strategy of corporate social responsibility has become an integral part of business practices to incorporate major stakeholder issues into their methods, while deriving economic and competitive benefits from doing so. While firms can respond to their stakeholders with responsible actions in economic, ethical, legal, and philanthropic areas (Carroll, 1979), strategies targeting the last dimension are the most likely to produce long-term benefits for both society and the firms (Jell-Ojobor, 2019). Anchored on the concept of creating shared value (Kramer & Porter, 2011), firms should develop new business models to enhance their competitiveness and simultaneously improve the economic and social conditions in the communities in which they operate. While no unified framework of sustainable supply chain management practices exists (e.g., Hong et al., 2018), such an approach to internal and external supply chain management practices demonstrates corporate social responsibility and creates shared value for all involved (Kleindorfer, Singhal, & Van Wassenhove, 2005).

*Coffee supply chains*

Increased productivity in food production across continents provides quality supplies to a growing population. Nevertheless, it does not eradicate hunger, is often inefficient and wastes food, and damages the environment in the most vulnerable parts of the world, particularly Sub-Saharan Africa (e.g., FAO, 2021; Lampridi et al., 2019). Hence, sustainable supply chain management in the agri-food industry aims to tackle the societal divide between industrialized and developing countries by transforming all of the stages of producing, processing, marketing, distributing, and consuming agricultural and food products (Borsellino, Schimmenti, & El Bilali, 2020).

There are about 50 countries worldwide that export coffee beans. These countries, located in the "Coffee Belt," have a favorable climate for growing coffee. Most of them are in Africa, Asia, South America, and North America. The market leader is Brazil, followed by Vietnam, and Colombia, which together account for about 61% of the total coffee production globally (Lewin, Giovannucci, & Varangis, 2004; Ponte, 2002). Due to several policy changes and the deregulation of the coffee export market in the 1980s and 1990s, power has shifted from coffee-producing countries to coffee-consuming countries, transforming coffee into a buyer-driven commodity (Ponte, 2002).

The actors in coffee supply chains are (1) growers or producers, (2) processors, (3) wholesalers, (4) retailers, (5) consumers, (6) traders/brokers, and (7) other parties (Kramer, Bitsch, & Hanf, 2021). Due to the dismantling of regulatory coffee boards and associations, such as the International Coffee Agreement (ICA) and the Association of Coffee Producer Countries (ACPC), coffee-producing countries are unable to compete with international traders, ceding market power to large international traders, such as Neumann Kaffee Gruppe, Ecom Agroindustrial, Olam, Volcafé, Louis Dreyfus Company, and Sucafina. Therefore, international traders sell either green coffee (unroasted coffee beans) or bulk instant coffee to buyers, either directly from its origin (producing countries) or via the spot markets in the United States and Europe. Because roasted coffee loses its freshness quickly, three powerful groups – Nestlé, JAB (Jacobs Douwe Egberts) Holding, and Lavazza – do most of the processing, such as the roasting, blending, and repackaging of bulk instant coffee. These large companies have massive investments in brand marketing and advertising and control the coffee chain in the consuming countries where they operate (Grabs & Ponte, 2019). Roasters then distribute the processed coffee to retailers, restaurants, or cafés.

Prompted by cause-conscious consumers and local communities concerned with the environmental impact and welfare of coffee farmers (Giovannucci & Koekoek, 2003), roasters, traders, manufacturers, and retailers have integrated sustainability practices into their operations, resulting in the creation of new business models and marketing strategies that we will explore in the following sections.

## Blockchain technology in agri-food supply chains

> We have proposed a system for electronic transactions without relying on trust.
> (Nakamoto, 2008)

Blockchain is a potentially disruptive technology that can transform the economy, society, and organizations alike (Kamilaris, Fonts, & Prenafeta-Boldú, 2019; Kramer, Bitsch, & Hanf, 2021; Pietrewicz, 2019). Its best-known application is Bitcoin, a peer-to-peer digital currency solution (Nakamoto, 2008). Blockchain is a software protocol that uses a distributed data storage facility for an evenly shared and constantly synchronized ledger distributed across locations and entities. It is based on distributed ledger technology, which is the umbrella term for blockchain technology. Like the role of DNA in biological organisms, which stores genetic information long term, blockchain stores transaction data long-term. Blockchain technology is comprised of intelligently combined IT solutions, creating a novel meta-technology. One of the key characteristics of blockchain is its consensus mechanism and the decentralization of the network architecture, enabling peer-to-peer transactions between untrusted parties, which eliminates the need for a coordinating trusted entity or intermediaries. Where the most important tasks of DNA are to enable cell growth through reproduction and cell repair, the consensus algorithm in blockchain technology confirms transaction data immutably. In doing so, it enables the reproduction of new transaction blocks, leading to a growing number of blocks in the blockchain. Due to its consensus algorithm, trust and transparency can be introduced into supply chains. The trust that is provided by the central authority in hierarchical organizations is replaced by the consensus algorithm because transactions can be executed only when the participants approve them. Other factors that promote trust are the visibility of the transactions, the immutability of chained data blocks, and the virtual anonymity of the trading entities. Blockchain is not limited to financial industries. Several industries have adopted the technology. Indeed, its application in the food industry, with its centralized supply chains, seems to be the most efficient utilization of this novel technology (Gartner, 2019; Kramer, Bitsch, & Hanf, 2021).

Blockchain technology has been designed with the intention of excluding a central authority coordinating the network. During its evolution in the first phase (Furlonger & Uzureau, 2019), private and consortium blockchain technology platform types emerged that provide centralized control, despite their decentralized architecture. As a result, three different blockchain platforms currently exist: public, private, and consortium. What all platforms have in common is the distributed ledger technology, peer-to-peer transaction capability, and a consensus mechanism. The platforms differ primarily in their access rights and rights to read from and write to the ledger. They also differ with regard to their governance mechanisms, such as incentives and consensus algorithms. Decision-making through consensus and incentives are governance categories, in both organizations and firms (Gulati, Nohria, & Zaheer, 2000) and in blockchain technology (Beck, Müller-Bloch, & King, 2018). Where the intensity of control in vertical, coordinated agri-food supply chains moves along a continuum ranging from the spot market to vertical integration, the blockchain governance continuum ranges from controlless to single command. Control in blockchain governance can therefore be described as a continuum in which the intensity of control ranges from no control in public networks to sole control by a single authority in truly centralized implementations (Kramer, Bitsch, & Hanf, 2022).

The choice of the appropriate blockchain technology platform in sustainable supply chain implementations will have a profound effect on the efficiency and, hence, on the sustainability of the agri-food supply chain network. There are studies examining the success of using various platforms (Groombridge, 2020). Findings indicate that the most successful implementations are in a vertically coordinated ecosystem and focus on providing provenance as well as tracking and tracing information. These factors are important in giving credence to companies in the agri-food supply chain. Blockchain implementations are primarily successful in private- and consortium-type platforms where the participation of firms is mandated by a centrally acting entity and mass consensus is excluded. However, the lack of public blockchain governance in private- and consortium-type blockchains can be compensated for by addressing intrinsic motivational factors (Kramer, Bitsch, & Hanf, 2021).

Given that blockchain technology is still in its infancy, the availability of tracking and tracing solutions in its first development phase does not reflect a complete blockchain solution. For example, tokenization and true decentralization capabilities have not been implemented yet (Furlonger & Uzureau, 2019). However, blockchain sustainable business models address the three areas of the triple bottom line. They meet social demands through consensus algorithms and coordination mechanisms that promote trust and behavioral intentions, as well as the use behavior of stakeholders. They meet environmental demands by using energy-efficient consensus algorithms. Finally, they meet economic demands by reducing transaction costs by eliminating intermediaries and exploiting intangible assets, such as trust and reputation. The advent of tokenization and true decentralization in phase two should increase economic sustainability even more.

## Theoretical framework

Grounded in the resource-based view (Barney, 1991; Conner, 1991; Nelson & Winter, 1982; Rumelt, 1984; Wernerfelt, 1984) and combined with strategic supply chain approaches (Hitt, 2011; Hult, Ketchen, & Arrfelt, 2007) and stakeholder management (e.g., Coff, 1999), sustainable coffee supply chain management practices are based on various resources and capabilities. International coffee manufacturers that align their business strategies with the needs of their primary stakeholders will be more effective in developing value-creating business models. For instance, sustainable business models of international coffee supply chains provide fair trade conditions to farmers, protect biodiversity in the country of origin, foster pollution-friendly production, and ensure product safety for consumers. Doing so leads to economic, social, and environmental value for supply chain stakeholders, such as premium prices for the coffee brand owner/manufacturer, quality coffee for consumers, better living conditions for farmers, and safeguards for the natural environment.

For sustainable coffee supply chain management practices to maintain their competitive advantage, these approaches need to be combined with complementary assets (Barney, 2002; Barney & Mackey, 2005; Teece, 1986). Figure 4.1 illustrates our framework indicating how brand differentiation and competitive advantage through blockchain-enabled dynamic capabilities are related to sustainable supply chain management practices in the international coffee industry.

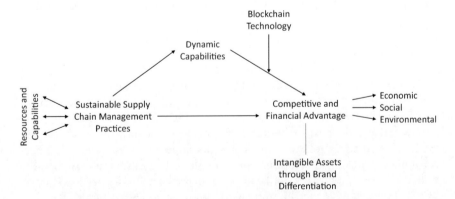

*Figure 4.1* Blockchain-transformed sustainable business model for international coffee supply chains

## Sustainable coffee supply chain management practices and inclusive value creation

International coffee manufacturers and their supply chain partners respond to critical stakeholders and combine their unique resources and capabilities to create sustainable supply chain management practices. These resources and capabilities comprise the effective deployment of a proactive strategy, an orientation toward learning and sustainability, the continuity of supply chain relationships, collaboration among supply chain partners, coordination/integration, and the risk management of supply chain activities (Beske, 2012; Beske, Land, & Seuring, 2014; Hong et al. 2018). Through effective exploitation throughout supply chain operations (Pagell & Wu, 2009), they become heterogeneous and tacit (e.g., Klassen & Whybark, 1999; Russo & Fouts, 1997).

Examples of sustainable coffee supply chain management practices and brands are Moyee Coffee and Solino Coffee. They have collaborated with external organizations, such as Moyee with the FairChain Foundation and Solino with local cooperatives, to proactively reverse the functions of their downstream value chains by investing in local infrastructure and the transfer of know-how for roasting and packaging coffee in Ethiopia, the origin of their coffee beans. In addition, many international coffee manufacturers use accreditations like ISO 65, ISO 9000, or ISO 14001, developed by the International Organization for Standardization (ISO), and other international standards certified by third-party auditors. They verify coffee production processes with regard to economic, social, environmental, and quality dimensions. This approach has gained momentum, evident in an annual 20% increase in certifications since 2000 (Reinecke, Manning, & Von Hagen, 2012). In 1991, Beyers Koffie, which belongs to the Sucafina Group, a global coffee-trading company, became the first FairTrade labeled coffee brand, and in 2015, the brand was labeled as a $CO_2$-neutral coffee. Nescafé and Nespresso, two coffee brands from the Nestlé Group, partnered with international associations like Rainforest Alliance, Fair Labor Association, Fairtrade International, and Technoserve to deliver sustainable coffee products to consumers, help meet the socio-economic challenges of farmers and their communities, and improve environmental issues in the countries of origin. Some large international coffee brands even developed their own sustainability standards. Examples include Starbucks' Coffee and Farmer Equity Practices Program (Starbucks C.A.F.E.) and Nestlé's Nespresso AAA Sustainable Quality. Large international wholesalers and retailers, such as Kraft (Philip Morris Group) and Albert Heijn, have also announced alliances with third-party certifications, such as Rainforest Alliance and UTZ Kapeh, for the purchase of certified coffee.

Overall, many downstream actors in the international coffee supply chain now guarantee production methods that preserve the soil without using synthetic chemicals (labeled "organic") and the natural environment (labeled "eco-friendly"). They also certify that they maintain direct trade relationships and minimum contract prices and labor standards with cooperatives or farmers (labeled "fair trade") in the coffee's country of origin. Such sustainable practices increase the international coffee supply chain's economic performance by improving operational efficiency and minimizing risk. They also meet a firm's commitment to corporate social responsibility through inclusive supply chain partner management and by reducing waste, pollution, and the use of natural resources. Thus, sustainable coffee supply chain management practices should have a positive effect on the international coffee supply chain's economic, social, and environmental performance.

*P1: Sustainable supply chain management practices will have a positive effect on economic performance throughout the international coffee supply chain.*

*P2: Sustainable supply chain management practices will have a positive effect on social performance throughout the international coffee supply chain.*

*P3: Sustainable supply chain management practices will have a positive effect on environmental performance throughout the international coffee supply chain.*

### Blockchain-enabled dynamic capabilities for brand differentiation and long-term competitive advantage

Sustainable coffee supply chains operate in a complex and dynamic environment that is driven by volatile stakeholder pressures and interconnected global markets with the instant spread of information. These supply chains also have geographically dispersed supply units (Teece, 2007), mainly located in developing and emerging countries (Cole, Stevenson, & Aitken, 2019; Kshetri, 2021). This challenging situation jeopardizes the competitiveness of sustainable coffee supply chains. It emphasizes the need to transform business models (Rocha, de Oliveira, & Talamini, 2021) by constantly reconfiguring resources and capabilities in the face of shifting markets, innovation, and the use of digital technologies (Kramer & Porter, 2011).

While sustainability strategies become public over time and hence, can be adopted by competitors, a firm's *proactive* decision to implement strategies for developing new resources and capabilities represents a dynamic capability that can give it a long-term competitive advantage (Barney & Mackey, 2005). Dynamic capabilities are developed by top management to "integrate, build, and reconfigure internal and external competences to address rapidly changing environments" (Teece, Pisano, & Shuen, 1997, p. 516). They can be classified into the three major categories of sensing, seizing, and reconfiguring of resources and capabilities (Teece, 2007; Teece, Pisano, & Shuen, 1997). They can be developed using complementary assets (Barney, 2002; Teece, 1986) to modify the supply chain's resource configuration (Eisenhardt & Martin, 2000), thereby releasing the value-creating potential of sustainable practices.

On the basis of Beske (2012), Beske, Land, and Seuring (2014), and Nandi et al. (2020), we maintain that dynamic capabilities in agri-food systems comprise the firm's ability to (1) manage the new and current knowledge of supply chain partners, (2) coordinate and develop supply chain partners, (3) re-conceptualize the supply chain, (4) co-develop new, synergistic products, and (5) reflect current sustainable practices and strategies. Hong et al. (2018) demonstrated that dynamic capabilities mediate Chinese manufacturing firms' ability to improve their economic, social, and environmental performance from sustainable supply chain management practices in different industries, including the food industry. These capabilities are indicative of the top management's proactive approach to innovation to improve their current sustainable coffee supply chain practices as markets change. Furthermore, studies have shown that investment decisions in complementary assets, such as lean practices, process innovations, and environmental management systems, have a positive effect on the relationship between sustainable practices and corporate performance (Christmann, 2000; Dey et al., 2019; Jell-Ojobor & Raha, 2022; Silva, Gomes, & Sarkis, 2019).

In practice, the adoption of blockchain technology represents an investment in such complementary assets. Blockchain technology connects international supply chain partners, allowing them to digitally share information on the distributed ledger about the farming, harvesting, processing, logistics and cold storage, and consumption of coffee supplies (Feng et al., 2020). Doing so makes it easier for all supply chain stakeholders to track and trace information in a transparent and efficient manner, leading to outcomes that are particularly important in the agri-food industry (Wang, Han, & Beynon-Davies, 2019).

As consumers increasingly demand transparency about their food quality and safety, a redesign of the agri-food supply chains driven by trust in product quality and food safety has occurred (Hanf, 2005; Saitone & Sexton, 2017). While existing certifications aim to convey a positive image regarding sustainable practices in coffee production to consumers in the United States, Canada, Japan, and Europe (Giovannucci & Koekoek, 2003), the fragmentation of these multiple certification standards makes it difficult for suppliers to comply with them and for consumers to understand them (Giovannucci & Ponte, 2005).

One of the key drivers to implementing blockchain technology in international supply chains, aside from increasing transparency about food quality, safety, and rapid recalls, is its potential to reliably track food items in real time and trace their movements backward across countries and supply chain stages. Doing so reduces unnecessary food waste caused by conditions like inappropriate storage and transport conditions, or inefficient inventory management. The Food and Agriculture Organization of the United Nations (FAO) estimates that around 14% of the food produced globally is wasted before reaching retailers' shelves (FAO, 2021). Therefore, blockchain has the potential to reduce food waste, while reducing operational costs and improving efficiency in agri-food supply chains (Li, Lee, & Gharehgozli, 2021).

While blockchain technology is a largely standardized, general-purpose asset accessible to any entity and applicable to any supply chain, it bundles critical dynamic capabilities that transform existing resources and capabilities into competitive business models. Its information-sharing capabilities improve a firm's ability to exchange knowledge throughout the international supply chain. Through such sharing, sustainable products, processes, and strategies can be constantly adapted and redesigned to fit the dynamic market environment. In addition, this information sharing helps coordinate supply chain operations across countries (e.g., Hald & Kinra, 2019) and promotes the achievement of high operational and product standards. Furthermore, the automated information and smart contracts that blockchain enables change in supply chain structures by eliminating the need for intermediaries (e.g., Saberi et al., 2019; Wang, Han, & Beynon-Davies, 2019), while strengthening existing relationships through external stakeholder participation. In addition, blockchain-enabled information tracking and tracing and other forthcoming features like tokenization and smart contracts enable the development of synergistic brand complements (e.g., Amit & Zott, 2001; Schlecht, Schneider, & Buchwald, 2021). For instance, consumers can directly donate to farmers or brand headquarters to invest in local training and infrastructure or communicate with farmers through digital meeting rooms, closed chat groups, or virtual reality meeting centers. Finally, the immutability, transparency, and tracking and tracing of blockchain-enabled information helps harmonize standards (e.g., Aldrighetti, Canavari, & Hingley, 2021), and monitor the efficiency of sustainability practices within the supply chain and revise them if needed.

Introducing blockchain into the international coffee supply chain should benefit consumers by giving them more trust in the safety and quality of the product. It should benefit farmers by providing them with the training to develop new skills. They can also earn more by eliminating the need to pay intermediaries. Thus, they will earn higher profits from selling premium coffee to consumers. The demands of international stakeholders will also raise awareness about and inspire participation in local sustainability initiatives that will help the natural environments of local communities to prosper from green practices. International coffee brand owners will profit from their customers' willingness to pay premium prices for coffee produced under such circumstances (e.g., Aldrighetti, Canavari, & Hingley, 2021). They will also develop operational and administrative efficiencies (e.g., Stranieri et al., 2021) in managing geographically and culturally distant suppliers along the supply chain, reducing its complexity (Hald & Kinra, 2019; Kshetri, 2021) and certification costs (Cole, Stevenson, & Aitken, 2019). Ultimately, blockchain-enabled dynamic capabilities promote coffee-brand differentiation, through, for instance, the creation of products complementing existing sustainability practices (Schlecht, Schneider, & Buchwald, 2021), such as authentic digital relational exchanges between stakeholders. These changes then create intangible assets (Hald & Kinra, 2019), such as reputation, trust, motivation, loyalty, and bonding along the supply chain. They distinguish sustainable international coffee brands from competitors and can be possible sources of long-term competitive and financial advantages. As a result, we hypothesize that the implementation of blockchain technology enables dynamic capabilities to radically reconfigure existing sustainability practices, resulting in improved performance and a competitive advantage. Specifically, blockchain technology is a moderator of dynamic capabilities. These dynamic capabilities mediate the relationship between sustainable coffee supply chain management practices and performance in terms of economic, social, and environmental responsibility.

> P4: Blockchain technology is a moderator of dynamic capabilities. These dynamic capabilities mediate the relationship between sustainable coffee supply chain management practices and performance in terms of economic, social, and environmental responsibility throughout the international coffee supply chain.
>
> P5: Blockchain technology is a moderator of dynamic capabilities. These dynamic capabilities mediate the relationship between sustainable coffee supply chain management practices and the creation of intangible assets, resulting in improved long-term performance and a competitive advantage for international coffee supply chains that utilize blockchain technology.

## Discussion

This study contributes to the novel literature on the increasing use of blockchain technology in sustainable international supply chains. Grounded in the dynamic capabilities of the resource-based theory, our framework explains how the adoption of blockchain technology provides benefits beyond transaction efficiency by helping differentiate business models of international coffee supply chains in a complex, changing environment. While blockchain technology is a standardized asset that may not guarantee firms a competitive advantage in the long run, its use reinforces the development of dynamic capabilities to modify existing sustainable practices. In doing so, it allows for combinations with complementary assets, such as the virtual technologies of Industry 4.0, which bond stakeholders – most importantly, consumers and farmers – to coffee brands from companies committed to corporate social responsibility. Blockchain technology helps companies demonstrate and actualize their commitment to these goals, providing them with intangible assets like reputation and loyalty that yield long-term economic, social, and environmental benefits throughout the international supply chain. Hence, adopting blockchain technology in the supply chain is the mechanism that unleashes the company's dynamic capabilities and helps it transform its business model into one of a differentiated sustainable coffee brand (e.g., Schilke, Hu, & Helfat, 2018). Overall, our study provides a framework describing how blockchain-enabled dynamic capabilities can transform the business models of sustainable international supply chains in the coffee industry. We thereby respond to the need for theoretical models to guide the adoption of blockchain technology in international supply chains in a way that creates value for the focal firm, and value that can be distributed among its stakeholders (e.g., Hald & Kinra, 2019; Nandi et al., 2020; Wang, Han, & Beynon-Davies, 2019).

Through blockchain-enabled supply chains, stakeholders in the coffee industry benefit from several advantages, such as the elimination of intermediaries, improved standardization of certification demands, and a standard tool to verify sustainability practices, all of which should increase the efficiency of sustainable supply chains and the trust in them (Cole, Stevenson, & Aitken, 2019; Feng et al., 2020; Wang, Han, & Beynon-Davies, 2019). In addition to the traditional benefits of efficiency, combining blockchain technology with the digital assets of Industry 4.0 can help transform business models (Hald & Kinra, 2019; Rocha, de Oliveira, & Talamini, 2021; Schlecht, Schneider, & Buchwald, 2021), allowing companies to differentiate themselves from their competitors, improve their reputations, and bind their stakeholders to them. Doing so should prompt customers to pay more (Kshetri, 2021) and allow rating agencies to give companies higher scores, giving these companies long-term financial benefits and a competitive advantage.

Beyond the creation of intangible assets, brand differentiation releases synergistic resources, capabilities, and assets at the farmer's level, which can help narrow the economic, social, and environmental value divide among the supply chain partners of developing and industrialized countries (Kshetri, 2021). For instance, the forthcoming tokenization in blockchain technology adds sustainable payments and donations to farmers, creating a "market for farmers." Stakeholders who can see where the products they are interested in come from can engage in traceable peer-to-peer transactions and interact with farmers through virtual exchange channels that can drive relational rents (Hald & Kinra, 2019). The achieved bonding between farmers and consumers will inspire the continuous development of know-how and improve product quality and environmental standards at the sourcing stage. Ultimately, these synergistic resources, capabilities, and assets – combined with novel, heterogeneous sustainable practices – can become the source of a long-term competitive advantage for international coffee brands.

Supported by the trend toward off-chain data storage, which shifts unstructured data away from permissionless public blockchain networks, thus reducing the amount of transaction data in the blockchain, these approaches are likely to stand out against private and consortium-based solutions with centralized control by a single or a few assigned entities (Aldrighetti, Canavari, & Hingley, 2021; Schlecht, Schneider, & Buchwald, 2021). In addition, the emergence of public trading platforms might provide opportunities to farmers located in countries with limited access to international trade (Kshetri, 2021). It increases the need for international coffee brands to develop innovative strategies that bond stakeholders such as farmers, consumers, and other stakeholders, to their supply chains. Given that off-chain data storage restricts access to complementary information that can affect decision-making (Schlecht, Schneider, & Buchwald, 2021), the value that blockchain technology brings to the brand to bond stakeholders is limited to the ecosystem created by private and consortium-based business models. Hence, international coffee supply chains should consider blockchain-enabled business model transformations as an opportunity (Saberi et al., 2019) to differentiate their brand, limit their competitors from gaining market share, and create long-term economic, social, and environmental value for their supply chain stakeholders.

# References

Aldrighetti, A., Canavari, M. and Hingley, M.K., 2021. A Delphi study on blockchain application to food traceability. *International Journal on Food System Dynamics*, 12(1), pp. 6–18.

Amit, R. and Zott, C., 2001. Value creation in e-business. *Strategic Management Journal*, 22(6–7), pp. 493–520.

Barney, J.B., 1991. Firm resources and sustained competitive advantage. *Journal of Management*, 17(1), pp. 99–120.

Barney, J.B., 2002. *Gaining and sustaining competitive advantage*, 2nd edition. Prentice Hall, Upper Saddle River, NJ, vol. 4, pp. 1–22.

Barney, J.B. and Mackey, T.B., 2005. Testing resource-based theory. In *Research methodology in strategy and management*. Emerald Group Publishing Limited, Bingley.

Beck, R., Müller-Bloch, C. and King, J.L., 2018. Governance in the blockchain economy: A framework and research agenda. *Journal of the Association for Information Systems*, 19(10), p. 1.

Beske, P., 2012. Dynamic capabilities and sustainable supply chain management. *International Journal of Physical Distribution & Logistics Management*, 42(4), pp. 372–387.

Beske, P., Land, A. and Seuring, S., 2014. Sustainable supply chain management practices and dynamic capabilities in the food industry: A critical analysis of the literature. *International Journal of Production Economics*, 152, pp. 131–143.

Borsellino, V., Schimmenti, E. and El Bilali, H., 2020. Agri-food markets towards sustainable patterns. *Sustainability*, 12(6), p. 2193.

Carroll, A.B., 1979. A three-dimensional conceptual model of corporate performance. *Academy of Management Review*, 4(4), pp. 497–505.

Christmann, P., 2000. Effects of "best practices" of environmental management on cost advantage: The role of complementary assets. *Academy of Management Journal*, 43(4), pp. 663–680.

Coff, R.W., 1999. When competitive advantage doesn't lead to performance: The resource-based view and stakeholder bargaining power. *Organization Science*, 10(2), pp. 119–133.

Cole, R., Stevenson, M. and Aitken, J., 2019. Blockchain technology: Implications for operations and supply chain management. *Supply Chain Management: An International Journal*, 24(4), pp. 469–483.

Conner, K.R., 1991. A historical comparison of resource-based theory and five schools of thought within industrial organization economics: Do we have a new theory of the firm? *Journal of Management*, 17(1), pp. 121–154.

Dey, P.K., Malesios, C., De, D., Chowdhury, S. and Abdelaziz, F.B., 2019. Could lean practices and process innovation enhance supply chain sustainability of small and medium-sized enterprises? *Business Strategy and the Environment*, 28(4), pp. 582–598.

Dyllick, T. and Hockerts, K., 2002. Beyond the business case for corporate sustainability. *Business Strategy and the Environment*, 11(2), pp. 130–141.

Eisenhardt, K.M. and Martin, J.A., 2000. Dynamic capabilities: What are they? *Strategic Management Journal*, 21(10–11), pp. 1105–1121.

Elkington, J., 1994. Towards the sustainable corporation: Win-win-win business strategies for sustainable development. *California Management Review*, 36(2), pp. 90–100.

FAO. 2021. *Tracking progress on food and agriculture-related SDG indicators 2021: A report on the indicators under FAO custodianship*. FAO, Rome. https://doi.org/10.4060/cb6872en.

Feng, H., Wang, X., Duan, Y., Zhang, J. and Zhang, X., 2020. Applying blockchain technology to improve agri-food traceability: A review of development methods, benefits and challenges. *Journal of Cleaner Production*, 260, p. 121031.

Furlonger, D. and Uzureau, C., 2019. *The real business of blockchain: How leaders can create value in a new digital age*. Harvard Business Press, Cambridge.

Gartner. 2019. *Gartner predicts 20% of top global grocers will use blockchain for food safety and traceability by 2025*. Available online: www.gartner.com/en/newsroom/press-releases/2019-04-30-gartner-predicts-20-percent-of-top-global-grocers-wil (accessed 10 January 2022).

Giovannucci, D., & Koekoek, F. J., 2003. *The state of sustainable coffee: A study of twelve major markets*. IISD, UNCTAD, ICO, London.

Giovannucci, D. and Ponte, S., 2005. Standards as a new form of social contract? Sustainability initiatives in the coffee industry. *Food Policy*, 30(3), pp. 284–301.

Grabs, J. and Ponte, S., 2019. The evolution of power in the global coffee value chain and production network. *Journal of Economic Geography*, 19(4), pp. 803–828.

Groombridge, D., 2020. *Unpacking blockchain myths from the reality*. Gartner Webinars, Gartner Inc., Stamford, CT.

Gulati, R., Nohria, N. and Zaheer, A., 2000. Strategic networks. *Strategic Management Journal*, 21(3), pp. 203–215.

Hald, K.S. and Kinra, A., 2019. How the blockchain enables and constrains supply chain performance. *International Journal of Physical Distribution & Logistics Management*, 49(4), pp. 376–397.

Hanf, J.H., 2005. *Supply chain networks: Analysis based on strategic management theories and institutional economics*. Paper presented at IAMO – Forum 2005, How Effective Is the Invisible Hand? Agricultural and Food Markets in Central and Eastern Europe, Halle, Germany, 16–18 June.

Hitt, M.A., 2011. Relevance of strategic management theory and research for supply chain management. *Journal of Supply Chain Management*, 47(1), pp. 9–13.

Hitt, M.A., Xu, K. and Carnes, C.M., 2016. Resource based theory in operations management research. *Journal of Operations Management*, 41, pp. 77–94.

Hong, J., Zhang, Y. and Ding, M., 2018. Sustainable supply chain management practices, supply chain dynamic capabilities, and enterprise performance. *Journal of Cleaner Production*, 172, pp. 3508–3519.

Hult, G.T.M., Ketchen, D.J. and Arrfelt, M., 2007. Strategic supply chain management: improving performance through a culture of competitiveness and knowledge development. *Strategic Management Journal*, 28(10), pp. 1035–1052.

Jell-Ojobor, M., 2019. Strategic CSR and the competitive advantage of franchise firms. In *Design and management of interfirm networks*. Springer, Cham, pp. 91–111.

Jell-Ojobor, M. and Raha, A., 2022. Being good at being good—The mediating role of an environmental management system in value-creating green supply chain management practices. *Business Strategy and the Environment*, 31(5), pp. 1964–1984.

Kamilaris, A., Fonts, A. and Prenafeta-Bold-, F.X., 2019. The rise of blockchain technology in agriculture and food supply chains. *Trends in Food Science & Technology*, 91, pp. 640–652.

Klassen, R.D. and Whybark, D.C., 1999. The impact of environmental technologies on manufacturing performance. *Academy of Management Journal*, 42(6), pp. 599–615.

Kleindorfer, P.R., Singhal, K. and Van Wassenhove, L.N., 2005. Sustainable operations management. *Production and Operations Management*, 14(4), pp. 482–492.

Kramer, M.P., Bitsch, L. and Hanf, J., 2021. The impact of instrumental stakeholder management on blockchain technology adoption behavior in agri-food supply chains. *Journal of Risk and Financial Management*, 14(12), p. 598.

Kramer, M.P. and Porter, M., 2011. *Creating shared value*. FSG, London, vol. 17.

Kshetri, N., 2021. Blockchain and sustainable supply chain management in developing countries. *International Journal of Information Management*, 60, p. 102376.

Lampridi, M.G., Kateris, D., Vasileiadis, G., Marinoudi, V., Pearson, S., Sørensen, C.G., Balafoutis, A. and Bochtis, D., 2019. A case-based economic assessment of robotics employment in precision arable farming. *Agronomy*, 9(4), p. 175.

Lewin, B., Giovannucci, D. and Varangis, P., 2004. *Coffee markets: New paradigms in global supply and demand*. World Bank Agriculture and Rural Development Discussion Paper, 3, Washington, DC.

Li, K., Lee, J.Y. and Gharehgozli, A., 2021. Blockchain in food supply chains: A literature review and synthesis analysis of platforms, benefits and challenges. *International Journal of Production Research*, pp. 1–20.

Nakamoto, S., 2008. Bitcoin: A peer-to-peer electronic cash system. *Decentralized Business Review*, p. 21260.

Nandi, M.L., Nandi, S., Moya, H. and Kaynak, H., 2020. Blockchain technology-enabled supply chain systems and supply chain performance: A resource-based view. *Supply Chain Management: An International Journal*, 25(6), pp. 841–862.

Nelson, R.R. and Winter, S.G., 1982. The Schumpeterian tradeoff revisited. *The American Economic Review*, 72(1), pp. 114–132.

Pagell, M. and Wu, Z., 2009. Building a more complete theory of sustainable supply chain management using case studies of 10 exemplars. *Journal of Supply Chain Management*, 45(2), pp. 37–56.

Pietrewicz, L., 2019. Blockchain: A coordination mechanism. *Proceedings of the Entrenova-Enterprise Research Innovation Conference (Online)*, 5(1), pp. 105–111, October.

Ponte, S., 2002. The Latte revolution? Regulation, markets and consumption in the global coffee chain. *World Development*, 30(7), pp. 1099–1122.

Queiroz, M.M., Telles, R. and Bonilla, S.H., 2019. Blockchain and supply chain management integration: A systematic review of the literature. *Supply Chain Management: An International Journal*, 25(2), pp. 241–254.

Reinecke, J., Manning, S. and Von Hagen, O., 2012. The emergence of a standards market: Multiplicity of sustainability standards in the global coffee industry. *Organization Studies*, 33(5–6), pp. 791–814.

Rocha, G.D.S.R., de Oliveira, L. and Talamini, E., 2021. Blockchain applications in agribusiness: A systematic review. *Future Internet*, 13(4), p. 95.

Rumelt, R.P. and Lamb, R., 1984. Competitive strategic management. *Toward a Strategic Theory of the Firm*, 26(1), pp. 556–570.

Russo, M.V. and Fouts, P.A., 1997. A resource-based perspective on corporate environmental performance and profitability. *Academy of Management Journal*, 40(3), pp. 534–559.

Saberi, S., Kouhizadeh, M., Sarkis, J. and Shen, L., 2019. Blockchain technology and its relationships to sustainable supply chain management. *International Journal of Production Research*, 57(7), pp. 2117–2135.

Saitone, T.L. and Sexton, R., 2017. Agri-food supply chain: Evolution and performance with conflicting consumer and societal demands. *European Review of Agricultural Economics*, 44, pp. 634–657.

Santa-Maria, T., Vermeulen, W.J. and Baumgartner, R.J., 2021. How do incumbent firms innovate their business models for the circular economy? Identifying micro-foundations of dynamic capabilities. *Business Strategy and the Environment*, 31(4), pp. 1308–1333.

Schilke, O., Hu, S. and Helfat, C.E., 2018. Quo vadis, dynamic capabilities? A content-analytic review of the current state of knowledge and recommendations for future research. *Academy of Management Annals*, 12(1), pp. 390–439.

Schlecht, L., Schneider, S. and Buchwald, A., 2021. The prospective value creation potential of Blockchain in business models: A Delphi study. *Technological Forecasting and Social Change*, 166, p. 120601.

Seuring, S. and Müller, M., 2008. From a literature review to a conceptual framework for sustainable supply chain management. *Journal of Cleaner Production*, 16(15), pp. 1699–1710.

Silva, G.M., Gomes, P.J. and Sarkis, J., 2019. The role of innovation in the implementation of green supply chain management practices. *Business Strategy and the Environment*, 28(5), pp. 819–832.

Stranieri, S., Riccardi, F., Meuwissen, M.P. and Soregaroli, C., 2021. Exploring the impact of blockchain on the performance of agri-food supply chains. *Food Control*, 119, p. 107495.

Teece, D.J., 1986. Profiting from technological innovation: Implications for integration, collaboration, licensing and public policy. *Research Policy*, 15(6), pp. 285–305.

Teece, D.J., 2007. Explicating dynamic capabilities: The nature and microfoundations of (sustainable) enterprise performance. *Strategic Management Journal*, 28(13), pp. 1319–1350.

Teece, D.J., Pisano, G. and Shuen, A., 1997. Dynamic capabilities and strategic management. *Strategic Management Journal*, 18(7), pp. 509–533.

Wang, Y., Han, J.H. and Beynon-Davies, P., 2019. Understanding blockchain technology for future supply chains: A systematic literature review and research agenda. *Supply Chain Management: An International Journal*, 24(1), pp. 62–84.

Wernerfelt, B., 1984. A resource-based view of the firm. *Strategic Management Journal*, 5(2), pp. 171–180.

# 5 Associativism as a promoter of sustainability in farmers and a driver for creating value for sustainable practices

The case of Socicana

*Rafael Bordonal Kalaki and Marcos Fava Neves*

## Introduction

The promotion of sustainable agriculture has been discussed in the world for years. Questions have arisen, such as the following: how to produce more using fewer resources; how production can have less of an impact on the environment; how to produce while respecting people and promoting well-being; how to equalize respect for the environment, people, and keep activities economically viable and profitable. These issues are on the minds of the leading business executives and are being grappled with by researchers, governments, students, and society. Also in this context, there is the issue of how to promote sustainability in agriculture directly with farmers, and how to create conditions and incentives for farmers to adopt increasingly sustainable farming practices.

In the city of Guariba, Bruno Rangel Geraldo Martins, the president of Socicana, an association of sugarcane growers, thought about future challenges and how the association, through collective actions, could generate value for its members and make them even more competitive and sustainable.

> The act of being part of Socicana is voluntary, that is, the grower only associates when he realizes the value. How could Socicana show that the benefit of participating in a collective action agency can benefit growers? How could Socicana help them increase sustainable development? What could Socicana do to show value to its members?
> 
> – *Bruno Rangel Geraldo Martins*

In the early 2000s, Paulo de Araújo Rodrigues, a sugarcane farmer, was in his farm office thinking about the challenges of sustainability, the demands that consumer markets had on products, and how he could demonstrate a more sustainable sugarcane production that would meet market demands and add value to his activity.

> Consumers are looking for products with greater sustainable appeal and I have been practicing it for generations. How can I show the world that

DOI: 10.4324/9781003223672-8

I have sustainable agriculture? How can I add value and differentiate my production based on my sustainable practices?

– *Paulo de Araújo Rodrigues*

Thinking about these dilemmas, Socicana had a challenge: What actions could it take to guide and assist farmers to increase their sustainable practices and how to generate value for farmers who already had sustainable practices recognized by the market? It was not an easy challenge, but it was within the scope of the work of a farmers' association to seek solutions to this challenge.

## The sugar-energy sector as a promoter of sustainability

The sugar-energy sector has been important for Brazil since the country's colonization (the fifteenth century). However, the consolidation of the sector began on November 14, 1975, when the Brazilian federal government created Pró-Álcool (National Fuel Alcohol Program), which aimed to stimulate the production of alcohol (ethanol), as well as to stimulate the production of cars fueled by ethanol, reduce and replace the consumption of petroleum products (which in that decade reached record prices), add anhydrous ethanol to gasoline, and reduce oil imports.

As stated initially, Pró-Álcool was created to stimulate ethanol production and mainly to reduce Brazil's dependence on oil. Today, the reasons for adopting ethanol go beyond this dependence. There is a worldwide focus on conscious consumption, reducing resources as well as greenhouse gas emissions. These concerns have led to global events to discuss these issues.

Among the global initiatives to discuss sustainability, it is possible to mention the 17 Sustainable Development Goals (SDGs) of the United Nations Agenda 2030, whose objective is to eliminate poverty, promote well-being and prosperity for all, combat climate change, and protect the environment. The ESG initiatives (Environmental, Social, Governance) and their indicators that guide companies in the search for sustainability are also worth noting.

For the sugar-energy sector, one of the initiatives that most directly impacted and will continue to impact the sector was the COP 21 event that took place in December 2015. COP 21 (21st Conference of the Parties) is a Framework Convention on Climate Change, which seeks to understand and find solutions to climate change. The Conference of the Parties is the principal decision-making body of the United Nations Framework Convention on Climate Change (UNFCCC).

Brazil has also reached an agreement, in which it proposes to reduce greenhouse gas emissions, mainly by increasing the share of renewable energy and bioenergy in its energy matrix. The commitments made by Brazil at COP 21 to increase the share of renewable energy will imply an increase in the demand for sustainable electricity and biofuels. In this scenario, the sugar-energy sector is seen as an important pillar of this growth since it offers ethanol, which is the biofuel produced from sugarcane, and bioelectricity generated in the industrial units using by-products of sugar and ethanol production[1].

For more than 40 years, Brazil has already promoted sustainability, replacing gasoline – which until that time had been the main fuel used in the country – with ethanol, a renewable fuel with greenhouse gas emissions up to 90% lower as compared to fossil fuel. It is important to note that, in that period, the incentive for adopting ethanol was to reduce dependence on oil imports. However today, the country continues to stimulate ethanol production and consumption, not because of the dependence on oil imports but because of all the benefits that the sector brings to Brazil, both social, economic, and mainly environmental benefits. Today, the incentive is sustainability (See note 1).

## Socicana

Socicana (Association of Sugar Cane Suppliers of Guariba) is an association formed by agricultural sugarcane growers in the Guariba region in the state of São Paulo. The association was founded in 1951 and is headquartered in Guariba-SP.

**Vision:** To be a reference organization for providing services to the associate, recognized as a leader in the articulation and management of initiatives that offer competitiveness to sugarcane growers.

**Mission:** Promote competitiveness and sustainable development for sugarcane growers, through services to the member, acting in defense of their rights and strengthening associativism.

### History of Socicana

Socicana was founded on February 15, 1951, in the city of Guariba–SP. The first president and one of the founders of the association was Antonio José Rodrigues Filho. The association was created because, in the view of the founders, only through strengthened representativeness it would be possible to implement advances in the sugarcane activity.

### Members

In the 2020/21 harvest, 913 condominiums of agricultural production were affiliated with the association and 1,143 members, with an approximate production of 6 million tons of sugarcane and an area of 72,000 hectares. The association's members are quite heterogeneous, especially regarding the size of the business. Most of the members are small farmers, and of the 913 associated condominiums, 706 are small farms (77.33%) and represent 21.11% of the production. There are 182 (19.94%) midsize farms, accounting for 44.54% of production. There are 25 (2.74%) large farms, representing 34.35% of production (Table 5A.1).

### Sector of activity, representativeness, and geographical scope

Socicana represents independent sugarcane farmers in the Guariba–SP region, operating within a 100-km radius of the municipality. The 100-km radius of the municipality of Guariba–SP encompasses 81 municipalities, 12 industrial units, and an area of 1,157 thousand hectares. Of the 1,157,000 hectares, the associates own 72,000 hectares, which is equivalent to 6.22%. Socicana's associates deliver to the 12 industrial units within 100 km.

### Services provided

Socicana's main objective is to offer representation for its sugarcane suppliers, offering greater competitiveness for its members. In addition to its representative function, it has a portfolio of services (free of charge) that it provides to its members. It is also divided into departments, and each department has a portfolio of specific services: agronomic technical services, a sucrose and inspection laboratory, project and sustainability services, legal services, and social and communication services.

### Governance and organizational structure

The highest decision-making body at Socicana is the General Meeting. The association still has, in its structure, the Fiscal and Administrative Councils for decision-making. The board and the executive manager serve as the administrator of the association (Figure 5.1).

### Associative fee

The contribution value of members is defined by a budget. An annual budget is built, based on the previous year's budget and adjusted according to the next

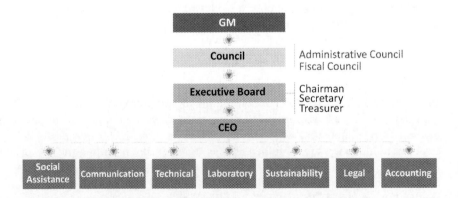

Figure 5.1 Governance and organizational structure of Socicana

Source: Socicana.

year's forecast. Based on the budget and the estimated production, the value of the contribution rate is calculated, dividing the budgeted amount by the total production and reaching a contribution value of R$/ton of sugarcane.

## Promoting sustainable development

Sustainable development programs at Socicana began in 2004, after the need arose for a seal that recognized good practices in the agricultural process by members. Thus, the president of Socicana at that time, Roberto Cestari, encouraged the search for alternatives in the market to resolve this issue, and the first contact with Bonsucro was made. In 2006, the association started raising awareness among members on the importance of a seal to show good practices in production. At first, making the farmer aware of such a topic was a difficult task, as some of them were not aware of the importance of the certification.

In 2010, the first contact between Socicana and Solidaridad took place and conversations began about the search for solutions to sustainable development and advising rural farmers. That same year, a partnership was signed between the parties.

A pilot project for Continuous Improvement was carried out in 2011 in a partnership among Socicana, Unica (Brazilian Sugarcane Industry Association)[2], Solidaridad[3], and industrial units. The project aimed to work on social, economic, and financial pillars.

With the success of the Continuous Improvement Program pilot project, in 2014, Socicana created the Projects and Sustainability department, which aimed to develop continuous improvement and sustainable development projects. In 2015, Socicana began developing its own environmental protocol, in partnership with Solidaridad, which is based on the world protocols of good sustainable practices for agricultural farmers. Following the development of its own environmental protocol, in 2016, the Top Cana Continuous Improvement Program was structured, advising about 120 farmers in the first year. Also in the same year, the association began the process of preparing its farmers for Bonsucro certification.

In 2017, Socicana started a pilot project in partnership with RSB for recognition and certification of small farmers (with fewer than 75 hectares) showing excellence in the management of sugarcane production. In that year, some of them obtained the Bonsucro certification. Also in 2017, Socicana developed its Environmental Management Plan.

In 2018, Socicana innovated with the Bonsucro certification, creating standards and a protocol that certified PSS (pre-sprouted seedlings), offering something new in the sector and certifying the first grower. That same year, a process of restructuring the Top Cana Program began.

In 2019, Socicana started to revise its Top Cana program, incorporating new indicators and readjusting the new needs of producers. In 2020, Socicana carried out the first worldwide commercialization of Bonsucro sugarcane credits on the Bonsucro digital platform. In this same year, Socicana began to develop a new project in partnership with Sicoob Coopecredi[4] aiming at a specific rural credit line for producers with sustainable practices. In 2021, the Crédito Rural Verde (Green Rural Credit) was launched, a rural financing destined for Socicana producers who are in one of Socicana's sustainable development programs (Bonsucro Certification, RSB certification, or Top Cana). Still in 2021, Socicana began utilizing Top Cana with its new protocol.

Socicana currently has three programs for the sustainable development of sugarcane: the RSB Certification Program, which includes small growers, the Bonsucro Certification Program, and the Top Cana Program, its own sustainable development program for sugarcane farmers.

### Top Cana Program

The TOP CANA Program[5] is a continuous improvement process aimed at farmers. Upon joining the program, farmers are told the strengths and weaknesses of their properties and given an improvement plan, which are worked to develop and qualify the technical, managerial, labor, environmental, good agricultural practice, and rural constructions areas, and with this, generate greater competitiveness for farmers. Top Cana's strategy is to provide farmers with technical assistance in terms of social and environmental issues as well as a portfolio of free services offered by the association. In the field, the monitoring takes place with Top Cana technicians making periodic visits to the farmers and their production areas.

The Top Cana program was created in 2016 as a partnership between Socicana and Solidaridad. Today, the program serves 120 farmers. The program is voluntary, free of charge, and tailored to the rural farm; it can be applied to the most diverse property profiles, from small to large, from family to business farmers.

After 2018, Socicana incorporated the Top Cana program, starting a review in 2019 to develop its own sustainability protocol, using internationally recognized certification protocols such as the Bonsucro certification standard, SAI certification standard, RSB certification standard, Brazilian legislation, Agenda 2030 of the United Nations (UN), and RenovaBio[6]. A digital tool began to be developed. Technician collects data with digital tool, and includes a database and desk data analysis board, aiming to automate the process and action plans, making it faster and allowing to serve more producers with the same resources. In 2021, the program had received an audit, aiming to validate the results and ensure transparency for all participating members.

The main objective of the program is to develop the rural grower concerning the promotion of sustainable agriculture, addressing the managerial, rural constructions and infrastructure, labor, technical, and environmental pillars, resulting in property management models that provide the sustainability of the production process, greater knowledge for the farmer about his business, thus helping in decision-making, knowledge of the risks of the activity, and the

*Associativism as promoter of sustainability, value for farmers* 107

search for greater productivity. The main specific objectives of the program are the following.

*Operational aspects*

In total, 120 farmers participated in the program. The program was advertised to all members, and those who showed interest in participating were selected. One cycle of the program lasts 12 months and focuses on working on management, labor, environmental, good agricultural practices, and rural construction pillars.

During the Execution Phase, farmers receive visits from extension technicians on their farms. Technicians make up to four visits over the 12-month cycle. Each visit has a different purpose and set of specific activities. Also during the execution, in addition to the four visits to the rural properties, the technicians have a day of office work, where they analyzed the collected data and build the customized improvement plan for each property. Details of the activities in each of the steps are described in Figure 5.2.

After the evaluation, they are classified into four levels according to the requirements: attention, bronze, silver, and gold. The rankings take into account compliance with the requirements, which may be essential, basic, and advanced.

*Main results*

Since 2015, Top Cana has traveled 37,467 km and performed 723 field visits. To raise their level, farmers relied on Socicana's assistance with the services offered, leading to 810 agriculture technical services, 75 legal services, 115 services in the laboratory, and 981 services of projects and sustainability. From 2021, its objective has been to expand on what it does by increasing the number of farmers served, reviewing program actions and initiatives, forming new partnerships, and improving its services.

Comparing the average overall performance of the participants between the years 2016 and 2019, the producers went from an overall performance average

*Figure 5.2* Execution steps of Top Cana Program

Source: Socicana.

of 74% of the fulfilment of the requisition to 88%. This is a considerable evolution in the sustainability of the farms.

### Bonsucro certification program

Bonsucro[7] is a global multi-stakeholder, non-profit organization. Bonsucro's goal is to promote sustainable sugarcane production, processing and trade around the world. The Bonsucro seal guarantees buyers, suppliers, and end consumers that sugar and ethanol have been produced in compliance with legislation, the environment, and human rights. The seal is valid for 3 years and, to achieve this, companies are evaluated, based on 48 sustainability, profitability, and competitiveness indicators. Sugar and ethanol producers, NGOs, and multinationals like Coca-Cola, Cargill, and Kraft Food are part of the certification board. Socicana was the first growers association in Latin America to occupy a seat on Bonsucro's Members Council, and it opened the doors for farmers to be certified as well.

### Operational aspects of the program

Seeking to assist producers to achieve Bonsucro certification, Socicana has developed a "Bonsucro Certification Management Model for Farms." In this program, farmers are certified in groups, in which Socicana is the manager of the group. Although the producers are certified as a group, each producer needs to be 100% compliant with the Main Indicators and be approved individually on the Bonsucro calculator.

In order to implement Bonsucro certification in its members, Socicana initially needed to become familiar with the materials and the Bonsucro certification process, described in the Guide to the Bonsucro Production Standard 2016, and adapt it to rural producers. Bonsucro has standards and criteria to be met but does not have a specific model for farmers. Thus, Socicana's primary function was to understand the rules and create a process, document, and management system. The Bonsucro Mass Balance Chain of Custody Standard was chosen to be implemented in the associates.

After understanding the certification, Socicana developed its "Bonsucro Certification Management Model for Farms," which consists of a process for managing actions and schedules, as well as a data management system in groups. The management model allows Socicana to manage a group of producers in the process of implementing the certification, assisting them in managing individual actions, as well as coordinating collective activities.

The main activities developed by Socicana to implement Bonsucro certification in its members are as follows:

- Develop an Internal Management System (GIS) containing the rules and responsibilities of Socicana and the farmers throughout the process and in monitoring the certification.
- Evaluate the farmers and the farm considering the criteria of the "Bonsucro Production Standard."

- Simulate filling in the Bonsucro calculator in order to check the farmer's suitability for certification.
- Assist in the development of the action plan for each farmer to conform to the Bonsucro standard.
- Accompany/monitor the development of the activities carried out by the farmer in the field.
- Manage the activities and actions of the associated farmers in relation to Bonsucro certification.
- Manage and monitor the development of the farmers' chain of custody.
- Develop the environmental management plan.
- Manage area conversion maps.
- Promote training and capacity building when necessary.
- Target the services of Socicana's portfolio.
- Monitor the position of interested parties via the questionnaire on access to stakeholders.
- Develop a list of pesticides registered for sugarcane and allowed by the standard.
- Organize and monitor the external audit.

When a new producer wants to join the certification group, he must show interest in the association, read and agree with the Internal Management System (GIS), and after that, the previous actions are all applied to him. These actions are carried out constantly throughout the year and are repeated the next year (Action 1 is reviewed).

Socicana has developed an online system (using Google's G Suite), where the shares of each farmer are inserted and are made available, individually, to each farmer. This platform also has a system to fill in the Bonsucro Calculator, Chain of Custody, Map Management, and Action Plan, and provide photos for the process Thus, the shares remain individualized and are then compiled into a result. In this way, Socicana is able to assist in the individual management of each farmer in the group, as well as manage the final results.

*Main results*

Socicana has five farmers with Bonsucro certification, representing a total production area of 9,617,2 hectares, in 108 agricultural funds and a total production of sugarcane (20/21 harvest) of 1,167,574.89 tons. Socicana's score, with the sustainability criteria of the Bonsucro certification, exceeds 94%. This is the highest certification rate in Brazil, even higher than the levels of mills that are between 80 and 85%.

### RSB certification program

Roundtable on Sustainable Biomaterials (RSB)[8] is a global initiative, which has established a voluntary certification system for the sustainable production of biofuels and biomaterials. The RSB standard represents a consensus of more than 100 organizations worldwide, including farmers, businesses, experts, governments, UN agencies, and non-governmental organizations. This multi-stakeholder initiative aims to ensure the sustainability of the production of biomaterials, providing tools that are easy to use by the industry to demonstrate compliance. With the support of Boeing Corporate Citizenship, RSB has funded the program to support smallholder farmers in Southeast Asia, South Africa, and Latin America.

The RSB (Roundtable on Sustainable Biomaterials) Certification Program is part of the "Sustainable Cane" project, carried out by Socicana, with support from RSB, financed in its first year by the Boeing Corporate Citizenship Project. Within the "Sustainable Cane" farmers have a comprehensive structure to achieve sustainability goals and market demands and have full support for improvements in their management and agricultural practices.

In 2013, RSB focused on the identification of barriers to market access and certification by small farmers and the development of strategies to overcome them, including the structuring of a specific RSB standard for groups of small farmers who, via a group certification system, would allow for its inclusion in the market of certified products. In Brazil, Socicana was chosen to team up with RSB, an organization that meets the requirements of a partner for the implementation of the project that will be a pilot in the country.

The project that aimed to create the RSB certification standard was called "Sustainable Cana." The RSB certification program is a group certification process aimed at small family farmers to qualify their internal and external management system to generate greater management capacity and expand negotiation power in the market by offering a product that they have in their chain custody practices, differentiating and highlighting the product in the sector.

Among the objectives of the program are to improve (1) the living conditions of small farmers, promoting sustainable practices based on the RSB standard and seeking a market for certified products; (2) professionalization of rural property; (3) contribution to the improvement of small farmers' production systems, encouraging safer and healthier production environments, in addition to promoting sustainability objectives in the economic, social, and environmental pillars; and (4) that future buyers will benefit from having their supply chain aligned with an internationally recognized standard, accepted by markets such as Europe.

*Operational aspects of the program*

The main activities developed by Socicana to implement Bonsucro certification in its members are as follows:

- Develop an Internal Management System (GIS);
- Identify groups of interested small farmers with the potential to implement sustainable practices, in accordance with the RSB standard;
- Conduct technical visits to understand the challenges facing farmers;
- Identify the paths – individual Diagnostic report;

- Plan for changes – individual Action Plan report;
- Monitor – monitor, advise, and train the farmer;
- Organize and monitor the external audit.

*Main results*

Socicana has seven small farmers in four agricultural funds of up to 75 ha, representing a total production area of 108,44 hectares and a total production of sugarcane (20/21 harvest) of 9,570.00 tons.

## Creating value through sustainability

By the year 2020, Socicana had already acquired expertise in the process of promoting sustainability in its members through its sustainable development programs (Top Cana, Bonsucro certification program, and RSB certification program). After about 4 years in the programs, the farmers who took part realized – albeit subtly – the benefits of the farm programs, but they lacked recognition for their sustainable practices, especially commercial and economic recognition.

> We were able to encourage and promote sustainability in the associated farmers. Despite this, we still needed to create value for these farmers with sustainable practices, directly recognize their practices and create motivations for them to continue their efforts, as well as create incentives for new farmers to be interested in the programs and adopt sustainable practices. How to do this? We needed to seek the direct financial valuation of the farmer, either through increasing revenues, which was a difficult path, or else looking for an alternative that could be through cost reduction, and thus, he would perceive direct economic value.
> Rafael Bordonal Kalaki, CEO at Socicana

In this scenario, Socicana was able to generate value for its associates with sustainable practices through two tools: the Rural Green Credit and the Bonsucro Sugar Cane Credit.

### Crédito Rural Verde

In recent years, green investments and so-called Green Bonds have started to become evident. These elements are especially important tools through which the market recognizes and encourages sustainable practices. Despite this, these credit offers use complex financial tools from the perspective of farmers, in addition to high financial volumes, which would make it impossible to reach mainly small- and mid-sized farmers. In this sense, another reflection emerged:

> If the path to obtain financial recognition via revenues for the sustainable practices of the farmers was difficult, then perhaps one way would be

to provide value by reducing production costs. Cheaper access to credit could be an interesting option for lowering money-raising costs. So, how to democratize access to sustainable credit for all farmers, in a simple and feasible way with their reality?

In this scenario, the Socicana and Sicoob Coopecredi – Free Admission Credit Cooperative of the Guariba Region – established a partnership for a new line of credit for the farmers. The Green Rural Credit, with cheaper interest rates, is dedicated to sugarcane producers that are part of environmental programs or have environmental certifications. The objective is to recognize the efforts of farmers that commit time and financial resources to sustainable agricultural practices. Therefore, the interest on this credit line to finance the production and renewal of the sugarcane field is up to 20% lower.

This initiative is pioneering in Brazil, as it democratizes sustainable financing by supporting small to large producers while simultaneously creating incentives for other farmers to seek better production practices, as this represents a lower cost of raising money.

The Green Rural Credit is similar to the regular rural credit. It offers a credit line to the farmers for sugarcane planting and ratoon as well. The difference between this credit line and traditional ones lies in the fact that it is specific for producers that have proven sustainable practices, via Bonsucro, RSB Certification, or participation in Socicana's Top Cana Program. With Green Rural Credit, the producer will save up to 20% in terms of the cost of a loan in 1 year. From the initial average of 5%, the rate may be reduced to 4%, according to the certification stage at Socicana. The farmers practicing sustainability and following a program aimed at certification represent less of a credit risk.

Having created the concept of the Green Rural Credit line, it was necessary to define which resources would be used to promote it. In other words, it was necessary that the credit cooperative had specific funding for this new line. Therefore, the Green CDR (Cooperative Deposit Receipt) was created.

The Green CDR is a low-risk, fixed-income investment with attractive remuneration rates in the long run. A company or individual investors will have a differentiated result when investing their money in Sicoob Coopecredi, with better profitability in the long run. This resource will revert to the farmers, and everyone should benefit. In this way, this fund allows not only farmers but also all of society in general to invest and encourage sustainability in agriculture.

*Operational aspects of the program*

For access to the Green Rural Credit, the sugarcane producer, a member of Socicana, must belong to one of the sustainable development programs of the association, such as Top Cana (own program), Bonsucro certification, or RSB (Roundtable on Sustainable Biomaterials). The farmer is also required to be already associated or in the process of becoming affiliated with Sicoob Coopecredi.

Therefore, the first stage of the project is to raise funds via Green CDR. The amount of funds raised is allocated entirely to the Green Rural Credit line. Funding can be done daily, as part of the credit union's activities and goals processes.

The Green Rural Credit line is available in two campaigns per year: the sugarcane planting campaign (October to January) and the ratoon cane campaign (March to November). During these campaigns:

- Farmers seek Sicoob Coopecredi with their credit projects.
- Sicoob Coopecredi tells Socicana about the farmer's interest in the credit line.
- Socicana issues a certificate to Sicoob Coopecredi attesting that the farmer is an associate, as well as detailing the sustainable development program in which the producer participates, as well as the total areas participating in the certification.
- Sicoob Coopecredi distributes the available resources proportionately to the interesting projects.

*Main results*

In January 2021, R$5.42 million (almost US$1 million) was already raised, an amount referring to investments made in the Green CDR of Sicoob Coopecredi. From this, a total of R$ 4.6 million (US$0.83 million) is the estimated potential of resources to be distributed to the producers with access in this first round. In January, nine producers were able to apply for credit: five with Bonsucro certification and four with RSB certification. In the next credit campaign for financing sugarcane ratoon, another 103 producers from the Top Cana Program will be included. Thus, we are talking about a total area of approximately 25,000 hectares. It is important to remember that the funds available for the Green Rural Credit line will depend on the volume of capital raised by the Green CDR.

**Bonsucro credits**

Bonsucro certification assures buyers that the products have been produced in compliance with legislation, environmental, and human-rights good practices. Until 2019, the transactions carried out were with physical products certified by Bonsucro, an exclusive relationship between producer and buyer, whether farmers to mills or mills to end users. However, in 2019, Bonsucro launched its Credit Trading Platform.

Bonsucro Credit Trading Platform[9] is a marketplace, that is, a digital platform for buying and selling credits related to products certified by Bonsucro, which connects sellers and buyers. Sugarcane, ethanol, molasses, and sugar credits certified by Bonsucro are traded on this platform. A Bonsucro credit, in the case of sugarcane, is equivalent to one ton of sugarcane produced in accordance with Bonsucro's Production Standard.

The sale is virtual and is not a physical transaction, and the volumes offered by the seller must be in accordance with the Bonsucro Mass Balance Chain of Custody Standard. The great benefit is that, at the same time, the farmer can continue to sell their physical cane normally to the mill. With the creation of this tool, the farmer is now able to sell his physical product with Bonsucro seal or if he sells it as a standard product, he can sell the credits related to this production on the Bonsucro platform.

Bonsucro's Credit Trading platform offers farmers an alternative reward for the efforts and investments necessary in the certification process. In this way, it validates all the work on the farm directed toward a more sustainable production every day. The credits also maximize the exposure of farmers in the market and add value to their remuneration; thus, the farmer now has one more option for revenue. In addition, this initiative allows the farmer to directly access end users and offer their differentiated production.

Credits are also an excellent deal for buyers, who can get past government restrictions imposed on trade in products derived from sugarcane, such as quotas. The transaction is a form of recognition from buyers and their support for the best environmental, social, and operational practices in the production of sugarcane. In this way, it encourages and practices the sharing of value created in the production chain.

Socicana manages the entire Bonsucro certification process for its members and also acts as a credit manager. On July 29, 2020, Socicana carried out the first worldwide transaction of Bonsucro-certified sugarcane credits on Bonsucro's Credit Trading Platform. The sale was made to the chocolate company Barry Callebaut.

*Operational aspects of the program*

The platform offers two forms of trading, the on-market trade and the off-market trade. In the on-market trade, sellers and buyers make offers based on volume and price. In the event of a match, the transaction is completed. In this way, buyers do not know or select sellers. The off-market trade, on the other hand, is a negotiation between seller and buyer, which takes place outside of the online platform, but after the agreement is concluded, the transaction is registered on the platform.

As Socicana is the manager of the group of certified producers, it was also responsible for managing the marketing of credits. Thus, the operational steps for Socicana are as follows:

Check the physical products sold under the Bonsucro seal and the availability of credits to be offered;

- Offer credits on the platform;
- Monitor the credit market;
- Negotiate with buyers in off-market mode;
- Validate the negotiations with certified producers;
- Finalize the transaction on the platform;

- Carry out the proportional distribution of credits sold among certified producers;
- Assist in administrative issues related to negotiation;
- Monitor the transactions.

*Main results*

Until March 2021, Socicana had sold a total of 183,000 sugarcane credits on the platform, equivalent to 183 thousand tons of certified sugarcane.

This system has advantages for farmers because they would not be able to trade alone: they either would have difficulty accessing markets or might not meet the volumes demanded by final buyers. Other than that, there is the whole administrative issue of international negotiations, as well as mechanisms for receiving international financial remittances and justification for Brazilian federal revenue. Socicana is the great facilitator for the commercialization of Bonsucro farmers' credits.

## Conclusion

Consumers increasingly demand sustainable products, which means agriculture with sustainable practices is necessary. On their own, farmers would have a hard time developing sustainable methods, often due to lack of knowledge, access to information, and technical assistance; this is especially true for small farmers. In this way, associations, as a form of collective action, can help to promote sustainable development among their associates, especially by taking the approach of continuous improvement, encouraging them, in their time and available financial resources, to promote improvements. The programs developed by Socicana play the role of promoting sustainability in the production of sugarcane.

Although it is extremely important to promote sustainability in the chain, it is also of fundamental importance to generate value for the farmers, recognizing their practices and creating incentives for them to continue these practices and also to attract new farmers to the programs. It's possible to generate value in different ways. In this case, Socicana generated value through additional revenues and reduced production costs via the lower cost of raising money.

The great challenges of the programs are still in convincing new producers to join the program and prove the benefits to those who participate. There is still a challenge for Socicana to maintain the program over the long term, as the program requires considerable financial resources.

## Teaching notes

*Overview*

This case study describes how Socicana, an association of sugarcane growers, sought to promote the sustainable development of its members through the creation of a continuous improvement program and the development of its sustainable protocol and the inclusion of producers in international certifications. In addition, it describes the efforts and programs developed to generate value for producers participating in sustainable development programs, seeking more benefits and incentives for them to continue and also for the association to attract new members for sustainable development and continuous improvement. It is a model of how associativism, as a tool for collective action, can seek solutions for sustainable agriculture and how private initiatives, in their various organizations, can contribute to each other in collective action.

*Statement of relevance*

This case is important because it shows the success of partnerships between the private sector and organized civil society to seek out sustainability solutions in agribusiness. It also opens up a discussion about strategy; after a delicate moment the Brazilian sugarcane associations faced, a strategy was created to generate value perception for the associate.

*Target market statement*

Teaching Objectives: discuss strategies on associativism and value creation in collective actions, as well as the challenges of promoting sustainable agriculture.

Target Audience: senior undergraduate course; graduate course; executive education.

*Suggested assignment questions*

- What strategy could an association, whose main function is representativeness, adopt to promote sustainable development?
- How should sustainable development protocols evolve and what should they address?
- How to financially maintain a sustainable development program?
- How to use partnerships to promote sustainable development in agribusiness and create value?
- Which stakeholders should be engaged to achieve to promote a sustainability agriculture?
- How to maintain a long-term program that does not generate direct revenue?
- How to generate value perception in associativism?
- How can farmers generate value with sustainable practices?

# Annexes

### COP 21 and the possible impacts on the Brazilian sugar-energy sector

The 21st Conference of the Parties (COP 21) seeks to understand and find solutions to climate change. It is the principal decision-making body of the

United Nations Framework Convention on Climate Change (UNFCCC). The goal of COP 21 was the commitment to reduce greenhouse gas emissions. During the event, 195 countries proposed individual commitment documents, called iNDC[10], which are action plans and targets submitted by each country aimed at reducing emissions of greenhouse gases.

Through its iNDC, Brazil presented measures in several sectors aiming at the reduction of GHG emissions. The Brazilian commitment implies initiatives from three sectors that had the largest share in Brazilian emissions in 2012: energy, land-use change and forests, and agriculture.

The Brazilian iNDC (see note 10) describes the measures adopted to achieve the goal of reducing greenhouse gas emissions by 37% in 2025 and 43% in 2030. Of these measures taken by the Brazilian government, some have direct impacts on the sugar-energy sector:

"i) Increase the share of sustainable bioenergy in the Brazilian energy matrix to approximately 18% by 2030, expanding the consumption of biofuels, increasing the supply of ethanol, also by increasing the share of advanced biofuels (second generation), and increasing the share of biodiesel in the diesel mixture. . .

iii) In the energy sector, achieve an estimated share of 45% of renewable energy in the composition of the energy matrix by 2030, including: . . .

to expand the domestic use of non-fossil energy sources, increasing the share of renewable energy (in addition to hydropower) in the supply of electricity to at least 23% by 2030, also by increasing wind, biomass, and solar."

Thus, it is necessary to understand the impact of these commitments in the sugar-energy sector, whether in the consumption of the main products, production, inputs, jobs, income generation, and taxes, among others.

## Socicana services provides

Technical department: crop loss assessment, planting quality assessment, pesticide application guidance and evaluation, IPM (MIP), machinery and equipment regulation, product monitoring, guidance on production costs, monitoring of new technologies, and lectures and training;

Sucrose and inspection laboratory: maturation analysis, analysis conference, truck weighing inspection, mill materials and equipment inspection, and Consecana's model audit and conference;

Projects and sustainability department: improvement of agricultural practices, improvement of financial management of rural properties, use of tools for better crop indicators, performance at social, environmental, and economic levels, Top Cana program, international certification processes (Bonsucro and RSB);

Legal department: environmental advice in relation to fires in sugarcane fields, advisory in contract analysis, land advisory, labor advisory, and representation in committees of the Mogi Guaçu Watershed.

Department of Social Assistance: provides collective health insurance products, dental health plans, monitoring and follow-up of accredited hospitals and physicians, guidance on care facilities, and health plan use.

Table 5A.1 Stratification of Socicana associates – 2020/21 harvest

| Production profile (size) Tons | Farmers' Numbers | | | Total Production | | |
|---|---|---|---|---|---|---|
| | Amount | % | Accumulated % | Production | % | Accumulated % |
| < 1,000 | 271 | 29.68 | 29.68 | 140,422.9 | 2.24 | 2.24 |
| 1,000–6,000 | 435 | 47.65 | 77.33 | 1,185,128.9 | 18.87 | 21.11 |
| 6,000–12,000 | 88 | 9.64 | 86.97 | 751,958.2 | 11.97 | 33.08 |
| 12,000–25,000 | 66 | 7.23 | 94.19 | 1,077,453.8 | 17.16 | 50.24 |
| 25,000–50,000 | 28 | 3.07 | 97.26 | 967,949.0 | 15.41 | 65.65 |
| 50,000–100,000 | 21 | 2.30 | 99.56 | 1,471,548.3 | 23.43 | 89.08 |
| > 100,000 | 4 | 0.44 | 100.00 | 685,464.9 | 10.92 | 100.00 |
| TOTAL | 913 | 100.00 | | 6,279,926.1 | 100.00 | |

Source: Socicana

*Associativism as promoter of sustainability, value for farmers* 119

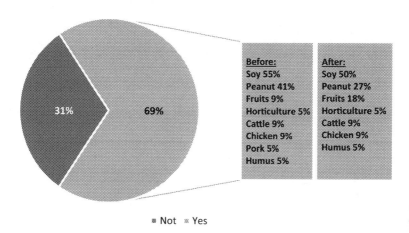

*Figure 5A.1* Governance and organizational structure of Socicana – the role of agents
Source: Socicana.

Communication Department: responsible for promoting information to members through printed material, newsletters, websites, SMS, WhatsApp messages, social fan page, and letters.

*GM*: The General Meeting is Socicana's highest decision-making body. The assembly is made up of associate farmers only and takes place once a year. In it, they make decisions regarding budget, definition of membership fees, and activity plans. During the assembly, each farmer is entitled to one vote, regardless of production size. In case of major and urgent decisions, an extraordinary general meeting may be convened.

*Administrative Council*: The council is made up of seven members, elected at the general meeting and serving a term of 3 years. It is responsible for drafting and planning norms for the development of the activities and the accomplishment of the company's general policy, such as setting guidelines, examining and approving budgets, setting work goals, and evaluating the performance of the council and CEO, among others. There are monthly meetings to discuss matters of the association, deliberation of actions to be taken, and decision-making.

*Fiscal Council:* This is formed by three associate members, elected at the general meeting. Its function is to oversee the acts and actions of officers and associates and the compliance with the bylaws. They hold monthly meetings.

*Executive Board:* This consists of three members elected from the seven of the Administrative Council. The board is composed of the president, secretary, and treasurer. It is a body subordinate to the Administrative Council, and its function is the executive management of Socicana, operational decision-making,

Table 5A.2 Top Cana farmer rating levels

| Requirements' Level | Attention | Bronze | Silver | Gold |
|---|---|---|---|---|
| Essential Requirements | Less than 100% | 100% | 100% | 100% |
| Basic Requirements | | 75% | 80% | 100% |
| Advanced Requirements | | | 50% | 75% |

Source: Kalaki et al., 2021.

Table 5A.3 Example of rating received by farmers

| Pillars | General Suitability | Classification |
|---|---|---|
| **Overall Performance** | **74%** | **Silver** |
| Management | 90% | Gold |
| Labor | 70% | Silver |
| Environmental | 95% | Gold |
| Good Agricultural Practice | 60% | Bronze |
| Rural Constructions | 45% | Attention |

Source: Kalaki et al., 2021.

and coordination of the CEO. They have monthly meetings. Board term of office is 3 years.

CEO: The CEO is responsible for the operational management of the association. This person is a market professional, hired by the board and not associates. The CEO has the role of planning, directing, controlling, organizing Socicana's activities, setting action policies, and monitoring development. He or she is still responsible for coordinating department managers and taking care of the entire team.

Departments: Socicana's activities were divided into seven departments: technical, laboratory, social, communication, sustainability, financial, and legal, and each of them has a responsible manager.

In addition to checking their suitability requirements for a certain level, farmers can track their progress with the assessment and levels within each pillar as well as a final result in terms of meeting the requirements. With this view, they can assess which pillar needs adjustments and also how much is left to level up.

### Top Cana general results

It is possible to find more details about the program, as well as a detailed analysis of its results at Kalaki, R. B. et al. Sustainability in the sugarcane production the case of Socicana and the Top Cana program. IN: Neves, M. F. and Kalaki, R.B. (org). Bioenergy from sugarcane. Available in: <http://socicana.com.br/2.0/wp-content/uploads/Livro_Bioenergy_From_Sugarcane_Fava_Neves_Kalaki-compactado.pdf>.

The analysis of the results was based on the checklist database applied to rural properties upon entering the Program (2013, 2015, and 2017) and on the last update of the checklist dated 2019, making it possible to check the evolution of the properties as a result of the Top Cana Program and the actions developed by Socicana. Thirty properties visited in 2019 out of 120 participants of the Top Cana Program were sampled.

*General data*

Sugarcane is the main source of income in 78.13% of farms, and family-based agriculture is present in 27.7% of the sampled properties. The female presence in the sugarcane activity was not very expressive, being about 16% of the properties are headed by women, in 28% there is female participation in cleaning, home, and cooking activities, and 13% have participation in administrative and office activities. Men predominantly occupy the agricultural area.

The average productivity of the properties is 88 tons of sugarcane per hectare against the national average of 73.49 tons per hectare (Conab 2018/2019). Crop diversification is present in about 68.75% of the properties, and this value has remained unchanged since the beginning of the Program.

Crop diversification is a favorable practice for farmers to remain in the sugarcane industry, especially in small and medium properties because it is possible to diversify income, make extra revenue from crop rotation, and lower costs.

The farms went from an overall performance average of 74% at the beginning of the program to 88% in 2019. As for the pillars, on average, growers also showed improvements in each of them.

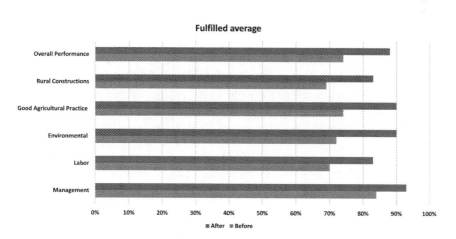

*Figure 5A.2* Crop diversification practiced by farmers participating in Topcana
Source: Kalaki et al., 2021.

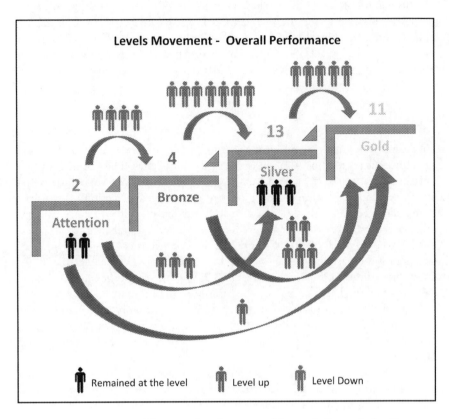

*Figure 5A.3* Comparison of the general performance of farmers before and after Topcana
Source: Kalaki et al., 2021.

Regarding the overall rating, most growers showed improvement in levels. No growers have dropped level during the program. Only five growers, out of the 30 analyzed, remained at the same level of classification, which does not mean that they did not evolve, because all had evolved, but probably the evolution was not enough to change levels. On the other hand, growers jumped more than one level and one grower jumped two levels in evolution, leaving the attention rating and going to the gold rating.

In the Overall Performance, all properties showed improvements due to the adjustments made to the farms, as indicated in the Improvement Plans. The table shows that, at the beginning of the Top Cana Program, more than half of the farms were in the Attention and Bronze levels, except for the Management Pillar. During the Program, there was significant migration to the Silver and Gold levels, currently consisting of 13 and 11 farms, respectively.

*Associativism as promoter of sustainability, value for farmers* 123

*Figure 5A.4* Evolution of Topcana participating farmers at different levels
Source: Kalaki et al., 2021.

*Table 5A.4* Number of farms before and after Top Cane Program

| Number of farms | Attention | | Bronze | | Silver | | Gold | |
|---|---|---|---|---|---|---|---|---|
| Pillars | Before | After | Before | After | Before | After | Before | After |
| Management | 5 | 2 | 4 | 2 | 14 | 10 | 7 | 16 |
| Labor | 12 | 3 | 9 | 12 | 7 | 9 | 2 | 6 |
| Environmental | 13 | 2 | 8 | 4 | 8 | 15 | 1 | 9 |
| Good Agricultural Practice | 12 | 0 | 9 | 3 | 6 | 16 | 3 | 11 |
| Rural Constructions | 15 | 5 | 3 | 5 | 9 | 6 | 3 | 14 |
| Overall Performance | 10 | 2 | 12 | 4 | 8 | 13 | 0 | 11 |

Source: Kalaki et al., 2021.

*Figure 5A.5* Simulation of the green rural credit line
Source: Socicana.

The evolution of the program participants was clear and evident, showing that the program, in fact, brought improvements to the development of the growers' activity and especially in relation to the development of sustainable agriculture.

## Projects recognized by Bonsucro Inspire Award

19 February 2018

The Bonsucro Inspire Award 2018 was awarded to Socicana for a project named Top Cana which was implemented in partnership with Solidaridad.

*Figure 5A.6* The awards received by the Top Cana Program

*Figure 5A.7* Top Cana Farmers' Awards Event

*Associativism as promoter of sustainability, value for farmers* 125

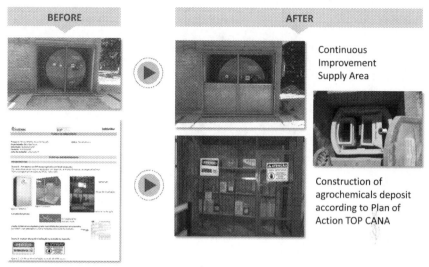

*Figure 5A.8* Examples of adjustments made by farmers in physical structure

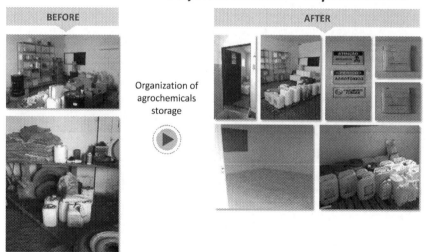

*Figure 5A.9* Examples of adjustments made by farmers in physical structure

126  *Rafael Bordonal Kalaki and Marcos Fava Neves*

*Figure 5A.10* Examples of adjustments made by farmers in farm organization

## Notes

1 More detailed information about social, economic, and environmental benefits of sugar-energy sector be found at: Neves, M.F. (org.), *O setor sucroenergético em 2030: Dimensões, investimentos e uma agenda estratégica*. Available in: <www.portaldaindustria.com.br/publicacoes/2017/8/o-setor-sucroenergetico-em-2030-dimensoes-investimentos-e-uma-agenda-estrategica/>; Neves, M.F., Kalaki, R.B., Pinto, M.J.A. and Gerbasi, T., Sugar cane as a promoter of development: The cases of Quirinópolis and Uberaba. In: Neves, M.F. and Kalaki, R.B. (org.), *Bioenergy from sugarcane*. Available in: <http://socicana.com.br/2.0/wp-content/uploads/Livro_Bioenergy_From_Sugarcane_Fava_Neves_Kalaki-compactado.pdf>.
2 UNICA (Brazilian Sugarcane Industry Association) is the representative body of a wide group of companies that produce sugar, ethanol, and bioelectricity in the Center-South region of Brazil. Available in: <https://unica.com.br/en/>.
3 Solidaridad is an international civil society organization with over 50 years of experience and operations in over 40 countries focused on the sustainability of value chains. In Brazil, Solidaridad operates in eight commodity chains, contributing to food security and the implementation of good agricultural practices in the context of climate change adaptation and mitigation. Available in: <www.solidaridadsouthamerica.org/brasil/pt>.
4 Free Admission Credit Cooperative of the Guariba Region, Sicoob Coopecredi, is one of the largest credit cooperatives in the country. It was created with the objective of providing financial support to farmers who worked with the cultivation of sugar cane in Guariba and region. Today, Sicoob Coopecredi is a free admission credit cooperative and has more than 5,000 members.
5 It is possible to find more details about the program, as well as a detailed analysis of its results at: Kalaki, R.B. et al., Sustainability in the sugarcane production the case of Socicana and Top Cana program. In: Neves, M.F. and Kalaki, R.B. (org.), *Bioenergy*

*from sugarcane*. Available in: <http://socicana.com.br/2.0/wp-content/uploads/Livro_Bioenergy_From_Sugarcane_Fava_Neves_Kalaki-compactado.pdf>.
6 RenovaBio is the National Biofuel Policy created by the Brazilian government. RenovaBio's main instrument is the establishment of annual national decarbonization targets for the fuel sector, in order to encourage an increase in the production and participation of biofuels in the country's energy matrix. The objectives of the program are to (1) provide an important contribution to the fulfilment of the commitments determined by Brazil under the Paris Agreement; (2) promote the adequate expansion of biofuels in the energy matrix, with an emphasis on regular fuel supply; (3) ensure predictability for the fuel market, inducing gains in energy efficiency and reduction of greenhouse gas emissions in the production, commercialization, and use of biofuels.
7 To learn more about Bonsucro. Available in: <www.bonsucro.com/>.
8 To learn more about RSB. Available in: <www. https://rsb.org/>.
9 To learn more about Bonsucro Credit Trading Platform. Available in: <https://credits.bonsucro.com>.
10 Intended Nationally Determined Contribution.

# 6 Social business models in agri-food

## An interview with Sara Rajabli, founder of Buta Art & Sweets

*Laman Baghirova, Elena Casprini, Niccolò Fiorini, and Maria Carmela Annosi*

**Introduction**

Social entrepreneurs *"need to simultaneously demonstrate their social and economic competence"* (Dacin et al., 2011, p. 1207). This need seems to suggest that social entrepreneurship should rely on more sophisticated business models that could balance both commercial and social sides.

Social entrepreneurship represents a new phenomenon (see Weerawardena and Sullivan Mort, 2006 for a review), which is gaining increasing importance in both developed and developing countries. However, whether there is a great deal of literature on social entrepreneurship and some specific aspects, such as its underlying theories (Ranville and Barros, 2022), social capital (e.g., Hidalgo et al., 2021), ecosystems (Diaz Gonzalez and Dentchev, 2021), and the motivations leading social entrepreneurs (Kruse et al., 2021), less is known about the social business models that help these social businesses to survive.

Literature on business models is in agreement, sustaining that business models are crucial in explaining a firm's performance (Foss and Saebi, 2017; Zott et al., 2011) and it is increasingly relevant to understanding how business models could be designed to pursue sustainable goals (Bocken et al., 2014). However, there are few empirical examples of social business models in comparison to, for example, for-profit businesses, even if the number of social enterprises is increasing around the world, capturing the attention of scholars (e.g., Wilson and Post, 2013; Santos et al., 2015; Carayannis et al., 2021; Tykkyläinen and Ritala, 2021). For the purposes of this chapter, two main elements should be considered as distinguishing social business models from other types of sustainable business models (e.g., Bocken et al., 2014). The first concerns the presence of social-profit objectives and shareholders (Yunus et al., 2010), which might shape, for example, the dimensions of a business model. Extant research has proposed several dimensions for business models (for a review, see Casprini, 2019), but probably the most diffused are those represented in the business model canvas (Osterwalder and Pigneur, 2010), namely, value proposition, customer segments, customer relationships, key resources, key activities, key

DOI: 10.4324/9781003223672-9

partners, channels, cost structure, and revenue stream. These dimensions need to be redesigned according to social-profit-oriented objectives, values, and key elements. In other terms, once the social value of the business is at the core of its mission, the same social value might influence one or more of these elements. The second element has to do with the role of the context where the social business emerges: local problems that need to be solved can inspire social entrepreneurship. Specifically, countries differ in terms of the focus placed on inclusion for the disadvantage, gender equality, culture and tradition, ethnic and/or political conflicts, and, broadly speaking, the economic situation. To this extent, we think that social business models could be particularly important in developing countries, where a scarcity of resources, such as physical and digital infrastructure, as well as social problems related to disabled people, women, refugees, and other disadvantaged groups in society, potentially exacerbated by war, political voids, etc. (Rosandic and Guluzade, 2018), could lead to entrepreneurs facing a variety of challenges in designing their business models.

We now present an example of the promotion and inclusion of disabled women in Azerbaijan, showing how *a young female social entrepreneur has developed a social business model integrating both economic and social values, thus successfully combining tradition, culture, and inclusion*. First, like other studies (Barney, 2004; Dunne and Martin, 2006; Alcaraz and Thiruvattal, 2010), we briefly present the background of the case and the whole interview conducted with this young social entrepreneur by one of the authors. Then, we discuss the main findings and takeaways from the interview.

## Background

Four years ago, in 2017, with a budget of approximately 80 euros (160 manat), Mrs. Sara Rajabli, a young Azerbaijani woman, decided to start her own enterprise to solve a social problem related to unemployment among women with special needs (i.e., women with mental or physical disabilities) in Azerbaijan. The name she chose was Buta Art & Sweets, which embraces the product type and has a strong link with art and culture.

The story of Buta Art & Sweets can be traced back to when Sara was studying in the bachelor's program for Tourism and Hotel Management in Azerbaijan. It was during her first year of her bachelor's degree that her interest in social entrepreneurship emerged. Sara was interested in the training sessions about social entrepreneurship organized by Oikos Baku[1]. After her studies abroad for a semester, Sara started a blog that become soon very successful, about social entrepreneurship. Her first idea was to sell sweets, honey, and *kelaghayi* (handmade silk scarves). Then, one of Sara's friends suggested she focus on only one product, adding social value to it. Therefore, Sara focused on sweets, thinking about the impact on society at the same time.

In doing some research, Sara recognized that about 300,000 women in Azerbaijan have some form of disability and almost all of them are unemployed.

The aim of Buta Art & Sweets became immediately clear: the problem of unemployment among women with special needs must be overcome, hence improving their place in the society. In fact, being a woman and having a disability are discriminating factors in both families and communities.

She wanted to learn how to help these women and how to successfully set up a social business. Therefore, she visited the homes of disabled women and collected data about them. This was useful for obtaining a comprehensive overview of their psychological conditions and personal stories.

Sara's objective was not to help them by offering money; instead, she preferred to choose a more sustainability-oriented approach. This is why she wanted to engage and motivate them. To do so, she told the disabled women about her desires and ambitions, with the purpose of enabling and empowering them to manage their own salaries. In this way, Sara gave disabled women a sense of dignity as self-entrepreneurs.

Upon establishing the company, Sara also aimed to represent the cultural values of Azerbaijan. Thanks to her project, Sara has won several awards, the most important being the "Youth Award" from the President of the Republic of Azerbaijan in 2019. Furthermore, Sara became the winner of Global Start-up Awards in 2020 and the Princess Diana Award 2021. Buta Art & Sweets has represented its products at high-level events in 17 countries. What's more, Buta Art & Sweets organizes master classes, thus having an even greater impact. Buta Art & Sweets provided small packages of mini national sweets with touching letters on behalf of women with special needs for political leaders and entrepreneurs during the High-Level Global Baku Forum in 2018, proving that limits only exist in people's minds.

Currently, 20 women with special needs are working for Buta Art & Sweets. Today, the social enterprise has a turnover of a minimum 350,000 dollars, by constantly investing profits in capacity-building programs for women with special needs. In 2021, Buta Art & Sweets organized, together with the Ministry of Education, the first project in Azerbaijan, officially certifying the confectionery skills of local women with special needs. During the COVID-19 crisis, Buta Art & Sweets redesigned their menu for vegan, gluten, and sugar-free sweets.

**Interview with Sara**

Laman Baghirova, at that time a master's student in International Accounting and Management at the University of Siena in Italy, conducted the interview in late 2020. Originally, the interview was planned in person in Azerbaijan; however, because of the travel restrictions due to the COVID-19 pandemic and, furthermore, because of limited Internet access for Sara Rajabli due to the war over Nagorno-Karabakh, in Azerbaijan, audio messages were the only way to replace a standard interview.

The purpose of the interview was to analyze the dimensions of the business model canvas (Osterwalder and Pigneur, 2010) as an example of social entrepreneurship. Specifically, we want to provide an in-depth analysis of how a social enterprise (1) addresses the value proposition and the benefits the product/service poses for customers and society; (2) determines customer segments; (3) identifies the partnerships that form the value network; and (4) explores how the social entrepreneur deals with customer relationships, (5) key resources, (6) key activities, (7) distribution channels, (8) revenue, and (9) cost models.

In aiming to do so, as a young female entrepreneur well known in Azerbaijan for the social impact of her idea, Sara represents an ideal choice of interviewee, as she gives us a window into understanding how the business model for a successful social enterprise (Buta Art & Sweets) was designed.

*Laman:* Which are the benefits of your product/service for a potential customer? How is the price chosen?

When thinking about the social enterprise, we did not want only for our clients to be a socially valuable brand. We also wanted to offer high-quality, fresh, and homemade sweets. So, people missing the home taste in sweets and who do not want to wait for long time could order from us, while also directly impacting local women with special needs, thanks to acquiring our sweets.

So, what are our value propositions and our uniqueness? First, fresh and handmade cruelty-free sweets, so unlike our competitors and supermarkets and cake shops, we do not sell any sweets that have been kept for more than one day. So, we prepare on the same day and we deliver to our customers. Second, our uniqueness is being handmade and homemade and using no animal ingredients. People who miss sweets that taste like home can order, of course, from a woman who prepares the sweets, but we are also adding new unique flavors which cannot be found in any other recipes, we are always innovating our products, we are always changing, and also we have vegan products, which cannot be easily found in local markets, so we are trying to be also handmade and homemade. Third, obviously, fast delivery, and customization for corporate orders because companies want to have customization and we also provide this, with also fast delivery, and special notes from our women. The last one is, of course, the social impact. We do not have standardized recipes for our sweets: this also makes us very different because every woman has her own recipes and they are not similar, they can have different tastes, and, according to the wishes and feedback from our customers, we can provide it. We have a special database listing the women's strengths. For example, one woman makes very good *pakhlava*, so we only order *pakhlava* from that woman. We do not order, for example, *shekerbura* because we know that she is not very strong and she likes to cook *pakhlava*. And, when we are talking with women we are asking actually, for example, one kilogram of *pakhlava* how much would be suitable for you? They do, for example, tell us the price for one kilogram of *pakhlava* with high-quality ingredients that they buy themselves. We do not provide those ingredients for them because we do not have enough team members to do provisioning for 20 women. They buy those products themselves from the supermarkets, and they are using high-quality products, so that is why it is not as cheap as the sweets in supermarkets. We use natural oil, natural milk products, nuts, especially for traditional sweets, and that is why it has an impact on prices.

The price depends on the sweets. If it is traditional, it is much more expensive. If it is not traditional, like simple cookies, it is much cheaper, but it also depends on the feedback of our customers. For example, if the customers do not want to have natural oil in the sweets, they can tell us, and we can offer much cheaper prices; generally, we do not provide any sweets without organic, natural products and ingredients, and actually it also adds some uniqueness and freshness and additional taste for our sweets. When we talk with those women, they tell us what they buy, and they also tell us the price and the expenses for products. We also ask for the receipts for those products in order to justify and add things up for ourselves.

When there are huge orders, we, of course, also offer discounts, but if there are some smaller orders, we give the original price, so, for example, if they tell us we are only making 1 kilo of *pakhlava* for 20 manat, we do not offer discounts, we tell our customers that 1 kilo of *pakhlava* is, for example, 25 manat. So, in this 5 manat, we are including our own commission, delivery costs, and also we are including prices for packaging and prices for sales, so actually we are giving many more opportunities for our women to earn, instead of reserving for ourselves, we are just covering the costs. Of course, if people buy only 1 kilo of *pakhlava*, this 5 manat for us will be very small amount, but generally, we receive huge orders, especially from companies, from people who are celebrating their parties in Novruz holidays, and so on. So, for us, these commissions are getting higher, and it gives us the opportunity to have an income, a profit, to reinvest into the social business.

*Laman:* How is the target customer identified? How does the target customer group influence your marketing?

In terms of the target customer group, it was a very specific and very challenging moment in our social business when we started because I did not know to whom we could sell our products. When I shared this idea with my parents, they did not agree. They told me that no one would buy those products just because people think that products handmade by women with special needs can never be of high quality so you cannot sell them in Azerbaijan. You can sell it in other countries, but you cannot sell it in Azerbaijan.

So, I was thinking that, if we cannot sell these products to individuals, we can sell them to organizations and companies that are interested in social responsibility, in promoting themselves by purchasing our products. Then, we reached out to companies in Azerbaijan, organizations, NGOs, and foundations, which plan different events and we called them every day. We reached a maximum of

30 companies per day through calls, emails, and networking events. We talked endlessly about our project and, of course, we gave them free sweets to try because, if you are in the food industry, it is so important for an entrepreneur to provide free samples of sweets of any food product in order to give an opportunity for potential customers to try those products before making any buying decisions so, for us, it was always important. Actually, my initial investment of 160 manat went to the women for trials, free samples of sweets; we actually went to companies, met with them, made presentations, and made our B2B business model in order to make sales. It was the best decision we made at the beginning because we knew that we could not reach individuals but we could reach companies, because they are interested, they can buy much more, and it would also be very beneficial for us. And when we reached companies, we gave them free samples. They liked them and immediately gave us the opportunity to sign contracts so we could provide the sweets for their events, corporate gifts, and any other occasions on a regular basis. So, for us it was a huge success as an early-stage entrepreneurship project because no one believed in us. For us, it was very important to have direct marketing and direct sales, by calling them, emailing them, and by going and talking to them. We also reached out to cafes and restaurants but, with cafes and restaurants, it was not really the right decision because they are not really interested in the quality of the food product, but rather in lower prices, so that is why we are not cooperating with cafes as much. We are working with companies and organizations mainly.

So, first, our customer segment is companies and organizations that are passionate about social responsibility and that have also shown great interest in the empowerment of women. For them, it was very important to support our social business by purchasing our products. The second customer segment is families and individuals – workers from those companies who once tried our sweets from the corporate gifts or from events and they also ordered from us in addition for their events, for their holidays, and for personal occasions. So, for us, businesspeople, entrepreneurs, office workers, and students are also our main customer targets because if we were to research the market for our cakes, we would see that the majority of customers or buyers of cakes are students, so we have also been focusing on students in order to provide those cakes and some different sweets. Corporate orders make up 80% of our sales with 20% coming from individuals.

With the B/business model, we rely on direct communications through emails, LinkedIn, calls, and networking events for B2B meetings. For individuals, we use social media, email, marketing, and also, of course, word of mouth. Word of mouth became also the most important part of our marketing because if one company liked our sweets, they could also recommend them to other companies and organizations and, for us, it was also a success to receive calls from unknown people, from unknown organizations, who got these recommendations by our customers. So, for us, it was also very important and also influenced our marketing in order to reach many more individuals. We also started using influencer marketing, collaborated with bloggers, and invited them for our video materials, video projects, so, for us, it was also very important to communicate with them.

*Laman:* What about the relationship between you and your customer group? How is it maintained and how does it influence the performance of social entrepreneurship?

Customer satisfaction and customer loyalty are the most important because customers are our main supporters. We do not get any sponsorships, any grants from anyone, and we understand the importance of customer relationships in every aspect. First, it starts from communicating with our women, whenever we are getting not so high-quality products, in terms of taste and appearance, even before ordering from them on constant basis, when we first meet with our women, we always tell them that if you are not preparing high-quality products, no one will buy them a second time. So, for us, it is so important in such a competitive market to be sustainable through maintaining these customer relations and keeping these high-quality products.

If our women give us low-quality products a second time, we do not buy those products from those women again. We explain that we'd already told them how important it was to keep the quality up, to not waste our time, give excuses. So if you are not taking care of the customer, the customer will also not take care of you, so he will just pay for the last order, and the second time he will just go to other competitors. So, we are not taking risks. We do not want to lose our customers: they are our friends, they are our main supporters, and we really appreciate them a lot. Especially for corporate orders, we offer discounts when we receive huge orders, we offer customized packaging, and we also send very touching letters on behalf of our women. I will tell you one story. When we organized those small packages of sweets for the High-Level Global Baku Forum, it was for VIP guests – all presidents, vice presidents, prime ministers, CEOs of companies, and heads of governments. They were in Baku, and we sent them special VIP packages of sweets with mini national sweets with special letters. So one of the VIP participants of this forum told me that he didn't open this small package of sweets in Baku because he wanted to take it back to the United States to show his son with autism that nothing is impossible when you see how special-needs Azerbaijani women prepare such great tasty amazing handmade national sweets. For us, it is very important to stir up emotions, memories, and experiences. It is very important to constantly listen to feedback. From accepting orders to after tasting our products, we always receive feedback about what they like, what they don't like, what they would change in our products, in our delivery services, which sweets exactly they like the most – because they can order different types of sweets – but which they like the most, and we will also work on those. It is also very important for us to give free sweets to our regular customers so they can try new sweets, and if they like them, they can order, so for us it is very important to keep this communication. We also use email marketing for updating them on our new offers, new campaigns, and new discounts, so we are making everything.

And we are also trying to just to talk with our customers. We don't even ask a lot of questions about our products or our services. We ask questions about their lifestyle, what they like the most, what their dreams are, how their work is going, and so on. So, for us, it is very important to know exactly who our customer is, not only at the beginning of marketing research but also in the process, so we are forming friendships, so people know our team members not only because of producing the sweets but also for maintaining this friendship. For us, it is very important and we are also keeping this database of our customers, we are taking note of their orders, we are taking note of their favorites, everything, so we are keeping this database and always making new changes to this database and we are always trying to maintain this loyalty with discounts, free gifts, and with touching letters on their birthdays, on special days, so that they also feel this warmth from our team members.

Customer relations play the most important role in the performance of social entrepreneurship, so if you do not have any customers, if you cannot keep these relationships, we cannot operate, we cannot keep growing, so, for us, customer relations is the most important and that is why I advise all entrepreneurs who would like to start a business to take into account the customer as a priority, not the investor, not the supplier, not the beneficiaries, but the customer because if you are satisfying your customer, you will grow and you will be sustainable as a business so it is very important to satisfy the customer, to be his friend, because, especially in the pandemic, we saw that our customers sent money. They could not buy our products but we kept up communications with them, so it was coming from our sincerity, our curiosity, what is happening around us, and what is happening in the lives of our customers.

That is why they choose us. They can't have these human relationships in every cake shop or with every sweet brand. Entrepreneurship is not about technology, sales, or marketing, but it is all about communication with people. This human factor, the emotions that humans have, can never be replaced by any technology or robots. We need to keep those emotions, which make us different. That was the biggest lesson that I learned from social entrepreneurship actually.

*Laman:* How do you reach your customers and what channels prove to be cost-effective?

To reach our corporate customers, we used channels like LinkedIn, calls, emails, networking events, and B2B meetings, and also, of course, our personal connections. As a social business, a strong network is needed to reach higher places and international organizations. I think it is very important to use all connections, use all resources, you have in your hand and when you are starting a social enterprise, it is so important to not be afraid to talk about your social enterprise.

I remember when I started, I was so shy to talk about us, because we did not have exact results and my family members were not satisfied with the work I was doing, so I was not self-confident, until getting the first sales and results. So it was also very important for us to get these results, and then I knew 100% that when we got these results, we would be much more confident, and we would be stronger in persuading others to purchase our products.

For corporate orders, we use channels, for individuals we use social media, word of mouth, rely on our friends, colleagues, events, charities, exhibitions, different social events, and events of NGOs, so we use everything. We use email, WhatsApp connections, and marketing, because we want to reach many more people, of course we have a niche market, we have specification of our target customer group because in the twenty-first century, and we can't reach everyone. You cannot build your business for everyone, but, if you want to just to raise awareness about your social value, you should use all your connections and all your channels, but, exactly if you are talking B2B sales, about customers, we use LinkedIn, which is a free resource, we use emails, which are also a free resource, we make calls, which is a little bit expensive because you need to call every month, every day, and so on. But we are trying to manage. It also means including the expenses of our budget, so there are not a lot of difficulties. We also use our personal connections, which are very valuable. I could never say this is free, and I could never put a price on this resource because much more in entrepreneurship, not only social entrepreneurship but, in general, in entrepreneurship, personal connections that work in different places, who can support you with contracts, with negotiations, they are much more important than getting investments, grants, or anything else, or international recognition. So, I think those personal connections should be also used. Thanks to personal connections, we were also able to collaborate with the first and only vegan shop in Azerbaijan, where we distribute our products.

In terms of individuals, we use social media, such as Instagram, Facebook, different groups, and word of mouth, which are free. If our customers are satisfied, they are actually your best sales manager and should not be forgotten.

*Laman:* Which are the key resources/assets and how does a social entrepreneur identify them?

Of course, our main resources are human resources. We can invest in technologies but the high quality of products (or services) depends on human resources. This is our main model, our main priority, and value, in running a social enterprise, so we are very much interested in developing our team members, we are always investing in their education, in developing skills and capacities. Therefore, the top resources are, of course, the special-needs women and other team members who are actively involved in the preparation of sweets, and in the delivery process, organizing orders, accepting orders, and bookings, in communication with clients and marketing.

The second important resources are, of course, the products necessary to prepare those sweets – ingredients. We plan these preparations with suppliers. We already have trusted suppliers, and we are already working with them. It depends on the ingredients for sweets, it is also about delivery in terms of, for example, couriers or taxi services, and it can be also related to packaging and also print materials. So, we are very interested in public relations, and our main key resources are, of course, our customers, if they are satisfied, there will be a lot of interest in spreading the word about our services and products, and, of course, there is social media and other marketing channels.

But if we are talking about main resources, I will always mention first human resources as the number one priority. The second are the ingredients necessary for our sweets. Third are print materials and packaging, and the fourth is, of course, our personal connections because without them, we cannot reach our customers. Five is, of course, our customers, who are our sales managers, who actually refer us. The next resources are our courier services and taxi companies. We have different discounts for regular orders, so we are collaborating with them. In addition, we also have volunteers, who support us a lot in organizing the quality controls, so, in the preparation process, they are checking, monitoring the preparation process of those sweets in order to take it to a higher level. And the last important resource for us is, of course, when we are talking about teamwork, Internet resources, especially during COVID, when we have internet. Especially during the conflict, we have had problems with the Internet, but we are trying to resolve them, and internet resources are some of the most important resources actually.

For a social entrepreneur, the identification of key resources is not only related to profit-making but also about the social impact, so whenever we are evaluating and taking into consideration the key resources or assets for social enterprise, we should always take into consideration both sides of social entrepreneurship, profit, and impact. If we are only focusing on one, the other side will be out of our focus and, therefore, it will not be sustainable. If we only focus on profit, we will lose our reputation which is one of the most expensive resources for a social entrepreneur. When you are only focusing on social impact, you are not sustainable because you cannot earn money, you cannot make a profit, and you cannot reinvest it. So, it is very important to keep this balance (profit and social impact), and which resources you can take into consideration. It is not only about material resources but also about everything you can have in your hands. It can also be the first, your capital in your pocket money, your old friends who call and support you, the small coffee shop where you can work that has a little bit of an inspiring atmosphere, and this coffee shop can bring you so much inspiration, so the most brightest ideas can come from this coffee shop. Resources are also very important, so we should consider everything that is related to profit and social impact.

*Laman:*   What are the main activities and how do you measure them?

When we are talking about the main activities, we should always take into consideration our values and our goals, so Buta Art & Sweets has the main mission of reducing the unemployment problem of special-needs women, so our main activities and measurement, and KPIs will be focusing on the **values** and the main goals and objectives related to our mission. To reduce the unemployment problem, we are trying to increase the sales of those homemade sweets and where are those homemade sweets prepared? In the homes of special-needs women. Why? Because women with special needs are not ready yet to go out of their houses because of family problems, because of their husbands, because of their children, or because of something else. They are happy to work in their homes.

In all of our activities, we try to take into consideration customer needs and the needs of our beneficiaries. To keep, this balance is important, because when you satisfy both sides of the social entrepreneurship model, it will be sustainable only in this case, so our main activities are related to, first, increasing the skills and capacities of our women, who are preparing those sweets. We always get feedback from our customers, especially loyal customers about their needs, about their trends, what they want from us, what their expectations are from our services and products. We are always updating this, always innovating our menu, and always trying to expand because, otherwise, we won't be sustainable in this competitive market. We hold various master classes and training programs for women because it is important for us to increase not only the capacities of baking but also soft skills. It is very important to take them to a higher level as entrepreneurs not only as employees.

The next activity is accepting orders, for sweets according to the database we have. For example, one woman only needs 3 days of advance notice about an order while another needs a week. It is very important to take that into consideration when we are accepting orders and when, based on the strengths of the women we are working with, to deliver those orders to those women. It is very important to do it in a systematic way: we have written communications with our women because if we only focus on calls, we won't accomplish anything. It is one of the most challenging groups of people you can work with. These people have different psychological problems, and they may have challenges in their daily lives. That is why whenever you are building a business or any project with people like this, it is very important to make the communication very clear, concrete, specific, and written for them, because otherwise it is impossible to explain anything to them, if it is only verbally or via calls. Of course, we are also working on written documentation, because without laws, rules, and protocols, without a systematic approach for documentation, we cannot have sustainable operations, and we cannot trust relationships even with governmental bodies. In order to not have any problems with the government, we have everything online and, in terms of payments, we have an account that can accept the online payment, so everything is visible through governmental systems and that is why when we are paying taxes, it is all visible in the system. If someone from a governmental institution wants to fine us because they have doubts about our transparency, we can prove they are not right because we accept all orders online, we can only accept the bank transfers (no cash), so that is why it is very important to make everything transparent. And actually, transparency makes your social business much more profitable for you as an entrepreneur, rather than only to work with cash, especially in developing countries, like Azerbaijan; it is very important to keep this transparency for everyone, if you are in social entrepreneurship. So, again, I will tell we can measure mainly via social impact, with the number of activities we are doing for our women, with the stories we can create for those women, and with the increase of income for some, if our sales are increasing, of course, the income for them is increasing. It is about expanding awareness among different countries and regions and also raising awareness via different media channels.

*Laman:* Who are your suppliers/partner network and how do you develop this network?

Whenever we are talking about sustainable models, we should always take into consideration our partners. Everyone who supports our social business – every customer, every woman working for us, all of our team members – is our partner. And we include everyone who is talking with us, working with us on a constant basis, who are taking even the smallest steps for us. When we are talking about suppliers, of course, it starts with ingredients, of the sweets, with packaging and print material [suppliers] we have been collaborating for a long time, we get discounts, and, of course. It is also about career and tax services, our trainers who hold master classes for our women. It is also about the places we work with for office space, when we have meetings with our team members. These offices give us the space for free or at a discount. We planned our first anniversary in a five-star hotel and, thanks to our personal connections, they gave it to us for free, and it was a huge surprise for us. We have also established partner relations with big companies who organized free gifts for our women on the first-year anniversary, and we will plan a huge event, after the pandemic, after everything is finished.

We are trying to do everything on a consistent basis, and when we are building partnerships, we are always thinking about win-win partnerships. Partnerships can be sustainable only when all sides get something for themselves; they have interest in this partnership, so when we are collaborating with companies with Corporate Social Responsibility, we do not want only to give them credibility or to give them the service for public relations or either advertisement; of course it is important for them, much more important is to have the high-quality products. So, whenever they think about buying this product they will think not only about social impact but about the quality, and competitive prices, they will also gain something for themselves in order to buy it again.

When we are talking about NGOs, they are also very interested in working with us, in partnering with us; because they understand that if they are giving this money to buy some sweets from the supermarket, they can also give this money to a social enterprise and especially when social enterprises and NGOs can create some great synergies for great projects, it will be much more useful for both sides.

We work with women with special needs. We should always consider that we are not here to only be compassionate about their challenges. Those women are responsible to be trustworthy, to be hardworking, to be passionate to learn, and to innovate. First, they do something for themselves, not for us. If they are responsible for their own lives and their families, then we will be assured that they will be interested in creating high-quality products. So, for us, if we are creating this opportunity for these women, we are also expecting something in return. We are not a charity, we are not a social project where we close down this project model after 6 months and that is all. We give reports to donors, that we want to make a sustainable and when you are thinking about the sustainability of your partnership, you should always be interested in getting something in return. If you are giving something to someone, it regards your suppliers, it regards your customers, and of course the beneficiaries as well. When we are talking about suppliers, our main suppliers are, of course, the suppliers of different ingredients, so we have partnership agreements with suppliers of different packages, print materials, couriers, taxi services, and products necessary for our sweets. Those are our main suppliers. Of course, we have some suppliers for outsourced services in terms of accounting, marketing, and different services we need, in organizing different projects, and, of course, we also take into consideration the places we are collaborating with when we are organizing different training sessions and master classes for our women.

*Laman:* What are the main costs of your social entrepreneurship?

The costs of Buta Art & Sweets include costs and expenses for products and ingredients necessary for the preparation of sweets, for commissions of our women, commissions for our team members, and for the taxes we are paying for each sale and every employee. It also includes logistical delivery service fees, packaging, print material expenses, participation in different exhibitions and events, the preparation of samples of the sweets, when we want to gain new customers and when we go to new places – you should always invest in that – and marketing costs. When we want to advertise some new campaigns, offers for people, our main costs include the costs of organizing training services, free educational programs for our women, our main costs also include, it is not all about money but also about the time and about the energy we are investing in developing the social enterprise, and I think, that can never be measured with any amount of money. Whenever you are passionate about your business even if some different employment opportunities arise, you always consider social impact as the most important thing and that is why it is very important for me to do something I love. And how are low costs maintained? Especially when you are building sustainable partnerships, you will always have discounts for regular orders, when you have bigger corporate orders, you can always negotiate with women who can decrease the expenses, for delivery services, for ingredients, whenever they can buy it from the suppliers. For us, it is very important to maintain this balance, to make it profitable, through delivering high-quality products because if you are delivering food products, it is very important and very risky at the same time when you do not provide high-quality products and fresh products for your customers. It is always important to keep that in mind, as when you deliver a product that isn't high quality, it can damage the health or even kill the person, so it is very important, very dangerous. The food industry is one of the most dangerous industries in the world: it is very risky. Could lowering costs damage customers' health? If we see that it does not damage the health of our customers, especially in packaging, print materials, or something else, we can lower the costs but if it is about, for example, using the fresh natural oil or not organic oil, we always ask this question of our customer because customers are different, the needs can be different, high-level customers won't ever eat the sweets with non-organic ingredients because they are used to everything natural and expensive. That is why you should always ask this question; otherwise, we can never be sustainable. As a business model, we should always focus on customer satisfaction.

*Laman:* What about the revenue streams of your social entrepreneurship? Is there income from non-market sources, such as donation and subsidies?

I am very proud to say that we are not dependent on any sponsorship, grants, and donations. So even when, as a social entrepreneur, I am implementing projects, I am not implementing it on behalf of Buta Art & Sweets, or any other social businesses, in order to maintain some cash flow. I had always considered it important to keep the sustainability through sales: this proves to everyone that social enterprise can be sustainable without being dependent on someone, on donors especially. So we do not get any grants, and we do not get any donations, so 100% of our revenue stream comes from sales of our products and services, and, in the future, we are expecting to increase the number of our services and products, so we also want to add some courses on vegan products, on the preparation of vegan sweets and products, very unique ones, with the participation of our women, so they will also get commissions for teaching. We will sell those courses online and everyone from any country can join and take these courses. They will be accessible and will also have social value for the new customer segment group and this customer segment group will consist of people who are passionate about exploring new recipes, to learn more about cooking.

Our revenue stream is the sale of our products and services. In our first year, we received some small grants (only 500 euros), for example, to organize our first masters classes for our team. But as soon as our sales increased, we were already not taking any grants or donations. We are proud to say that we are self-sustainable selling our products. This is actually social entrepreneurship: when you can be independent while you can make a sustainable social impact.

## Discussion

The case of Buta Art & Sweets well represents an illustrative example of what social entrepreneurship and social business models are (Dacin et al., 2011; Seelos and Mair, 2005; Yunus et al., 2010). We described a case of a young female social entrepreneur who has developed a social business model in a developing context, distinguishing the two phenomena. On the one hand, there is a social enterprise where a woman has been able to make a profit and to have a sustainable and successful business, able to compete in the market (a trait that is typical of for-profit businesses), while also making a social-oriented profit, as represented by her mission to empower women and eliminate unemployment for disadvantaged women. On the other hand, she has developed a social business model that goes beyond social-profit-oriented shareholders and specifies social-profit objectives (as Yunus *et al.*, 2010 advance), also making clear the importance of involving a broader 'social ecosystem'.

As it survived the pandemic, we think that Buta Art & Sweets' social business model can be defined as successful. The social business has been able to balance, on the one hand, the production (and sales) of high-quality products at good prices. On the other hand, it allowed women with special needs to rely on an income that, during the pandemic, often represented an important source of sustainment. We think that the elements that have made for the success of Buta Art & Sweets can be traced back to an enlightened entrepreneur who has been able to clearly define the boundaries of both profit and social impact, and the capacity of establishing long-lasting partnerships where mutual benefits are at the core. Figure 6.1 presents the social business model canvas of Buta Art & Sweets, adapting the dimensions of the business model canvas developed by Osterwalder and Pigneur (2010).

Extending what previous research has supported, that is, the dichotomy between economic and social value (Santos, 2012), we distinguish among five types of values: economic, social, environmental, emotional, and cultural. The *economic* value is from the revenues generated by Buta Art & Sweets. The *social* value is created by the employment of women with disabilities and special needs and who, for cultural prejudices, are usually thought to be unable to work. The *environmental value* consists of using cruelty-free and eco-friendly ingredients for the preparation of sweets and packaging. The *emotional* value is critical for building a relationship with the customers, and, moreover, attempting to maintain regular contact with them: Buta Art & Sweets tries, through the women it employs, to build a personal and close relationship also thanks to particular after-sales contact and to a friend-like relationship that the women always strive for. Finally, there is a fourth value dimension, that is, the *cultural* value: working for Buta changed the mindset of many people, employees included. This is of critical importance for Sara, since, thanks to this, Buta Art & Sweets is able to indirectly influence society with its work. Moreover, due to the production of high-quality sweets, the women can prove their value to the society.

Social business models in agri-food 143

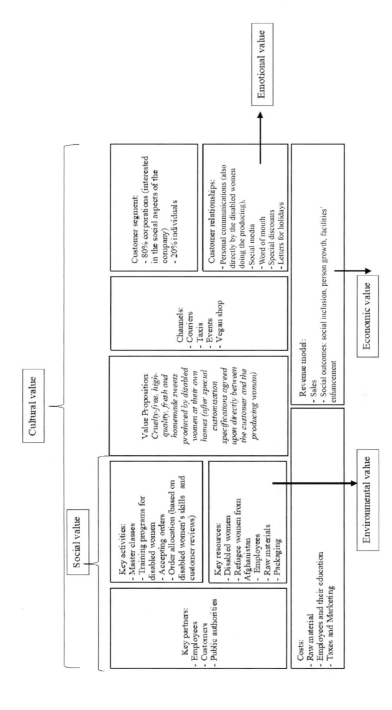

Figure 6.1 The social business model canvas of Buta Art & Sweets
Source: Adapted from Osterwalder e Pigneur, 2010.

We think that the social business model is also successful thanks to *female intrapreneurship*. Antoncic and Hisrich (2001) identified four dimensions of intrapreneurship (i.e., entrepreneurship within the organization): the creation of new businesses related to the 'mother' organization; the creation of new products/services; a self-renewal dimension in terms of reformulating strategy; and a proactiveness dimension. These elements are somehow present also in our case. In fact, in the case of Buta Art & Sweets, the women employed are considered and practically act as real entrepreneurs. They are in charge of choosing the best ingredients to fulfil the needs and wants of customers, with which they maintain direct and indirect personal communications. Women are in charge of setting the prices too. The value is added mainly by the employees, which are considered more partners than simple employees by Buta itself. Hence, we could say that the successful business model of this social entrepreneurship lies in the fact that it enables intrapreneurship. Buta Art & Sweets oversees the main activities, such as conference and meeting participation, brand awareness, documentation and data management, coordination, and general management. However, daily work, production, and value and emotion generation are mainly done by the disabled women involved in this business. This kind of structure also helps women in redeeming themselves and in proving to the society they can successfully contribute, being at the same time independent. These women work from their homes, organizing themselves autonomously. The aim of improving the workplace, which is a crucial aspect according to Sara, is linked with the importance for the women to improve their conditions too.

## Conclusion

This chapter has presented an interview with a social entrepreneur who has applied a social business model that elevates the status of disabled women. From the case of Buta Art & Sweets, we have understood that the ability of a social entrepreneur is crucial to creating social value and launching social innovation with an entrepreneurial perspective.

Social entrepreneurship is more complicated than "pure" profit-oriented entrepreneurship because of the need to balance revenues and non-measurable (or not easily measurable) social value.

The good balance of economic profits and the social impact has allowed the social business to remain independent from donations or subsidies, thus making the women financially sustained.

There is still scarce knowledge of social entrepreneurship in society. There is a need to educate students, communities, and rural regions on social entrepreneurship: this would improve the overall understanding and, therefore, the attention to social entrepreneurship. Furthermore, it would allow achieving increased social responsibility in society.

Social enterprises, as shown by the case of Buta, are important and inspiring examples for further potential social entrepreneurs.

From a theoretical point of view, the analyzed case of Buta Art & Sweets helps in understanding *how a social entrepreneur develops a social business model*. We think that the core element is related to the employees' intrapreneurship (in the specific case of Buta Art & Sweets it is pursued by disabled, disadvantaged women) and the role of the social enterprise (Buta Art & Sweets, in this case) as acting as the brand-creator and orchestrator of this intrapreneurship. In fact, while Buta Art & Sweets is in charge of some services, such as logistics, other pivotal activities and decisions (e.g., production, communication with customers, and price setting) are carried out by the employees/partners/intrapreneurs. This might appear a mere administrative and managerial aspect; however, it is of critical importance from the social perspective. Enabling them as entrepreneurs contributes to increasing redemption for people otherwise poorly considered by society (and often by their families too). Thanks to this business model, the social impact of the main enterprise is significantly augmented. Moreover, the emotional value associated with the company is increased, too, making it more attractive for companies looking at CSR issues, which then might want to move from "pure" customers to real partners.

Furthermore, this chapter provides interesting implications for practitioners and public institutions. Even if there is not much need for legislation on social entrepreneurship, since it is possible for social enterprises to legally use the rules for pure-profit ones, establishing legal forms of social entrepreneurship in the country's legislation may indicate the importance of social entrepreneurship for the state. Specific dedicated rules for social enterprises might also help them in obtaining more governmental and institutional support, which is, however, needed in some cases.

Social entrepreneurs can mitigate social problems, such as gender equality issues or the discrimination of disadvantaged people, as seen in the case of Buta Art & Sweets. Examples such as the one described definitely help in reaching the sustainable development goals of Agenda 2030.

Of course, it would be interesting to compare multiple cases to expand this research, but at national and international levels.

## Note

1 Oikos Baku is the Azerbaijani's chapter of the Worldwide global community Oikos; it is focused on sustainable economics and management, and it represents a "leading reference point for the environmental sustainability."

## References

Alcaraz, J. M. and Thiruvattal, E. (2010), "An interview with Manuel Escudero The United Nations principles for responsible management education: A global call for sustainability", *Academy of Management Learning & Education*, vol. 9, no. 3, pp. 542–550.

Antoncic, B. and Hisrich, R. D. (2001), "Intrapreneurship: Construct refinement and cross-cultural validation", *Journal of Business Venturing*, vol. 16, no. 5, pp. 495–527.

Barney, J. B. (2004), "An interview with William Ouchi", *Academy of Management Perspectives*, vol. 18, no. 4, pp. 108–116.

Bocken, N. M. P., Short, S. W., Rana, P. and Evans, S. (2014), "A literature and practice review to develop sustainable business model archetypes", *Journal of Cleaner Production*, vol. 65, pp. 42–56.

Carayannis, E. G., Grigoroudis, E., Stamati, D. and Valvi, T. (2021), "Social business model innovation: A quadruple/quintuple helix-based social innovation ecosystem", *IEEE Transactions on Engineering Management*, vol. 68, no. 1, pp. 235–248.

Casprini, E. (2019), *Beyond servitization: New managerial challenges for manufacturing firms*. CEDAM Wolters Kluwer.

Dacin, M. T., Dacin, P. A. and Tracey, P. (2011), "Social entrepreneurship: A critique and future directions", *Organization Science*, vol. 22, no. 5, pp. 1203–1213.

Diaz Gonzalez, A. and Dentchev, N. A. (2021), "Ecosystems in support of social entrepreneurs: A literature review", *Social Enterprise Journal*, vol. 17, no. 3, pp. 329–360.

Dunne, D. and Martin, R. (2006), "Design thinking and how it will change management education: An interview and discussion", *Academy of Management Learning & Education*, vol. 5, no. 4, pp. 512–523.

Foss, N. J. and Saebi, T. (2017), "Fifteen years of research on business model innovation: How far have we come, and where should we go?", *Journal of Management*, vol. 43, no. 1, pp. 200–227.

Hidalgo, G., Monticelli, J. M. and Vargas Bortolaso, I. (2021), "Social capital as a driver of social entrepreneurship", *Journal of Social Entrepreneurship*, available at: https://doi.org/10.1080/19420676.2021.1951819.

Kruse, P., Wach, D. and Wegge, J. (2021), "What motivates social entrepreneurs? A meta-analysis on predictors of the intention to found a social enterprise", *Journal of Small Business Management*, vol. 59, no. 3, pp. 477–508.

Osterwalder, A. and Pigneur, Y. (2010), *Business model generation: A handbook for visionaries, game changers, and challengers*, John Wiley & Sons.

Ranville, A. and Barros, M. (2022), "Towards normative theories of social entrepreneurship: A review of the top publications of the field", *Journal of Business Ethics*, vol. 180, pp. 407–438.

Rosandic, A. and Guluzade, M. (2018), *Social economy in Eastern neighbourhood and in the Western Balkans*, Country Report, Azerbaijan, pp. 1–34.

Santos, F. M. (2012), "A positive theory of social entrepreneurship", *Journal of Business Ethics*, vol. 111, no. 3, pp. 335–351.

Santos, F., Pache, A. C. and Birkholz, C. (2015), "Making hybrids work: Aligning business models and organizational design for social enterprises", *California Management Review*, vol. 57, no. 3, pp. 36–58.

Seelos, C. and Mair, J. (2005), "Social entrepreneurship: Creating new business models to serve the poor", *Business Horizons*, vol. 48, no. 3, pp. 241–246.

Tykkyläinen, S. and Ritala, P. (2021), "Business model innovation in social enterprises: An activity system perspective", *Journal of Business Research*, vol. 125, pp. 684–697.

Weerawardena, J. and Sullivan Mort, G. (2006), "Investigating social entrepreneurship: A multidimensional model", *Journal of World Business*, vol. 41, no. 1, pp. 21–35.

Wilson, F. and Post, J. E. (2013), "Business models for people, planet (& profits): Exploring the phenomena of social business, a market-based approach to social value creation", *Small Business Economics*, vol. 40, no. 3, pp. 715–737.

Yunus, M., Moingeon, B. and Lehmann-Ortega, L. (2010), "Building social business models: Lessons from the Grameen experience", *Long Range Planning*, vol. 43, no. 2–3, pp. 308–325.

Zott, C., Amit, R. and Massa, L. (2011), "The business model: Recent developments and future research", *Journal of Management*, vol. 37, no. 4, pp. 1019–1042.

# Part III
# The role of innovative technologies in sustainability

# 7 The role of innovative technologies in sustainability

*Francesca Checchinato, Cinzia Colapinto, Vladi Finotto, and Alena Myshko*

**Introduction**

The diffusion of new technologies entails finding a relationship between their potential and the schemata individuals use to make sense of the world (Garud & Karnoe, 2003; Hargadon & Douglas, 2001). Thus, regardless of the inherent revolutionary character of a novel solution, innovation needs to be framed and made intelligible via social construction processes (Cornelissen & Werner, 2014). Frames having to do with the improvement of the social and environmental contexts we inhabit have been frequent in history and have become increasingly more important in the past 20 years, and at the same time inequality and pollution have reached unprecedented peaks. Policymakers welcome and use frames that combine narratives on the economic potential of new technologies – incentivizing profit-seeking organizations and entrepreneurs – with those focused on the social and environmental benefit technologies bring about. This framing is a matter of interaction and reciprocal influence between the discourses structured in different fields, most often the academic debate feeding the public discourse with data and analyses, and the policymaking one, taking stock of the former to set agendas and the allocation of resources.

Smart agriculture and industry 4.0 in the food sector are no exceptions. They are labels that denote an assortment of technologies and a policy-driven discourse aimed at triggering novel models of collaboration and coordination among firms, public actors, and research entities (Reischauer, 2018). Sophisticated sensors, limitless computational capacity, end-to-end integration of data, algorithms to optimize decisions – all these and other features are usually mentioned in analyses on, and calls for, the adoption of industry 4.0 technologies (Coco et al., 2021). Smart and 4.0 technologies, on the one hand, could help firms increase their productivity and their competitiveness in general; on the other hand, they allow for sustaining profit-making with the improvement of workers' conditions, the reduction of emissions, and environmental impacts on fields and production plants, reducing the overall footprint of the industry. Moreover, a combination of the new digital tools with the already integrated automated technologies, such as drones and smart tractors, is supposed to support farmers to "be more precise with inputs (i.e. seeds, water, fertilizers and

DOI: 10.4324/9781003223672-11

pesticides) while enhancing their knowledge of agro-ecological conditions (including weather and landscape interactions and soil and plant health)" (Rotz et al., 2019, p. 112). Industry 4.0, probably more than any other technological trend, is both a label for a portfolio of technologies and applications and a policy-driven discourse aimed at inspiring novel models of collaboration and coordination among firms, public actors, research entities, and organizations (Reischauer, 2018).

At the same time, the agri-food sector has been facing serious pressure from global sustainability challenges. The sector is expected to increase food quality and quantity and thus resolve problems of food insecurity; in parallel, it is expected to decrease emissions and the environmental impact of its operations. The growing environmental, social, and economic risks, as well as institutional conditions, have highlighted the need for integration of the environment and development, which is conceptualized as "sustainable development." In the last decade, sustainable development in general and sustainable development goals (SDGs) in particular have been central in the focus of a variety of supranational organizations, institutions, and their initiatives. One of the most prominent initiatives is an action plan called Agenda 21, which was introduced at the Earth Summit in 1992. Agenda 21 presents an action plan for sustainable development, which is a response to the urgent need to integrate the environment and development issues more extensively.

The 2005 World Summit was a milestone in terms of developing the idea of sustainability and rebuilding concepts around it. At the summit, world leaders introduced three pillars of sustainability (or sustainable development), bringing together the environment, economic development, and human well-being. The agenda of the Summit and its final report was largely criticized by both researchers and policymakers. First, for its misinterpretation of sustainable development as "a label for environmental issues" (Wilkins, 2008, p. 171), which is partially responsible for ongoing limited understanding of sustainability as mostly an environmental agenda. Moreover, among other policy initiatives, it is frequently carried out with the concept of sustainable development as opposed to "sustainability," thus shifting the emphasis on the development process.

While approaching sustainability by categorizing its issues and themes into three (or more) pillars can be perceived as "an inherently political act" (Boyer, 2016, p. 3), this research utilizes the potential of a holistic and integrated understanding of such a complex and multi-layered phenomenon as sustainability. In other words, it appropriates the triple bottom line framework with the institutional dimension in order to analyze the variety of sustainability issues and, more importantly, the interconnections and interdependencies among them. The search for the most appropriate solution and its effective implementation requires a wide-ranging, complex overview of challenges related to sustainability in various industries, informing the decision-making process. In fact, one of the solutions to sustainability challenges involves introducing technological advancements and Industry 4.0 in different sectors. The benefits of innovative technologies have already been changing the agricultural and agri-food sector and its supply chains by optimizing processes and reducing the ecological impact.

This chapter aims to understand the role of innovative and digital technologies for sustainability in the agri-food sector through analyzing technological applications and responses to various sustainability challenges and dimensions. Through the investigation of the application of innovative and Industry 4.0 technologies to implement sustainable practices and increase economic, environmental, social, and institutional sustainability, this chapter uncovers the pathways between technological development and sustainability in agri-food. Specifically, this chapter aims at shedding further light on the interaction between digital technologies and sustainability in the context of the agri-food industry. In particular, this research unpacks the application of digital technologies in the sector by analyzing the reasons for technological advancement, the part of the sector or supply chain and actors involved (or affected) in the application, and sustainability achievements through its dimensions.

This chapter utilizes the methodology of a systematic literature review to collect existing research, both theoretical and practical, on the connections between digitalization of the sector and its sustainability issues. In such a way, the review provides a range of technological implementations and their input on the sustainability of the sector, which should be useful to inform not only future research on sustainable agribusiness but also policy initiatives. We assume, in fact, that policymaking and the scientific community are reciprocally influencing each other, and thus a systematic analysis of the scientific literature might give us a representation of the determinants of public policy's focus on the sustainability potential of digital technologies.

This chapter is organized as follows: it begins with the introduction of the analytical framework of sustainability and its pillars, or dimensions, to investigate the existing research on innovative and digital technologies and their role in sustainability in agri-food. The second part is dedicated to the description of the methodology of this systematic literature review. In the third part, the results of the research are presented and discussed within the adopted analytical framework of sustainability. This chapter closes with conclusions and avenues for future research.

## Theoretical framework

Sustainability is a large complex phenomenon, which has been approached by policymakers, researchers, and experts and conceptualized in a variety of ways. Being articulated in many discourses, often contradictory, has contributed to the concept's development, as well as to its broad ambiguity and fuzziness. One of the widespread approaches to sustainability, presented in both academic research and the policy sphere, is the triple bottom line framework, which is based on the three pillars – environment, economy, and society, or planet, profit, and people. Therefore, this framework encompasses three dimensions of sustainability – environmental, economic, and social, which are interconnected and create the basis for sustainable communities and industries. An investigation into the conceptual origins of sustainability by Purvis et al. (2019) uses "pillars" to address its complex nature, with sustainability at the intersections of society, economy, and environment. The authors mentioned a variety of notions used to present those pillars, such as dimensions, components, aspects, etc., and stated their interchangeable use. We have not developed a specific preference for any of these terms; therefore, we use them as synonyms in our research. At the core is the perception of the complex nature of sustainability, which encompasses several dimensions and their interconnectedness.

Due to the framework's roots in the policy dimension, it lacks an extensive theoretical basis but has been applied to numerous areas and investigations. The adoption of the framework for the analysis of the role of innovative technologies in sustainability in agri-food is based on the original ideas of developing sustainability as a complex phenomenon and agenda with interconnected dimensions and structures. According to Clune and Zehnder (2020, p. 1001), the three-pillar approach is more practical and solutions-oriented by supporting "the creation of new economic and political institutions that embed (from start to finish) the key inputs, stakeholders, and incentive structures necessary for sustainability planning and projects to be feasible, successful, and socially accepted." This research recognizes the "extended" framework with the fourth pillar – the institutional one as a set of (particular) institutions and institutional conditions. In such a way, the sustainability framework provides an opportunity to analyze the impact of technology implementation for sustainability in the sector as a whole or as a segment, not only generally speaking but also with social, ecological, economic, and institutional conditions. Furthermore, some research extends the framework by exploring culture as an independent aspect of sustainability (e.g., Birkeland, 2008; Soini & Birkeland, 2014) and presents it as a fourth pillar. Nevertheless, within this review, culture is not articulated as a distinct pillar or dimension.

The economic understanding of sustainability is often associated with economic growth and an increase in efficiency, which presupposes that resources are allocated to their highest valued use and, consequently, there is a rise in productivity and capital assets (Elliott, 2005). Then, environmental, or ecological, sustainability in agriculture focuses on the continued productivity and functioning of ecosystems, which includes a range of factors from resource base quality, the preservation of physical conditions and resources and of biological diversity to productive capacities and climate change mitigation (Yunlong & Smith, 1994).

While the meaning and, therefore, the practical application and measurement of two sustainability pillars – environmental and economic – are relatively clear and elaborated in research and policy, social sustainability is more challenging, having even been referred to as "a missing pillar" (Bolstrom, 2012). The social sustainability pillar most definitely requires more clarification, especially as a dimension of sustainability as an analytical framework. The challenges of analysis and implementation, in projects and policies, of social sustainability are caused by, first of all, the roots of the sustainability agenda in "specific forms of environmentalism based in models of global capitalism that thrive upon the exploitation of natural and human capital" (Boyer et al., 2016, p. 2). In such a way, historically the sustainability agenda has placed its focus on green and nature-related issues instead of devoting more attention to social inequalities. Social issues, urban and rural complexities, in turn, are highly complex to be fully addressed and described by existing social science's methods, both qualitative and quantitative. Therefore, social issues and the corresponding sustainability dimension appear to be frustrating for researchers and policymakers to objectively measure, describe, and integrate into policy decisions.

Social sustainability can be defined through the human appropriation of the environment and focuses on the availability of access to social resources by current and future generations, represented in intra- and inter-generational equity, respectively (De Gennaro & Nardone, 2014, p. 25). Social, or societal, aspects of sustainability are largely based on broad stakeholder input and include, but are not limited to, animal welfare, values and responsibilities of consumers (as citizens), (un)documented labor conditions and issues, public engagement, and others (von Keyserlingk et al., 2013). A review of the literature on the social pillar of sustainable development by Murphy (2012) resulted in a conceptual framework, which is based on the concepts and policy objectives outlined in the research, which identifies four comprehensive social concepts: public awareness, equity, participation, and social cohesion.

Moreover, a review by Boyer et al. (2016, p. 2) suggests that research into the social pillar provides it with a range of roles, from a stand-alone objective to a "fully integrated, locally-rooted, and process-oriented approach to sustainability." The authors conclude that the latter role is the most prospective not just for the development of the social pillar itself but for the whole of sustainability theoretical and practical research as well as policymaking. We second their call for efforts "that recognise how environmental, social, and economic values overlap" and the need for a systematic, integrated, and holistic approach to sustainability, which does not separate or prioritize its pillars (Ibid., p. 13). Figure 7.1 provides a classical visual representation of interconnectedness of the three pillars with sustainability at the center, which can be found in various academic and policy sources (e.g., Petrisor & Petrisor, 2014; Purvis et al., 2019; von Keyserlingk et al., 2013, to name just a few).

Additionally, some research goes beyond the classical framework with three pillars by adding more dimensions to sustainability to emphasize its complex nature. While in the literature stream adopting the "extended" framework, the fourth pillar is the cultural one (not least due to its explicit representation in Agenda 21), several researchers focus on the role of institutions and distinguish institutional sustainability pillar. Hosseini and Kaneko (2012) follow the approach of Hak et al. (2007) and present a dynamic concept of sustainability composed of four interlinked and integrated pillars. They identify causalities among those "sustainabilities," which show, among other interlinks, that "improvement in environmental conditions can strongly improve the social

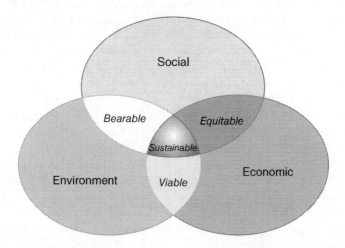

*Figure 7.1* Visualization of the "classical" three pillars of sustainability approach
Source: Petrisor & Petrisor, 2014, p. 180.

variables directly, and positively affect institutional development indirectly through the social pillar" (Ibid., p. 200).

To continue, Clune and Zehnder (2018, 2020) highlight the role of laws, governance, and regulations since sustainability depends on all levels, from local to international, "upon matching the scope and scale of law and governance to social and ecological contexts" (p. 226). The authors highlight that, despite being a simplification of a complex system, the three-pillar model does still provide "an effective structure and analytic rigor related to key points of support and contribution," which is significant for the promotion of multidisciplinary projects (Ibid., p. 214). Though the institutional dimension is primarily characterized by consistency between norms and laws, on the one hand, and the levels of governance, it also has to be aligned with other sustainability dimensions.

Broadly speaking, institutional sustainability can be understood as "the ability of institutions under particular conditions, to guide actors to reach desirable goals," for example, such as adaptation to and mitigation of climate change (Kajembe et al., 2016, p. 27). Within the context of governance for sustainable development, institutional sustainability consists of the institutions' capabilities and activities related to coordination and "the facilitation of decision making and implementation of sustainability policies," often in order to achieve sustainability goals (Pfahl, 2005, pp. 83–84).

As well as for the other sustainability dimensions, academia and policymaking saw various attempts to define, measure, and access institutional sustainability. A number of policy actions and documents on sustainable development (and SDGs) included a set of sustainable indicators. Spangenberg (2002) and Spangenberg et al. (2002) outline that sustainability indicators are supposed to be general, indicative, sensitive, and robust, and have different levels of details depending on the level of decision-making, therefore, be organized in a hierarchy. However, one of the major challenges for a comprehensive methodology has been a lack of (shared or common) understanding of institutions in the first place, as Pfahl (2005) points out, which are not equal to organizations or regimes. It should be noted that most of the research on measurement of institutional sustainability operates within the sustainable development paradigm.

Therefore, institutional sustainability provides actors with a framework to achieve other sustainability dimensions, on the one hand, and is influenced by the state of these dimensions, on the other hand. It is important to emphasize that institutions, both formal and informal, are not static but dynamic (if they are liveable); they constantly evolve and change over time and also act as an indicator of change. A lack of attention to the role of institutions is misleading "since the concept of sustainable development attributes a central role to institutions as a tool for its implementation," especially as articulated in Agenda 21 (Pfahl, 2005, p. 80).

Despite several benefits and perspectives brought by the three-pillar framework, some authors point out its drawbacks. One such criticism is the very practical orientation of the framework without having developed a solid theoretical basis. While the approach has been shared as a "common view" for at least two decades, it is difficult to trace its original urtext (Purvis et al., 2019, p. 685). Because it originated from policy-oriented research, that might explain, on the one hand, a wide practical application of the paradigm and, on the other hand, a shortage of theoretical background. The application of the framework to a specific sector such as agriculture and agri-food offers an overview of sustainability as a complex system with different dimensions and structures. At the same time, the research can benefit from breaking down the ambiguity of the sector's sustainability into more localized issues, which are interconnected within a system. In such a way, the framework provides opportunities to develop research and policy interventions, which, on the one hand, address localized issues and, on the other hand, can be incorporated into a holistic and comprehensive approach.

Broadly speaking, research on the three pillars of sustainability often either perceives them as distinctive perspectives, that is, focus on one of them or attempt a systematic approach by stressing their integration and interconnectivity. Within a system approach, "there lacks a commonality in how interactions are treated, whether trade-offs occur or mutual reinforcements are made" (Purvis et al., 2019, p. 692). Despite the co-existence of the three pillars, and interlinks among them, the economy "circle" and economic pillar come to the forefront, in both academic and policy-oriented researches. One of the reasons is a blurring of the separation line between concepts of "sustainability" and "sustainable development," where the latter has often been associated with economic development ("such that economic development remained an implicit, but inadequately formulated, part of sustainability" (Purvis et al., 2019, p. 692)). We understand sustainability as both a process and an aim, but, at the same time, we should avoid direct correlations between "sustainability" and "development" in policy connotations.

In the agri-food sector, most research concentrates on economic and/or environmental sustainability, while the social dimension and its role in agriculture's development have been undeservedly underdeveloped. Some authors even point out that the focus of most of the studies on the topic has been on the ecological and environmental aspects of sustainability. For instance, Hubeau et al. (2017, p. 52) specify that in the existing sustainability studies the ecological aspect of sustainability in agriculture is mainly presented through resource use efficiency and "lack of embedding the agri-food system in the wider socio-ecological environment." In that way, the problem of the existing imbalance among the sustainability pillars, which is present in research and policy, has been perpetuated in agriculture and agri-food. Yunlong and Smith (1994) promote sustainable agriculture, which combines the three dimensions and warn against the focus on only one pillar. The concentration on one or two pillars without interlinking them with social conditions and institutional environment leads, in turn, to a narrow understanding of the sector's transformation under digitalization and the adoption of innovative technologies.

In such a way, to analyze the role of innovative and, in particular, digital technologies, our research was driven by these main research questions:

RQ1: Why is technology being introduced, or what is the aim of applying a specific technology to the agricultural and agri-food sector in general or to specific operations?
RQ2: Which operation(s), or stage in the sector or supply chain is the technology applied to?
RQ3: Which actors are involved in technology's application or are affected by its implementation?
RQ4: Which dimension of sustainability (one or more) do these technologies tackle?

Our investigation is based on a holistic approach to sustainability as a complex phenomenon, which includes such dimensions as economic, social, and environmental (or ecological), as well as characteristics of the institutional environment. This systematic literature review attempts to describe and discuss not only each aspect of sustainability on its own how they are presented in the studied literature but also mainly to understand these dimensions as a whole system – in sustainable agriculture or the agri-food system.

## Methods

To investigate the outlined research questions and the general aim of this research, we have adopted the methodology of a systematic literature review. The research follows guidelines developed by Fink (2010) and Tranfield et al. (2003) for conducting an evidence-informed systematic literature review with a high level of transparency and reduced distortion. Following the steps in this review, the research questions and bibliographic database were selected, and then at the conceptualization step research terms were defined. Web of Science (WOS) was selected as the main database to investigate the relevant literature for the analysis, with a parallel search carried out using the same keywords on Google Scholar. The methodology took advantage of some existing relevant literature reviews, for example, on the three pillars of sustainability during COVID-19 (Ranjbari et al., 2021), the relationship between technology and sustainable development (Annosi et al., 2020), and digital transformation and environmental sustainability (Feroz et al., 2021), just to name a few. This investigation focused on terms related to, first, the agri-food sector, and, second, smart technological development within the connection to sustainability (and sustainable development). We have also applied both practical and methodological quality screens (Fink, 2010).

The search and data download were performed on October 6, 2021. We used the following key search: (agri* OR agri-food OR agrifood OR food OR agribusiness OR agri-business) AND (industry 4 OR smart OR smart-agri* OR agri-tech OR agritech) AND (sustainab*). The search was limited by the topic parameter (title, abstract, and keywords). Moreover, we analyzed only the articles under the WOS social-science index (including management) as shown in Figure 7.2.

Within the database of 500 articles, we dismissed 62 articles, which did not focus on agriculture or agri-food sector; therefore, they were irrelevant for our review. Then, we selected 88 articles, which investigated sustainability issues but did not cover them in regard to smart or digital technologies. These articles were dismissed from the analysis but were still considered for the framing of sustainability and its pillars (for the theoretical framework). In such a way, we allocated a final selection of 350 papers, which is at the heart of the analysis and discussion. The papers in the selection included all the search parameters, that is, smart technological advancement and sustainability in agribusiness.

To analyze the selected articles, we applied the three-sustainability pillar framework to the process of implementation of innovative and smart technologies in agri-food. To collect and analyze the data from the papers, we have developed an approach based on three general categories: smart technology,

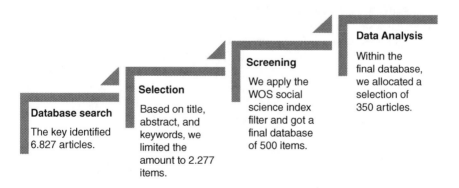

*Figure 7.2* The research flow

supply chain, and sustainability. In this way, in each article, we have identified, first of all, a type of digital and innovative technology, which has been applied in the agri-food sector. The category also included the rationale or justification behind a choice of an innovation in general and the particular technology. Along with the identification of a technology or digital tool, the use of a research framework, where applicable, was included in the analysis. Second, we looked at the sector or node of the supply chain, the phase of the extended production and activity system at which a technology is implemented. Then, we selected the actors, who are engaged in, or affected by, the technological implementation. Third, we identified the so-called sustainability challenges. Finally, we considered the achieved results of technological application, or what impact technology has on increasing sustainability. These inputs were classified according to the four sustainability pillars, considering the interlinks among these dimensions. All these general categories and subcategories were the basis for grouping and coding the extracted data.

## Discussion

To discuss how digital technologies increase sustainability, the research applied the three-pillar analytical framework, which is extended with the institutional dimension. While there is a range of academic and policy work investigating sustainability and its pillars in agriculture, only a few of them link sustainability and digitalization. To demonstrate, the review by Annosi et al. (2020) investigated various challenges faced by agribusinesses to implement digital technologies, as well as challenges to sustainable development. Another systematic review by Feroz et al. (2021) identifies "disruptions driven by digital transformation in the environmental domain" (p. 1). Furthermore, Annnosi and Brunetta (2020, pp. 2–6) investigated "potential managerial factors affecting firms' reactions to digitalization waves," as well as "the use of technology to meet the objectives of economic and environmental sustainability." Considering a significant actual input and potential of digitalization for the sector, a better understanding is needed of the ways the smart technologies enhance sustainability and its various aspects. However, while most of the research focuses on environmental and economic sustainability, this chapter aims to embrace the existing research under the umbrella of an integrated and complex approach to the phenomenon. To be useful for research and practice, our analysis has to offer actionable insights and points of departure for further investigations. We thus look at sustainability in a detailed way through its dimensions and how it is connected to digitalization in the agri-food sector. We consider in particular the drivers and issues behind the application of innovative technologies to specific components of supply chains and which actors they involve.

### *Description of results*

Based on the results' analysis performed by Web of Science, all the articles in the final database of 500 items were published between 2010 and 2021. The

*The role of innovative technologies in sustainability* 159

popularity of the topics presented in our key has been steadily increasing year after year, especially since 2016. The largest publication input was in 2020 (135 items, 27%) and 2021 (123 papers, 25%). In this way, more than half of the research has been published in the last 2 years. Although the topics in the focus of the current review have been clearly gaining unprecedented attention in the last few years, they are rooted in the earlier research on digitalization and, especially, the sustainability of the agricultural and agri-food sector.

The top three areas of published research are Environmental Sciences Ecology (297 papers), Science Technology and other topics (181), and Agriculture (68)[1]. Therefore, the overwhelming majority of research lies within environmental and technological studies. Both environmental studies and science and technology studies (STS) are principally interdisciplinary fields, which emerged from the confluence of a variety of disciplines and disciplinary subfields and utilize their theoretical and methodological stands. The largest number of articles (115) comes from *Sustainability* journal; the second and third main sources are *Journal of Cleaner Production* (22) and *Land Use Policy* (19).

### Factors behind innovative technological implementations

To start with, a significant number of papers in the array discussed smart technological transformation of the sector within a framework of climate-smart agriculture and climate change adaptation (in total, 156 from 338 papers). The understanding of it is helpful to analyze the digital transformations tackling sustainability challenges in the right light since it is the most spread framework[2] in the database. Climate-smart agriculture (CSA) can be understood as a transformative and sustainable agriculture

> that tries to increase efficiency (productivity) in food security and production systems, using a combination of the pillars of climate change (adaptation, resilience, and mitigation) as well as smart and new technological knowledge, that do not only build capacity of farmers

in terms of farming techniques but also increases profit, reduces vulnerability of the systems as well as their results (farm products/animals), through the reduction of GHG emissions (Adesipo et al., 2020, pp. 10–11). CSA rests on its three main pillars, such as agronomic and economic productivity, resilience and adaptive capacity, and climate change mitigation. This type of agriculture specifically highlights the necessity to address the challenges of both food security and climate change, which are interlinked. It is a type of an integrated approach in agriculture, which deals with managing the landscape (e.g., livestock, croplands). In such a way, it already has a restricted perspective of analyzing the sector since it focuses on only one stage of it. Moreover, according to the Climate Change Action Plan 2016 by the World Bank, this agricultural approach has three main aims: (a) increased productivity of food quantity and quality; (b) enhanced resilience and reduced vulnerability to climate-related risks; and (c) reduced emissions (in food production).

In such a way, a particular body of research focuses on two major challenges – climate change and food (in)security. Both challenges are very complex and do affect various spheres of life and industrial sectors, although climate change has traditionally been perceived primarily as an environmental threat. These papers embrace social conditions and institutions as well, although do focus largely on the environmental side of sustainability. In such a way, on the one hand, environmental sustainability comes to the forefront in this research, which can be also understood as a drawback of the framework. On the other hand, the application of the framework still allows researchers to investigate the role of social and institutional conditions, which provides more coherent research than those focused on only one sustainability pillar. Nevertheless, the risk is that the focus of this approach might overshadow the role of social and institutional factors in sustainability's expansion.

Another crucial challenge in agriculture is land use and degradation, which incorporates various factors such as soil quality, land management, and others. Degradation of land has been intensified by "problems related to the unsustainable use of land resources, rural – urban migration, farm marginalization and regional disparities" (Smiraglia et al., 2016, p. 598). Land use and land cover changes, which include soil erosion, malnutrition, and desertification, have been identified as key drivers of global change. Likewise, the issues of water management and energy use (in particular, GHG emissions) require urgent development of more sustainable utilization, which can be advanced by innovative technologies. Therefore, the main factors driving the implementation of digital technologies, as research identifies, lie primarily within the production stage, or farming. While some research considers challenges which occur at other nodes of a supply chain, farming conditions are at central stake for both researchers and policymakers.

A significant portion of research addresses, directly or indirectly, the differences in application of climate-smart agriculture (CSA) and climate change adaptation/mitigation in developed and developing countries. Table 7.1 represents the distribution of research in general and the adaptation of CSA framework in particular by geographical area[3].

The analysis was conducted on the basis of the set of articles including both sustainability and novel technologies in agriculture. The table shows that the largest proportion is represented by papers without specific geographical focus or which aim at cross-national investigation. The next largest set of articles focuses on Africa with the vast majority of it adopting the CSA framework. The second largest piece of research on CSA is based on Asian countries' cases. On the contrary, areas of developed countries, such as Europe, North America, Australia, and New Zealand, have the smallest proportion of CSA research compared to their total numbers.

This dispersion should be considered when discussing the context and conditions of technological applications. Some research assumes that "the way that climate change challenges are addressed, through either mitigation (mostly for the developed countries) or adaptation and productivity-increase lenses" are

Table 7.1 Distribution of research by geographical area

| Geographical location of research | Top countries (with number of articles) | Total amount of articles[4] | Amount of articles adopting CSA and climate change adaptation/mitigation framework |
|---|---|---|---|
| **Africa** | Africa (9); Malawi (9); Southern Africa (9); Kenya (7); others (44) | 78 | 66 |
| **Asia** | China (14); India (8); Pakistan (6); others (23) | 51 | 17 |
| **South/Latin America** | Brazil (6); rest (5) | 11 | 8 |
| **North America** | US (5) | 5 | 1 (along with cases from Sub-Saharan Africa) |
| **Middle East** | Turkey (3); Iran (2); others (2) | 7 | 4 |
| **Australia and New Zealand** | Australia (7); NZ (2) | 9 | 1 |
| **Europe** | Europe or several countries (20); Spain (5); others (37) | 63 | 10 |
| **Other or No specification** | Developing countries/ emerging economies (5); MENA region (1); Rep. of Moldova (1) others (122) | 129 | 49 |
| **TOTAL** | | 353 | 156 |

strongly dependent on the national economic development ratio (Totin et al., 2018, p. 12). Moreover, the research from low-income countries addresses also the crucial challenges of poverty and land inequality, which are reinforced by climate change conditions (Rampa et al., 2020). Last but not the least, the issues of energy use and energy poverty differ in developed and developing countries, particularly in energy availability and accessibility.

Thus, the major body of the analyzed research, both theoretical and empirical, focuses on climate change, food (in)security, productivity growth, and land use as the main factors behind the application of digital technologies. These grounds are partly rooted in the CSA framework and its application, which, in turn, derives from policy institutions, initiatives, and documents. In fact, these conditions are discussed as global challenges, not only for agriculture but also for humanity in general, and digital technologies are one of the ways to tackle them.

### Mapping the sector: nodes of the agri-food supply chain

This research is interested in the input of different smart technologies in terms of the enhancement of sustainability and sustainable agriculture. In the papers, a great deal of attention is paid to the use of smart technologies in farming or the production stage. Some research specifically highlights optimization of agricultural production processes as one of the major challenges in the sector, as well as the reason behind application of novel technologies. The enhancement of farms is particularly important since they "are the engine to support rural employment and to make a considerable contribution to territorial development" (Lezoche, 2020). The implementation of smart technologies at the production stage can be united under the umbrella of smart farming, which "connects farm equipment to software platforms that track on-farm data and enable analyses of soil and climate conditions in specific locations" (Clapp & Ruder, 2020, p. 49). Smart farming technologies, in turn, can be divided into three main categories: "farm management information systems, precision agriculture systems, and agricultural automation and robotics" (Balafoutis et al., 2020).

Crop operations and management can be largely supported by a variety of digital technologies, such as big data, internet of things (IoT), robotics, sensors (or remote sensing), 3D printing, system integration, artificial intelligence, digital twins, blockchain, and others. Their uses for specific operations related to minimizing emissions, water management, energy consumption, waste collection, and more are mainly discussed in relation to farming. Moreover, the analysis of the technological contribution to social issues and labor relations (part of social sustainability) is significant for farmers but is not limited to them. Whereas the contributions brought by these technologies are complex and various, one of the main transformations is the integration of operations and aspects into smart connected systems. These innovations link operations with a farm as a unit into a system and then can include it into a larger data-driven system of units, or system of systems.

One of the most widely spread innovations is the application of robotics for production and crop management. While the majority of the papers analyze its use during the farming stage, some research suggests the technology's capabilities be applied at other nodes of the supply chain. Robotics is one of the technologies, which has a wider impact on sustainability, the research implies, since it affects its three dimensions. The use of robots reduces material costs and human labor, and it also tackles harsh working conditions and difficult work in farming. Another popular technology used at the production stage is remote sensing, which has been largely applied to water management (reduction of water losses, estimation of crop water requirements, and more) and to estimate soil erosion (Adamides, 2020). This technology's use has an impact on environmental and economic sustainability, especially through control of resources, but its effect related to social conditions is not widely discussed.

The concept of smart farming should not be confused with the idea of smart agriculture or Agri-food 4.0. While smart farming, as shown earlier, transforms farm operations, smart agriculture

> offers the opportunity to farmers, technology and service providers, governance agencies and other impacted stakeholders (financial organization,

investors, traders, etc.) to share their experiences and preoccupations in the optimization in the farming supply chain with the close respect of production sustainability.

(Lezoche et al., 2020)

Therefore, smart agriculture also includes both traditional suppliers of farm inputs (packing, machinery, chemicals, and else) and digital services providers. Nevertheless, the farming supply stage, as well as distribution, as wide fields for technological advancement is out of focus in the analyzed research. Moreover, the role of distribution, both wholesale and retail, is crucial for the integrity and continuity of agri-food supply chains. It provides a large room for technological improvement and sustainability development, ranging from labor operations to tracking and transport services. The integration of smart technologies in agri-food logistics can reduce food losses along production and supply chains (Vernier et al., 2021). Other investigations in the literature on sustainability and logistic processes and strategies in food chains define it as limited and incomplete (e.g., Seccia, in De Gennaro & Nardone, 2014). They add value to the topic of production and are included in sustainable supply chain management but are not part of the focus of digital technology applications for sustainability. Evidence from research shows that "supply chain performance will improve when chain transparency and customer-oriented supply chains are created with associated operational coordination mechanisms" (Ibid., p. 45).

In a nutshell, the review of technological applications in agri-food supply chains sheds light on disproportional research and policy interest in the production stage or farming. While the incorporation of innovative technologies on farms and for crops is crucial for both increasing productivity and decreasing the ecological impacts, the other components of supply chains similarly require input from research and policy fields. One of the most under-investigated processes in agri-food chains is logistics and distribution. This gap is crucial to address since distributors are an integral part of the supply chain and operation of the sector as a whole, and they also have an observable potential for technological refinement and sustainability input (for example, reverse logistics). In such a way, the use of many technologies is not limited to the covered applications and they have a larger potential to boost not only effectiveness but also sustainability in agribusiness as a whole.

## *Mapping the sector: the role of actors*

As has been demonstrated earlier, the analyzed research largely focuses on farming and farms as units within supply chains and networks. Nevertheless, various investigations into farming and increase in its sustainability do not necessarily lead to adopting a complex approach to farmers as subjects or actors in supply chains. In other words, the research pays more attention to farming as a supply chain's node than farmers as actors and their role in the sector's operations. However, among other groups of actors within the supply chain, farmers and smallholder farmers are the most investigated group, with a few exceptions. For instance, the analysis of barriers to the adoption of CSA in Europe by Long et al. (2016) considers, among others, the challenges for technological innovation providers and technology users. However, its focus is limited by innovation providers and does not reflect on the links between other providers (e.g., of machinery) and sustainability.

One of the main reasons behind this disproportion is the framework of climate-smart agriculture, which identifies the main issues and threats to climate change as located at the production stage. As was shown previously, this framework focuses on technological advancement and improvement at the production stage, which is based on the producers – farmers. To specify, Collins (2017) addresses the three core pillars for CSA (as articulated by the World Bank): "sustainably improve agricultural productivity and enhance food security, increase farmers' resilience and adaptation to climate change, and reduce and/or remove greenhouse gas (GHG) emissions where possible" (p. 5). In such a way, the policy-oriented framework has a specific target group, which receives wide recognition and certain resources through various plans and projects. This highlight of farmers is consistent within the framework since it focuses on challenges of climate change and food security, which, in turn, rely primarily on crop production and management. At the same time, food losses and waste contribute to food insecurity, which, in turn, can be improved by technological advancement in logistics and distribution.

Within the body of research in sustainable and smart farming, some works examine farmers' motivations, as well as drivers and existing barriers to adopt novel technologies. These papers highlight the need to investigate deeper these conditions in order to develop a more complex understanding of farmers' knowledge and attitudes to digitalization. The farmers' relationship with technologies, knowledge, and trust in them, as well as the competencies to use them, are at heart of success and effectiveness of smart farming and its contribution to sustainable development.

Selected articles demonstrate that often policymakers and institutions encourage farmers to adopt smart technologies, especially in developing countries. In such a way, it is rather a top-down than bottom-up approach, which contributes to the challenges that farmers experience with the digitalization of the sector. These challenges and barriers also include (lack of) knowledge of particular technologies, their application and maintenance, and the following transformations of operations. Accordingly, on the basis of their assessment of correlations among smart agriculture (SA)-related knowledge, attitude, and adoption among farmers, Chuang et al. (2020) suggest that "agricultural R&D institutes should concentrate on improving market access for established and valuable SA technologies."

Moreover, the analytical review by Lajoie-O'Malley et al. (2020) finds out that "many of the texts also mention the importance of farmers' trust in the technologies themselves," where "trust in one technology can . . . also generate trust in others." The research suggests that digital tools can be, on the one

*The role of innovative technologies in sustainability* 165

hand, technologies themselves and, on the one hand, means to engage farmers to define their needs and concerns (for example, ICTs). At the same time, several researchers emphasize the growing concerns related to unequal access to technology and its reproduction, specifically among farmers, in particular, if adopted "within existing knowledge power structures" (Ibid.). To paraphrase, an increase in technological advancement in agri-food can widen the so-called digital divide by expanding the existing access and not providing sufficient new opportunities.

To add, due to the lack of research on other groups of actors within a supply chain, it is difficult to debate the barriers and drivers they experience. Although, based on the extensive interdisciplinary research beyond this database, the assumption is that technological knowledge and competencies, attitude and trust are also crucial for other actors to implement smart technologies effectively. Moreover, actors' cross-engagement and exchange of knowledge and experiences in technological advancement can influence its acceptance and distribution.

In general, the analyzed research investigates different components of a supply chain with a particular focus on farming, especially within the framework of climate-smart agriculture and challenges of climate change and food (in) security. At the same time, it tends to under-investigate the role of actors in the supply chains' operations in general and their input in the increase in sustainability and spread of technological applications. Innovative technologies can definitely transform operations along the whole supply chain and contribute to improving the resources conditions and use, labor performance, and analysis of information and data. However, their establishment, provision, and implementation are vastly dependent on the actors. To specify, crucial is not simply a particular group of actors, such as farmers, but all the variety of actors, including institutional actors, distributors, service and machinery providers, consumers, and others. Hence, an analysis of technological advancement in the agri-food sector requires a comprehensive approach, which includes all supply chain nodes and all groups of actors.

### *Sustainability: toward a comprehensive approach*

The analyzed research highlights the significant contribution of innovative technologies to sustainability development in agriculture, notably within the discourse of climate change and food insecurity global challenges. Despite the fact that only a few papers conceptualize sustainability through the application of the triple bottom line framework, the existing research tends to investigate more than one dimension. In other words, most of the papers do address more than one pillar, even without referring to the set of conditions as such.

The main focus of the research is on the environmental set of issues in agri-food, although it has been considered in relation to other conditions, in particular, economic and social. Such attention to the ecological dimension was predicted because, first, of the roots of the sustainability concept, and, second, the utilization of the climate-smart agriculture framework. One of the major achievements brought about by smart technologies is control of resources and their more effective use, which is, at the same time, linked to economic sustainability. Although, in a number of countries (often developing countries), the concern also refers to primary unequal access to resources and land in particular. A large share of papers refers to adaptation and mitigation of climate change (156 in total) brought about by innovative technologies, for example, through the reduction of greenhouse gas emissions (mainly considered in farming). The energy use, which includes energy efficiency and renewable energy, lies in the overlapping of economic and environmental sustainability.

Economic sustainability is enhanced through, first of all, the optimization of operations, resource management, and an increase in productivity (in particular, crop productivity). Precision or smart farming can not only boost productivity but also decrease the damage and waste. Agricultural data analytics contributes to more effective planning of operations through data-based decision-making. Moreover, particular technologies such as robotics are said to transform labor operations and costs. The research points out the input of blockchain technology into traceability and transparency of transactions and processes, which raises the economic return. Overall, the technologies affect the rise of productivity and capital assets through resource allocation to their highest valued use, but under the conditions of global challenges and environmental crisis. In such a way, the economic profit is linked to the sector's engagement with environmental conditions. Moreover, implementation of smart technologies throughout the supply chain can ensure the continuity of economic sustainability.

Social sustainability is an essential part of agricultural sustainability, which, first of all, refers to food safety and controls to ensure its both quantity and quality and production of healthy food (Hrustek, 2020). Also, it embraces social equity, which can be conceptualized, first, through labor conditions and relations. The review shows that one of the most notable roles in increasing social sustainability is performed by robots. Robots are capable of undertaking dangerous and difficult tasks, performing under harsh working (and weather) conditions, and reducing medical hazards. Moreover, they can tackle the high costs of production that derive from increased labor costs, the aging of rural populations, and the observed shortages of laborers (Adamides, 2020). An important social threat to the sector is rural population aging, which affects not only social but also economic conditions. Another challenge is shared with other industries and is the sector's gender inequality(ies) and imbalances that might arise through the application of new technologies (Collins, 2017). While the risks have to do with the increase in technological advancement itself (such as potential access imbalances), the way corporate actors utilize the language and framework of CSA can lead to the reinforced perpetuation of gender inequality in agriculture as a whole.

Last but not least, the institutional dimension of sustainability is addressed in the papers mostly through the institutions, which are often presented through their policies and policymaking, or political institutions. Some papers stress the need for policy and institutional strategies "to be locally context specific

The role of innovative technologies in sustainability 167

in order to ensure success and sustainability of scaling processes" in agriculture through a regulatory and policy support framework (Makate, 2019, p. 46). Rampa et al. (2020) argue that "communities/groups should also be a subject of tenure security recognised by other sources (such as local, regional, central governmental and legislative institutions)" to ensure their stability. The ecosystem-based approach to climate-smart agriculture includes the analysis of institutional requirements, which are important for its application and effectiveness (e.g., Akamani, 2021). While the selected research highlights the importance of policies and regulatory frameworks for technological spread and implementation, it does not provide a clear image of its enablers and constraints or barriers and how they act toward digitalization in agri-food. For example, knowledge gaps and institutional barriers, as shown by Dougill et al. (2017, p. 25), "influence land management decision-making and constrain conservation agriculture uptake." The knowledge of such context, as demonstrated by Totin et al. (2018), contributes to the research design and supportive policy (for technological sustainability-oriented implications).

This research suggests that the blurred and scattered incorporation of institutional framework into smart and sustainable agriculture can be rooted in limited utilization of the concept of institutional sustainability (or a pillar). As it was presented in the framework, several authors assembled institutional factors within a so-called fourth sustainability pillar. On the contrary, we suggest distinguishing institutional environment and institutional sustainability. The latter can be understood as a characteristic of the institutional environment, which ensures its stability and creates opportunities for accomplishment of other sustainability dimensions. In such a way, we propose conceptualizing the institutional factors not as another pillar but as a determining environment for sustainability enhancement, as shown in Figure 7.3. The institutional factors

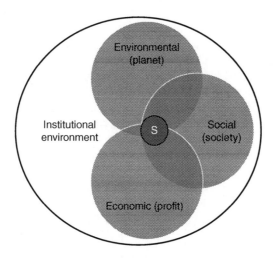

*Figure 7.3* Proposal for the extended sustainability framework

affect technological implementations at all stages of the supply chain, as well as transactions and interactions among actors and stakeholders, which, in turn, predeterminate the development of particular sustainability dimensions.

Overall, the existing research on the innovative technological development and sustainability in agriculture and agri-food, in particular, is relatively imbalanced. It represents extensive technological implementation based on digital and precise innovations within the focus on farmers as actors and farming or production as the phase in the supply chain. Certainly, the potential for transformations at the production stage is immense, yet the other actors and nodes of supply chains could benefit from technological interventions. Moreover, the role of technologies in increasing the environmental sustainability has been in the spotlight of analyzed research, with attention also paid to their input in terms of economic sustainability. One of the factors behind this limited approach is the employment of climate-smart agriculture framework by corporate actors and firms, policymakers, and researchers. This review highlights the importance of social and institutional factors for development of sustainability in agri-food by addressing their presence in the analyzed literature. Nevertheless, those factors are mostly not conceptualized as sustainability dimensions or aspects and are mostly conceptualized through economic and environmental sustainability.

## Conclusion

This chapter researched the existing literature on topics of sustainability and digitalization, or smart technology implementation, in the agricultural and agri-food sectors. To analyze the selected dataset, the research adopted an analytical framework of three sustainability pillars (economic, environmental, and social), which was extended by the institutional environment. The utilization of the framework allowed us to analyze inputs brought by innovative technologies to enhance agricultural and agri-food sustainability through its dimensions. However, these dimensions were reviewed not separately but as interconnected pillars within a complexity of sustainability as a phenomenon.

The interconnections between sustainability dimensions can be seen, for example, in the analysis of transformations in labor relations and conditions. The application of innovative technologies in agri-food, for example, can shift the performance of dangerous tasks and address unequal power relations and entrenched inequalities (social aspect), as well as tackle the high cost of production (economic aspect). Also, technologies can encourage and support farmers' ability to adapt to climate change (environmental dimension). Wherein all these aspects are in close interrelation and when carried out together, it increases the sector's sustainability as a whole.

Sustainability in agriculture can (and should) reasonably be analyzed and treated as a complex system with interconnected subsystems. In other words, while the ecological and environmental sustainability of the agricultural sector is clearly important, it will not be understood without its connections

*The role of innovative technologies in sustainability* 169

to economics, social sustainability, and the institutional environment. Thus, a holistic approach to agriculture as a system is perceived to be the way of advancing its understanding. Moreover, it requires more investigations into the social impact of innovative technologies, which includes both intended and unintended consequences associated with them. This so-called double-edged nature of technology affects the distribution of power as well, for example, increasing the risk of suppressing environmental side effects and "further concentrate power in the hands of corporate actors in ways that undermine farmer autonomy" (Clapp & Ruder, 2020, p. 64). Moreover, spread of innovative technologies in agriculture risks intensifying the existing so-called digital divide by reproducing the power relations and access (to resources, information, technology).

This research highlights the importance of examining the factors and conditions behind the choice and application of particular innovations and digital strategies. The identification of issues and aims for each case in agribusiness is supposed to assist the choice and implementation of innovation, the node of supply chain, and actors involved. However, to achieve a pervasive transformation in agri-food, which will lead to a turning point in fighting the global sustainability challenges, the existing efforts might not be enough. The application of innovative technologies requires a more strategic, or systematic, and comprehensive approach, which focuses on all supply chain nodes and actors (or sector as a whole), on the one hand, and on tackling different sustainability dimensions, on the other hand.

Moreover, the recognition of the role of the institutional environment for technological advancement is crucial for advising the decision-making and creation of supportive policies and research. A set of particular institutions constitutes an environment, where a variety of relations, including those regarding technological development, are executed. While a (smart) technology has a particular set of common features and implementations, its performance and outputs will vary from context to context depending on the existing enablers and constraints and the way they impact that implementation. In such a way, the technology's utilization and the following contribution to sustainability and its dimensions will change in different contexts. Hence, the extension of the three pillars framework with the institutional dimension (but not as an extra pillar) provides a more comprehensive approach to sustainability. Furthermore, the analysis of the institutional environment can also contribute to understanding the factors behind innovative technological implementations.

This chapter has identified some gaps for future research avenues. First of all, the sector requires more research to understand the role of novel technologies in different components of supply chains. The analyzed research covered various technologies and their input in terms of sustainability in the sector, paying special attention to technological advancement at the production stage, or digital and precision farming. Without downplaying the contribution of farming to fighting global challenges, the input of the other nodes of the supply chain is valuable. To specify, logistics' role to support supply chains and their continuity is crucial, and also there is a plenty of potentials for smart technological advancement to enhance its sustainability, for example, through reverse logistics. Last but not least, the institutional framework and its role in the development of agricultural sustainability through digitalization requires more investigations.

## Notes

1 Articles were assigned to one or more areas of research.
2 Climate-smart agriculture can be understood as both a framework and an agriculture type.
3 To clarify, it refers to the geographical location (continent's subregion, region, country, etc.) of investigations, not the researcher's or publication's origin.
4 Some papers included cases from more than one area; therefore, this total number exceeds the total number of analyzed papers.

## References

Adamides, G. (2020). A review of climate-smart agriculture applications in Cyprus. *Atmosphere*, vol. 11, issue 9

Adesipo, A. et al. (2020). Smart and climate-smart agricultural trends as core aspects of smart village functions. *Sensors*, vol. 20, issue 21, https://doi.org/10.3390/s20215977

Akanami, K. (2021). An ecosystem-based approach to climate-smart agriculture with some considerations for social equity. *Agronomy*, vol. 11, issue 8, https://doi.org/10.3390/agronomy11081564

Annosi, M.C., Brunetta, F. (2020). *How is digitalization affecting agri-food? New business models, strategies and organizational forms*. Taylor & Francis, Routledge

Annosi, M.C., Brunetta, F., Capo, F., Heidelved, L. (2020). Digitalization in the agri-food industry: The relationship between technology and sustainable development. *Management Decision*, vol. 58, issue 8, pp. 1737–1757

Balafoutis, Athanasios T., Van Evert, Frits K., Fountas, Spyros. (2020). Smart farming technology trends: Economic and environmental effects, labor impact, and adoption readiness. *Agronomy*, vol. 10, issue 5, p. 743.

Birkeland, I. (2008). Cultural sustainability: Industrialism, placelessness and the reanimation of place. *Ethics, Place and Environment*, vol. 11, Issue 3, pp. 283–297

Boström, M. (2012). SSPP: A missing pillar? Challenges in theorizing and practicing social sustainability: Introduction to the special issue. *Sustainability: Science, Practice and Policy*, vol. 8, issue 1, pp. 3–14

Boyer, R.H.W. et al. (2016). Five approaches to social sustainability and the integrated way forward. *Sustainability*, vol. 8, issue 9, pp. 1–18

Chuang, J.-H., Wang, J.-H., Liou, Y.-C. (2020). Farmers' knowledge, attitude, and adoption of smart agriculture technology in Taiwan. *International Journal of Environmental Research and Public Health*, vol. 17, issue 19, https://doi.org/10.3390/ijerph17197236

Clapp, J., Ruder, S.-L. (2020). Precision technologies for agriculture: Digital farming, gene-edited crops, and the politics of sustainability. *Global Environmental Politics*, vol. 20, issue 3, pp. 49–69

Clune, W.H., Zehnder, A.J.B. (2018). The three pillars of sustainability framers: Approaches for laws and governance. *Journal of Environmental Protection*, vol. 9, no. 3, pp. 211–240.

Clune, W.H., Zehnder, A.J.B. (2020). The evolution of sustainability models, from descriptive, to strategic, to the three pillars framework for applied solutions. *Sustainability Science*, issue 15, pp. 1001–1006

Coco, N., Colapinto, C., Finotto, V. (2021). Supporting pervasive digitization in Italian SMEs through an open innovation process. In A. Hinterhuber, T. Vescovi, F. Checchinato (Eds.), *Managing digital transformation: Understanding the strategic process* (pp. 259–269). Routledge.

Collins, A. (2017). Saying all the right things? Gendered discourse in climate-smart agriculture. *The Journal of Peasant Studies*, vol. 45, issue 4, pp. 1–17

Cornelissen, J.P., Werner, M.D. (2014). Putting framing in perspective: A review of framing and frame analysis across the management and organizational literature. *Academy of Management Annals*, vol. 8, issue 1, pp. 181–235, https://doi.org/10.1080/19416520.2014.875669

De Gennaro, B.C., Nardone, G. (eds.) (2014). *Sustainability of the agri-food system: Strategies and performances*. Proceedings of the 50th SIDEA Conference Lecce, Chiostro dei Domenicani, 26–28 September, Universitas Studiorum

Dougill, A.J. et al. (2017). Mainstreaming conservation agriculture in Malawi: Knowledge gaps and institutional barriers. *Journal of Environmental Management*, vol. 195, pp. 25–34

Elliott, S.R. (2005). Sustainability: An economic perspective. *Resources, Conservation and Recycling*, vol. 44, pp. 263–277

Feroz, A.K., Zo, H., Chiravuri A. (2021). Digital transformation and environmental sustainability: A review and research agenda. *Sustainability*, vol. 13, issue 3, p. 1530. https://doi.org/10.3390/su13031530

Fink, A. (2010). *Conducting research literature reviews: From the Internet to paper*, 3rd ed. Sage Publications.

Garud, R., Karnoe, P. (2003). Bricolage versus breakthrough: Distributed and embedded agency in technology entrepreneurship. *Research Policy*, vol. 32, issue 2, pp. 277–300, https://doi.org/Pii

Hak, T., Moldan, B., Dahl, A.L. (2007). *Sustainability indicators: A scientific assessment*. SCOPE Project. Island Press

Hargadon, A. B., Douglas, Y. (2001). When innovations meet institutions: Edison and the design of the electric light. *Administrative Science Quarterly*, vol. 46, issue 3, pp. 476–501, https://doi.org/10.2307/3094872

Hosseini, H.M., Kaneko, S. (2012). Causality between pillars of sustainable development: Global stylized facts or regional phenomena? *Ecological Indicators*, vol. 14, pp. 197–201

Hrustek, L. (2020). Sustainability driven by agriculture through digital transformation. *Sustainability*, vol. 12, p. 8596

Hubeau, M., Marchand, F., Coteur, I., Mondelaers, K., Debruyne, L., Van Huylenbroeck, G. (2017). A new agri-food systems sustainability approach to identify shared transformation pathways towards sustainability. *Ecological Economics*, vol. 131, pp. 52–63.

Kajembe, G.C. et al. (2016). Institutional sustainability in the face of climate change: Empirical insights from irrigation institutions in the Iringa Rural District, Tanzania. In R. Lal et al. (Eds.), *Climate change and multi-dimensional sustainability in African agriculture climate change and sustainability in agriculture*. Springer

Lajoie-O'Malley, A. et al. (2020). The future(s) of digital agriculture and sustainable food systems: An analysis of high-level policy documents. *Ecosystem Services*, vol. 45, p. 101183

Lezoche, M. et al. (2020). Agri-food 4.0: A survey of the supply chains and technologies for the future agriculture. *Computers in Industry*, vol. 117, p. 103187

Long, T.B., Blok, V., Coninx, I. (2016). Barriers to the adoption and diffusion of technological innovations for climate-smart agriculture in Europe: Evidence from the Netherlands, France, Switzerland and Italy. *Journal of Cleaner Production*, vol. 112, pp. 9–21

Makate, C. (2019). Effective scaling of climate smart agriculture innovations in African smallholder agriculture: A review of approaches, policy and institutional strategy needs. *Environmental Science and Policy*, vol. 96, pp. 37–51

Murphy, K. (2012). The social pillar of sustainable development: A literature review and framework for policy analysis. *Sustainability: Science, Practice and Policy*, vol. 8, issue 1, pp. 15–29

Petrisor, A.-I., Petrisor, L. (2014). 25 years of sustainability: A critical assessment. *Present Environment and Sustainable Development*, vol. 8, issue 1, pp. 175–190

Pfahl, S. (2005). Institutional sustainability. *International Journal of Sustainable Development*, vol. 8, issue 1–2, pp. 80–96

Purvis, B., Mao, Y., Robinson, D. (2019). Three pillars of sustainability: In search of conceptual origins. *Sustainability Science*, vol. 14, pp. 681–695

Ranjbari, M. et al. (2021). The three pillars of sustainability in the wake of Covid-19: A systematic review and future research agenda for sustainable development. *Journal of Cleaner Production*, vol. 297, p. 126660

Rampa, A. et al. (2020). Land reform in the era of global warming – can land reforms help agriculture be climate-smart? *Land*, vol. 12, issue 9, p. 471

Reischauer, G. (2018). Industry 4.0 as policy-driven discourse to institutionalize innovation systems in manufacturing. *Technological Forecasting and Social Change*, vol. 132, pp. 26–33, https://doi.org/10.1016/j.techfore.2018.02.012

Rotz, S. et al. (2019). Automated pastures and the digital divide: How agricultural technologies are shaping labour and rural communities. *Journal of Rural Studies*, vol. 68, pp. 112–122

Smiraglia, D. et al. (2016). Linking trajectories of land change, land degradation processes and ecosystem services. *Environmental Research*, vol. 147, pp. 590–600

Soini, K., Birkeland, I. (2014). Exploring the scientific discourse on cultural sustainability. *Geoforum*, vol. 51, pp. 213–223

Spangenberg, J.H. (2002). Institutional sustainability indicators: An analysis of the institutions in agenda 21 and a draft set of indicators for monitoring their effectivity. *Sustainable Development*, vol. 10, pp. 103–115

Spangenberg, J.H., Pfahl, S., Deller, K. (2002). Towards indicators for institutional sustainability: Lessons from an analysis of agenda 21. *Ecological Indicators*, vol. 2, pp. 61–77

Totin, E. et al. (2018). Institutional perspectives of climate-smart agriculture: A systematic literature review. *Sustainability*, vol. 10, issue 6

Tranfield, D., Denyer, D., Smart, P. (2003). Towards a methodology for developing evidence-informed management knowledge by means of systematic review. *British Journal of Management*, vol. 14, issue 3, pp. 207–222

Vernier, C. et al. (2021). Adoption of ICTs in agri-food logistics: Potential and limitations for supply chain sustainability. *Sustainability*, vol. 13, p. 6702, https://doi.org/10.3390/su13126702

Von Keyserlingk, M.A.G. et al. (2013). Invited review: Sustainability of the US dairy industry. *Journal of Dairy Science*, vol. 96, pp. 5405–5425

Wilkins, H. (2008). The integration of the pillars of sustainable development: A work in progress. *McGill International Journal of Sustainable Development Law & Policy*, vol. 4, issue 2, https://ssrn.com/abstract=2623221

Yunlong, C., Smith, B. (1994). Sustainability in agriculture: A general review. *Agriculture, Ecosystems and Environment*, vol. 49, pp. 299–307. doi:10.1016/0167-8809(94)90059-0

# 8 Sustainability in agribusiness
## What is still in the works

*Maria Carmela Annosi, Francesco Paolo Appio, and Federica Brunetta*

### Concluding remarks and what is still in the works

Sustainability is a key element in the agribusiness sector. The most relevant arguments for implementing sustainable management practices affect multiple levels of analysis; ecosystems (macro-level), organizations (meso-level), and individuals (micro-level) have all to make sure that their practices converge toward a more sustainable approach to agribusiness. Of particular importance is understanding how and to what extent changes and innovations in agribusiness can contribute to solve urgent societal challenges, accomplish the largest number of sustainable development goals, and leverage upon the most recent technological advancements.

Back in the 1950s, the term "agribusiness" was coined to identify and describe how the international and national pressures for internal development were driving transformations at the socio-economic and technological level (Ioris, 2018). It turned out that agribusiness gradually favored a short-term logic centered on legitimizing intensive agri-food systems and increasing financial gains over a long-term vision centered on nutrition and health (Ioris, 2018). With this Handbook, we hope to shed some light on this conundrum.

The relevance of agribusiness is evident in terms of values for international trade, output, and employment. The production of sufficient quantity and quality food to keep the population healthy is the main scope of the agribusiness sector. Companies operating in the agribusiness are extremely active in producing and commercializing food, with an increasing internationalization rate mainly targeting China, the United States, and Germany as top three markets by revenues. While this is a sign of a healthy and constantly revitalized operational and commercial apparatus, it is disconcerting that other fundamental properties of the agribusiness system, namely, nutrition, farmers' well-being, the preservation of traditional practices, and the biological equilibrium of the ecosystem, lose ground in favor of profit, lower costs, and consumer satisfaction imperatives (Ioris, 2018). It suffices to think about the quantity of food sold in plastic boxes, its low quality, the difficulties in tracking the activities and contributions of all the actors in the value chain, and an increasing level of pollution (e.g., Bajan and Mrówczyńska-Kamińska, 2020). Concerning the latter, the

DOI: 10.4324/9781003223672-12

Institute for Agriculture and Trade Policy (IATP[1]) recently released a report on the environmental impact of the agri-food industry, concluding that "the top-10 emitters in the dairy and meat industries produce more greenhouse gases than many major OECD countries including Germany, Canada or France." The study compares the combined annual emissions of the five major meat and dairy emitters to the emissions of three major oil companies such as BP, Shell, and Exxon Mobil. Combined, the selected food companies (i.e., Cargill, Dairy Farmers of America, Fonterra, JBS-Friboi, and Tyson Foods) emit 573 million tons of greenhouse gases, which is more than any of the three oil companies. Accordingly, companies in the agri-food sector must work hard to decrease their emissions and support the effort against global warming.

It is not a coincidence that the EIT Food[2], a Europe's leading food innovation initiative having a challenging mission of building a future-fit food system that produces healthy and sustainable food for all, briefly identified and described these challenges as among the top five European food trends in 2022: (1) food systems will be a pivotal discussion and decision-making climate-change-related issue, especially in the run-up to COP27; (2) regenerative farming practices will be increasingly adopted by large-scale farms and corporations; (3) a growth is expected in the European alternative proteins market; (4) members of younger generations will increasingly be covering the roles of food activists and act as change agents; and (5) front-pack environmental labeling will be adopted by more brands in 2022. They all point in the direction of coming up with a more sustainable approach to agribusiness (e.g., Ioris, 2018; Pani et al., 2020; Spann, 2017; Joshi et al., 2020; Nasution et al., 2020; Dentoni et al., 2020). However, it is increasingly clear that accomplishing sustainability in the agribusiness sector is a challenge that both developing and developed countries are facing (Bajan and Mrówczyńska-Kamińska, 2020; Joshi et al., 2020). A closer look at the sectors shows that it is becoming increasingly complex, multifaceted, and has broad implications when it comes to achieve more sustainable outcomes. The main challenge resides in understanding to what extent this is happening, the multiple ways it can help addressing the sustainable development goals[3] (e.g., SDG 2 = zero hunger, SDG 5 = gender equality, SDG 8 = decent work, SDG 12 = responsible consumption and production, SDG 13 = climate action).

Nonetheless, notwithstanding the aspirations of policymakers, institutions, and consumers for environmentally friendly and socially viable methods of production, the question remains is agribusiness getting serious about sustainability. Although the quantity and quality of sustainable-oriented agribusiness are increasing, and preliminary results appear promising, sustainability for agribusiness remains a challenge (Malorgio and Marangon, 2021). In fact, a number of critical factors, such as technical inefficiencies, seem to constrain agribusiness to perform below the most sustainable options. Food preferences and habits of the end consumers (Linnemann et al., 2006) impact food waste and at the same time, suppliers and retailers are moving toward a long-term perspective, recognizing that the longevity of their businesses is dependent on natural resource capital. As a consequence, it is clear that *all* agribusiness sector participants must "find new ways to reduce inputs, minimise waste, improve management of resource stocks, change consumption patterns, optimise production processes, management and business methods, and improve logistics" (Europe, 2020)[4]. Lack of transparency is another issue that plagues sustainable efforts, despite the effort in recognizing it as a pivotal element fostering conversation between suppliers and consumers. Thus, companies are making efforts to enhance transparency, for example, through corporate sustainability reporting, and joining programs such as the "Carbon Disclosure Project"[5] or the "Center for Food Integrity,"[6] whose mission revolves around improving the diffusion of information and consumer trust. Partnerships between science and industry are also drivers of accountability, transparency, and accuracy. According to a recently published BCG report[7], agribusiness can certainly lead the shift toward sustainability conditional to raise awareness and embracing new regulations to make the industry greener (e.g., European Green Deal, in particular, the F2F policy) and targeting the entire agriculture value chain; shift value pools in the industry exploiting opportunities provided by seed innovation, novel biological products, new formulations of conventional products; but also adopting a range of new digital services and tools helping farmers generate better results while reducing the amount of chemicals used, and rethinking business models by adjusting the portfolios of initiatives accordingly and placing a higher value on value rather than volume, which means that agribusiness success should no longer be conceived as stemming from the use of inputs such as fertilizer and the productivity of a given field through a nearly linear relationship. Farmers, indeed, have become more conscious of the environmental impact of chemicals, and they must maximize output per hectare while using lower chemical volumes. Aspects related to production optimization, waste minimization, and nutrition promotion, deployment of production systems capable of taking responsible care of natural resources, value creation and value sharing along the value chain, respecting workers', producers', and consumers' rights, acting in accordance with the law (national and international regulations and standards), investing in the development of small producers' capacities, and in the implementation of good practices for sustainable production at all level, are all aspects that still deserves urgent attention.

This Handbook helps explain how to reconcile multiple dimensions of contemporary agribusiness. Improving the sustainability of agribusiness endeavors means dealing with environmental and socio-economic issues. Furthermore, business model innovations are recognized as key drivers of sustainability. Also, the assessment of sustainable accomplishments in the agribusiness sector has oftentimes been carried out from a qualitative perspective, neglecting the important contribution quantitative indicators can provide. Then, interpreting the evolution of the agribusiness sector in embracing the sustainable paradigm requires the adoption of different lenses such as the societal challenges, technological advancements, and development goals.

Overall, we specifically tackled five research questions: How can we conceptualize the link between agribusiness and sustainability? What are the drivers and barriers for the agribusiness sector to become sustainable? Which business models can favor the implementation of sustainable goals? How can we measure the extent to which the agribusiness sector is becoming more sustainable? How can the agribusiness sector leverage recent technological advancement and pave the way to achieving the sustainable development goals? Each chapter provides a comprehensive answer to these research questions, opening novel research avenues and emphasizing (nonetheless) the importance of conducting more in-depth studies on the role of the sustainability pillars.

In this vein, we do hope inspiring academics engaged in innovation management, who are interested in the applications of these theories for the understanding of innovation and other performance outcomes; also, academics engaged in sustainability research, who are interested in understanding and deepening knowledge on solving important societal challenges through specific actions in the agribusiness sector; practitioners and managers in the agribusiness sector, coping with digitalization strategies and implementation. This will inevitably lead to an interdisciplinary academic effort, as well as an open debate between scholars around the world.

## Notes

1. www.iatp.org/
2. www.eitfood.eu/
3. https://sdgs.un.org/goals
4. www.eea.europa.eu/policy-documents/a-resource-efficient-europe#:~:text=A%20resource%2Defficient%20Europe%20%E2%80%93%20Flagship,economy%20to%20achieve%20sustainable%20growth
5. www.cdp.net/en
6. https://foodintegrity.org/
7. www.bcg.com/publications/2022/agribusiness-and-the-shift-to-sustainable-farming

## References

Bajan, B., and Mrówczyńska-Kamińska, A. (2020). Carbon footprint and environmental performance of agribusiness production in selected countries around the world. *Journal of Cleaner Production*, 276: 123389.

Dentoni, D., Bijman, J., Bossle, M.B., Gondwe, S., Isubikalu, P., Ji, C., Kella, C., Pascucci, S., Royer, A., and Vieira, L. (2020). New organizational forms in emerging economies: bridging the gap between agribusiness management and international development. *J0ournal of Agribusiness in Developing and Emerging Economies*, 10(1): 1–11.

Ioris, A.A.R. (2018). The politics of agribusiness and the business of sustainability. *Sustainability*, 10(5): 1648.

Joshi, S., Singh, R.K., and Sharma, M. (2020). Sustainable agri-food supply chain practices: Few empirical evidences from a developing economy. *Global Business Review*, in press.

Linnemann, A.R., Benner, M., Verkerk, R., and van Boekel, M.A.J.S. (2006). Consumer-driven food product development. *Trends in Food Science and Technology*, 17: 184–190.

Malorgio, G., and Marangon, F. (2021). Agricultural business economics: The challenge of sustainability. *Agricultural and Food Economics*, 9(6): 1–4.
Nasution, A.H., Aula, M., and Ardiantono, D.S. (2020). Circular economy business model design. *International Journal of Integrated Supply Management*, 13(2–3): 159–177.
Pani, S.K., Jena, D., and Parida, N.R. (2020). Agricultural sustainability and sustainable agribusiness model: A review on economic and environmental perspective. *International Journal of Modern Agriculture*, 9(4): 875–883.
Spann, M. (2017). Politics of poverty: The post-2015 sustainable development goals and the business of agriculture. *Globalizations*, 14(3): 360–378.

# Index

Note: Page numbers in *italics* indicate a figure and page numbers in **bold** indicate a table on the corresponding page.

21st Conference of the Parties *see* COP 21
2030 Agenda for Sustainable Development 64

Agenda 21 150
agribusiness: changes and legitimacy of 15–17, 21, **22**; definition 32; impact on sustainable development goals (SDGs) 4
agribusiness sustainability *see* sustainability in agribusiness
agricultural research 48–50, 52–53
agriculture: climate-smart 37–38, 51, 159–161, **161**; fragility of 11; role in ending poverty 35–36; role in greenhouse gas emissions 42–43
artificial intelligence 6
associativism 6, 101–126

big-data analytics 6
biomass conversion into gas 39
biotechnologies 49, 51
Bitcoin 88
blockchain technology 5, 166; characteristics of 88–90; model in coffee industry supply chain 85–96, *90*
Boeing Corporate Citizenship 110
Bonsucro 105–106, 108–109, 113–115
Brazil: and impact of COP 21 116–117; as promoter of sustainability 102–126
business ecosystems 5–6
business models 5–6; social 128–145
Buta Art & Sweets 5, 6, 129–145; activities of 138–139; communication channels with customers 135–136; costs of 140–141; customer relationship 134–135; key resources/assets 136–137; product pricing 131–132; revenue streams of 141; suppliers/partner networks 139–140; target customer group 132–134; values of 142, *143*

carbon footprint 44
certification 16–17; in sugarcane industry 105–111
circular economy 1, 47
circular production 34, 46–48
civic and green communication 16
climate change 34, 42–44, 51, 102, 116–117, 159–161, **161**, 164, 166, 174
climate-smart agriculture 37–38, 51, 159–161, **161**
coffee industry 5, 23; sustainable supply chain management practices 91–92; transforming supply chains in 85–96
communication, civic and green *versus* domestic 16
community-based entrepreneurship 20
cooperatives 25, 91
COP 21 102, 116–117
COVID-19 pandemic 24
crop diversification 121, *121*
CSA *see* climate-smart agriculture
cultural entrepreneurship 19, 25
cultural value 142, *143*

deforestation 42, 47
de-globalization 24
digital divide 165, 169
digital technologies 6, 49–50, 51, 85, 151
digitization *see* digital technologies
domestic communication 16

## Index  179

ecological sustainability 1, 2, 26, 152, 165
economic sustainability 1, 4, 6, 65, 86, 152, *153*, 156, 166, *167*
economic value 142, *143*
EIT Food 174
emotional value 142, *143*
entrepreneurship: community-based 20; cultural 19, 25; social 6, 128–145
environmental sustainability 1, 4, 6, 64, 86, 152, *153*, 156, 160, 165–166, 168
environmental value 142, *143*
ethanol as a biofuel 102–103

FairChain Foundation 91
Farmer Equity Practices Program 91
farm mechanization 36, 37–38, 48, 53
FDA 17
food (in)security 159–160, 164
food production 22, 32–33, 40–41, 45; holistic *versus* atomistic view 45–46; requirements 40, 41
food system: definition 45; holistic *versus* atomistic view 45–46; reforming 33–34, 45–52; sustainable 46, 174
farm to fork 85
frugal innovation 38–39

gasification technology 39
gender equality 4–5, 39–40, 64–76; in Italian agri-food companies 65, **69**, 69–75, **70–71, 72, 73, 74**; in sustainability disclosures 67–69
genetically modified organisms (GMOs) *see* GMOs
geographical information system (GIS) technologies 34, 49–50
geospatial technology 49–50
global reporting initiative (GRI) standards 67–68, **70–71**, 70–75, **72**
glocalization 16
GMOs 16–17, 36
governance structures of organizations 19–20
Green Bonds 111
Green CDR 112, 113
greenhouse gas emissions 34, 42–43, 102, 117, 159, 174
green revolution 40
Green Rural Credit 111–113, *123*

ICT technologies 49
iNDC 117
Indigenous peoples as stakeholders 16, 21

industry 4.0 technologies 6, 95, 96, 149–151, 162
Information and Communication Technology *see* ICT technologies
innovation 6–7, 36–39, 48–50, 53, 149–170; frugal 38–39
institutional sustainability 153–155, 160, 166–168, *167*, 169
intangible assets 5
Italy and gender equality in agri-food companies 65, **69**, 69–75, **70–71, 72, 73, 74**

JAB Holding 88

land conservation 51
land degradation 41, 160
land scarcity 41
legitimacy of agribusinesses 15–17, 21–22
life cycle assessment 44

mechanization of farming 36, 37–38
microfinance 36
micro-irrigation 37
Millennium Development Goals (MDGs) 33
Monsanto 17
moral legitimization 16, 21–22

natural resource depletion 41–42
NGOs 16, 19, 24
nongovernmental organizations *see* NGOs

organizational change 17–18, 22–23, **23**

poverty: demographics of 34–35; reducing/ending 20, 33–37, 51, 64, 102
Pró-Álcool 102

Rainforest Alliance 91
Rajabli, Sara 6, 129–145
renewable energies 50, 51
robotics 6, 162, 166
Roundtable on Sustainable Biomaterials (RSB) 109–110, 112
RSB Certification Program 105–106, 109–111, 112

SDG 1 4, 34, 35, 41, 51
SDG 2 4, 33, 35, 41, 51, 174
SDG 3 4, 34, 51
SDG 5 4, 34, 64, **70**, 70–75, **72, 74**, 174
SDG 6 33, 51

180   Index

SDG 7 34, 51
SDG 8 4, 174
SDG 10 4, 34
SDG 11 51
SDG 12 4, 33, 34, 51, 174
SDG 13 4, 34, 51, 174
SDG 14 34
SDG 15 4, 33, 34, 51
SDGs 4, 32–53, *65*, 102, 150, 174 *see also* specific ones; and gender equality 64, 66–75, **70–71, 72, 73, 74**; and global reporting initiative (GRI) standards 67–68, **70–71**, 70–75, **72**, **74**
Sicoob Coopecredi 106, 112, 113
smart agriculture 6, 34, 37–38, 51, 149, 159–165, **161**
smart farming 162–163
smart technologies: and farmers' role in adopting 163–165; and the supply chain 161–163, 169
social business models 6, 128–145
social entrepreneurship 6, 128–145; case study 129–145
social movements 17
social sustainability 1, 2, 4, 6, 64, 86, 152–153, *154*, 160, 166, *167*
social value 142, *143*
Socicana 5–6; and Bonsucro Sugar Cane Credit program 114–115; and Green Rural Credit 112–113; history, members, and structure of 103–105, *104*; promoting sustainable development 105–111; services and structure of 117–120, **118**, *119*; Top Cana Continuous Improvement Program 105–108, *107*, 112, **120**, 120–124, *121–126*; using associativism 101–126
soil-sensing technology 38–39
solar-powered pump 39
standards 16–17; in the coffee industry 91; voluntary 18, 24
sugarcane industry 5, 6; certification in 105–111; and impact of COP 21 116–117; overview 121–122; as promoter of sustainability 101–126
supply chain: and smart technologies 161–163, 169; sustainable 18–19, 23–24, **24**, 86–87, 91–92; transformation in coffee industry 85–96
sustainability: dimensions of 151–156, *154*; ecological 1, 2, 26, 152, 165; economic 1, 4, 6, 65, 86, 152, *153*, 156, 166, *167*; environmental 1, 4, 6, 64, 86, 152, *153*, 156, 160, 165–166, 168; institutional 153–155, 160, 166–168, *167*, 169; social 1, 2, 4, 6, 64, 86, 152–153, *154*, 160, 166, *167*; strategical 2
sustainability disclosures and gender equality 67–75; case study of Italian agri-food companies **69**, 69–75, **70–71, 72, 73, 74**
sustainability in agribusiness 173–176; contributing to sustainable development 20–21, 26, **26**; differences in U.S. and European environments 16; dimensions of 151–156; future research in 21–26, **22**; generating value via credits 111–115; innovative technologies in 6–7, 36–39, 48–50, 53, 149–170; literature overview 11–27, *13*, *14*; measuring 44; and organizational change 17–18, 22–23, **23**; promoted by Socicana 105–111; social business models 128–145; Socicana case study 101–126; sustainable value chains in 18–19; viability of the enterprise 19–20, 24–25, **25**
"Sustainable Cane" program 110
sustainable development 1, 4, 6, *15*, 20–21, **26**, 26–27, 64, 86, 105–111, 150, 154–156 *see also* SDGs; case study 105–116
sustainable development goals (SDGs) *see* SDGs
sustainable supply chains 18–19, 23–24, **24**, 86–87, 91–92
sustainable value chains 18–19, 23–24, **24**
sustaincentrism 17, 23

technologies in agribusiness 6–7, 36–39, 48–50, 53, 149–170; literature review 156–170, *157*
Top Cana Continuous Improvement Program 105–108, *107*, 112, **120**, 120–124, *121–126*
transglocal value chains 18

UNFCCC *see* United Nations Framework Convention on Climate Change (UNFCCC)
United Nations Framework Convention on Climate Change (UNFCCC) 102, 117

values 142, *143*; cultural 142; economic 142; emotional 142; environmental 142; social 142

wastewater treatment 39

water: management of 37, 42, 160; wastewater treatment 39; withdrawal and degradation 42

watershed development 37

women: barriers in agriculture 11; disabled women as entrepreneurs 6, 129–145; empowering 39–40; equality in agribusiness 66–76, **69**, **70–71**, **72**, **73**, **74**; and gender equality 4–5, 34, 39–40, 64–76

zero waste 34, 46–48

Printed in the United States
by Baker & Taylor Publisher Services